Leading for Literacy

Leading for Literacy

A Reading Apprenticeship Approach

Ruth Schoenbach
Cynthia Greenleaf
Lynn Murphy

JB JOSSEY-BASS™
A Wiley Brand

Published by Jossey-Bass
A Wiley Brand
One Montgomery Street, Suite 1000, San Francisco, CA 94104-4594—www.josseybass.com

The contents of this book were developed under a grant from the U.S. Department of Education, Investing in Innovation (i3) Program, grant number U396B10025. However, these contents do not necessarily represent the policy of the Department of Education nor endorsement by the federal government.

Library of Congress Cataloging-in-Publication Data

Names: Schoenbach, Ruth, author. | Greenleaf, Cynthia, author. | Murphy, Lynn, author.
Title: Leading for literacy : a Reading Apprenticeship approach / Ruth Schoenbach, Cynthia Greenleaf, Lynn Murphy.
Description: San Francisco, CA : Jossey-Bass; Hoboken, NJ : John Wiley & Sons, 2016. | Includes index.
Identifiers: LCCN 2016027834 | ISBN 9781118437261 (pbk.) | ISBN 9781119321309 (ePDF) | ISBN 9781119321675 (epub)
Subjects: LCSH: Literacy programs. | Reading promotion.
Classification: LCC LC149 .S39 2016 | DDC 379.2/4—dc23 LC record available at https://lccn.loc.gov/2016027834

Cover Images and Author Photos: © WestEd
Cover Design: Christian Holden

Printed in the United States of America

FIRST EDITION

PB Printing   10 9 8 7 6 5 4 3 2 1

Contents

List of Close-Ups

List of Team Tools

These resources are available to be downloaded from the Reading Apprenticeship website, http://readingapprenticeship.org/publications/downloadable-resources/. Permission is given for individuals to reproduce these for use in leading Reading Apprenticeship professional learning. No other reproduction of these materials is permissible. (See explicitly the copyright page of this volume.)

Foreword

I AM ALWAYS happy to find people in our field who combine theory and practice as part of their professional DNA. And I am especially pleased when that work has a clear focus on empowering students through critical literacy — needed now more than ever. This book, the result of several decades of work by the authors and their colleagues, is rooted in a critical literacy approach they call Reading Apprenticeship, which deeply integrates theory and practice. The work this book describes also happens to have a long record of research showing positive impact for student learning, which of course is another strong plus.

While everyone agrees that all students deserve great teaching and that all teachers will benefit from meaningful support, we also know that we must invest our professional learning dollars and time wisely. Those of us who have long advocated for professional learning know that there are qualities that set highly effective teacher learning efforts apart from traditional professional development. The Reading Apprenticeship approach builds on teachers' own knowledge and expertise, challenges teachers with new research-based insights, and provides structured opportunities for them to explore their own reading and comprehension processes as a foundation for apprenticing students to reading, writing, thinking, and speaking in the different disciplines. Ultimately, this approach expands teachers' visions of their students' capabilities.

The authors of this book bring us something rare in their lively tour of schools, districts, college campuses, and larger networks. Rather than instances where teachers simply learn a set of strategies, the authors offer powerful examples of professional learning communities engaging in deep inquiry into the many ways of reading and responding to texts in different disciplines. They show us how these reading inquiries can lead not only to profound changes for students in individual classrooms but also across schools, systems, and state-wide networks.

Teacher leaders, administrators, and others interested in building strong inquiry communities to strengthen disciplinary literacy will find many practical steps, examples, and insights for adapting their own Reading Apprenticeship work. Readers will also find stories of teachers' and administrators' resourcefulness and persistence throughout this book.

As someone who has advocated for this kind of embedded and reflective professional development for years, I especially appreciate several of the themes the authors explore in *Leading for Literacy*:

- Building teachers' *generative knowledge* — beyond learning to employ a set of reading strategies in classrooms, teachers become able to make the kind of moment-to-moment professional judgments needed to help students develop dispositions necessary for academic engagement and success;

- Creating clear structures for collaborative work among teams of teachers who are working to improve their practice, and grounding that work in classroom-based formative assessment;

- Encouraging teachers to spend time not only discussing student work and lesson designs, but also to focus on close examination of their own reading processes, with challenging texts in their disciplines;

- Emphasizing the importance of teacher leadership, teacher–administrator collaboration, and administrators' involvement to support and sustain a new intervention, like the Reading Apprenticeship Framework; and

- Acknowledging the real impact of initiative fatigue and helping educators understand how Reading Apprenticeship is at the leading edge of school improvement initiatives and can serve to bring other initiatives together.

Stepping into the stories and hard-won lessons of this book, I found myself encouraged by visions of hopeful futures for our middle schools, high schools, and colleges — with vibrant professional learning at the core. I hope you will find some of that same inspiration here.

Stephanie Hirsh
Executive Director
Learning Forward

Preface

WHAT DOES it take to organize and promote a culture of literacy throughout a school, a district, or a college campus? How can one person or a committed small group get started, engage others, and sustain a focus on improved disciplinary literacy? And what can be learned from the experiences of others who have successfully spread deep change in classroom practice across many different contexts?

This book provides tools, examples, and some principles to help spread the benefits of a research proven instructional approach—Reading Apprenticeship —that sparks students' engaged reading and thinking across disciplines and from middle school through college. As a companion to the landmark *Reading for Understanding*, this book guides teacher leaders and administrators through the nuts and bolts, benefits and challenges of creating Reading Apprenticeship communities that can extend a culture of literacy beyond individual classrooms.

In *Leading for Literacy*, we explain how to generate authentic buy-in from teachers and administrators, use the Reading Apprenticeship Framework to turn reform overload into reform coherence, and create literacy teams, professional learning communities, and Reading Apprenticeship communities of practice that sustain an institutional focus on a student-centered, strengths-based culture of literacy.

Key insights from Reading Apprenticeship practitioners across the country address getting started, building momentum, assessing progress, and building partnerships and networks across schools, districts, campuses, and regions. Tools and approaches developed by WestEd's Strategic Literacy Initiative provide concrete help for building knowledgeable teams and creating coherence across system priorities:

- How to integrate Reading Apprenticeship with existing reform efforts;

- How to use formative assessment to promote teacher and student growth;

- How to coach and empower teachers;

- How to cultivate literacy leadership; and

- How to provide support for a strong, long-term, content-literacy program.

Nationwide classroom research on Reading Apprenticeship[1] has shown that the approach promotes literacy, content knowledge, and motivation — leading to better student outcomes that reach beyond classroom walls.

What You Need to Know Before Reading This Book

Many readers may be familiar with Reading Apprenticeship through our website www.readingapprenticeship.org or our book about classroom practice—*Reading for Understanding: How Reading Apprenticeship Improves Disciplinary Literacy in Secondary and College Classrooms*. Others may have participated in some related professional learning. And still others may be picking up this book as a general introduction for leading school- or system-level literacy improvements. Whatever the case, this book, like the Reading Apprenticeship Framework, suggests a unique *approach* to enacting change—not a regimented program or particular set of materials. In diverse settings and across a wide range of situations, the Reading Apprenticeship Framework is a powerful tool for designing classroom and professional learning. Its implementation is a continuous process of inquiry and reflection and is most successfully accomplished in the company of others.

What Is the Reading Apprenticeship Framework?

A full explanation of the Reading Apprenticeship Framework can be found on the Reading Apprenticeship website[2] and in Chapter Two of our earlier book, *Reading for Understanding*.

The Reading Apprenticeship Framework emphasizes these approaches:

- Making students' reading processes, motivations, strategies, knowledge, and understandings visible to the teacher and to other students;

- Helping students gain and learn to use insight into their own reading processes;

- Helping students develop a repertoire of problem-solving strategies for overcoming obstacles and deepening comprehension of texts from various academic disciplines; and

- Making the teacher's discipline-based reading processes and discourse knowledge visible to students.

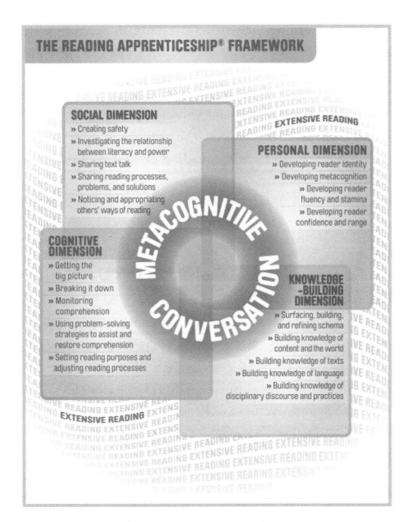

Figure 1   The Reading Apprenticeship Framework

Figure 1 is a snapshot of the Framework's key elements. The Framework's four interacting dimensions of learning—social, personal, cognitive, and knowledge-building—reflect the importance of supporting learners' affective as well as cognitive learning processes.

The Social Dimension addresses community building in the classroom, including recognizing the resources brought by each member and developing a safe environment for students to be open about their reading difficulties.

The Personal Dimension includes developing students' identities and self-awareness as readers, as well as their purposes for reading and goals for reading improvement.

The Cognitive Dimension focuses on developing readers' mental processes, including their problem-solving strategies.

The Knowledge-Building Dimension supports students in identifying and expanding the kinds of knowledge that readers bring to a text and further develop through interaction with that text.

Within and across these dimensions, the Framework promotes metacognitive conversation: through internal metacognitive conversation, students learn how to monitor their reading comprehension; through external metacognitive conversation, students learn from the reading processes of others and collaborate to build knowledge.

All of this takes place in the context of extensive in-class opportunities for students to practice reading in more skillful ways.

How Have Educators Been Involved in the Development of Reading Apprenticeship?

For more than twenty-five years, teachers have been our partners in thinking about the Reading Apprenticeship Framework, in trying out tools for best implementing it, in helping to define the elements of effective professional learning, and by participating in numerous research studies that lend validity to and guide the continuous improvement of Reading Apprenticeship.

In the past decade, WestEd's Strategic Literacy Initiative, the developer of Reading Apprenticeship, has won five multiyear federal grants to increase and study the reach of Reading Apprenticeship. The largest of these, Reading Apprenticeship Improving Secondary Literacy (RAISE), was designed to study a five-state scale-up of Reading Apprenticeship. RAISE impacted close to 2,000 teachers and over 600,000 students. Secondary schools in the study worked to sustain a focus on disciplinary literacy while increasing and sustaining Reading Apprenticeship implementation with fidelity for multiple years. Many RAISE teachers and administrators share their experiences in this book.

Other voices in these pages are those of teachers and administrators whose schools or districts have contracted with us, the Strategic Literacy Initiative at WestEd, for professional development and coaching services. The community college practitioners represented here include instructors who helped us design our first forays into postsecondary settings, as well as more recent partners and faculty members who are now helping design campus-wide first-year experience programs, tutoring programs, acceleration programs, and a range of curriculum reform efforts.

Administrators, too, have contributed to our learning about how to effect literacy improvement and education change. In the most successful implementations of Reading Apprenticeship, administrators are active, knowledgeable participants on literacy teams and advocates for long-term support of teacher learning. You will hear from many of them.

How Is This Book Organized?

In this book we address questions about how to implement deep changes in teaching—Reading Apprenticeship in this case—and we present ideas about multiple implementation paths. Broadly speaking, the book offers three chapters that explore guidelines and examples for successful Reading Apprenticeship implementation (Chapters One, Two, and Seven), one chapter that grounds the rationale for our approach to professional learning (Chapter Three), and three chapters that present tools for implementation (Chapters Four, Five, and Six).

Chapter One, "How to Start?" sketches paths schools and colleges have taken toward implementation. These include models where teachers lead, where impetus for change comes from administrators, and where external pressures can be used to meet internal goals. Chapter Two, "Partnering for Leadership," considers the roles of administrators and teacher leaders in promoting buy-in for deep, school-wide change. Chapter Three, "The Role of Inquiry in Reading Apprenticeship Professional Learning," presents the rationale and theoretical foundation for the approach to professional learning we advocate and describe in the following three chapters.

The first of these tools chapters is Chapter Four, "Setting the Social and Personal Foundations for Inquiry." It offers guidelines for creating conditions for productive adult learning. Chapter Five, "Exploring Reading as Colleagues," moves to the core practice that distinguishes Reading Apprenticeship professional learning. We urge readers who are committed to implementing Reading Apprenticeship to make this chapter the center of their work. We believe that when school leadership teams attempt to work on system-level change without practicing the core Reading Apprenticeship routine of *making your thinking visible* with varied types of texts, the implementation loses power. A more typical and very important aspect of professional exchange, talking about teaching, is the focus of Chapter Six, "Exploring Instruction as Colleagues." Included are many protocols for looking closely at practice and at student work and for building pedagogical knowledge.

Chapter Seven, "Building Capacity, Momentum, and Sustainability," addresses some of the most challenging—and productive—aspects of implementing Reading Apprenticeship at a systemic level. Here we offer examples of districts and schools where this work is playing out in ways unique to local contexts and with lessons, we hope, for others.

Acknowledgments

We like to think of the Strategic Literacy Initiative as a professional learning community where staff members' good will, good humor, and dedication to our collective work contribute to all we do. These particular past and current staff were instrumental in supporting the development of this book: Willard Brown, Irisa Charney-Sirott, Gayle Cribb, Gina Hale, Heather Howlett, Rita Jensen, Margot Kenaston, Diane Lee, Cindy Litman, Kate Meissert, Mary Stump, and Lorelle Wien. We also include our partners at home, Lynn Eden, Paul King, and Peter Shwartz, who encourage us without fail in devoting ourselves to this work that we love.

For particular participation in the life of this book, we thank Nika Hogan, who coordinates our community college work, for her invaluable insights and introductions to the growing network of college faculty implementing Reading Apprenticeship. We also call special attention to the roles played by our colleagues in the five-state, five-year federal Investing in Innovation (i3) grant—Reading Apprenticeship Improving Secondary Education (RAISE)—multistate coordinator Cathleen Kral, and statewide coordinators Susan Kinney and Melissa Devlin of Pennsylvania, Bill Loyd of Michigan, and Donna Walker of Indiana. The warm professional relationships they developed over many, many statewide RAISE teacher leader meetings and visits to schools and classrooms gave us access to those same schools and classrooms for dozens of the interviews for this book, not a few of which Sue and Bill conducted.

More than anything, *Leading for Literacy* represents the work and feedback of hundreds of teachers and administrators who directly helped us think through the challenges of building learning communities in which the Reading Apprenticeship Framework guides a sustained focus on literacy. We thank them deeply—for their generosity allowing us into their schools and classrooms, for their teaching chops, and for the difference they make in the lives of their students.

Contributing Teachers and Administrators

The educators listed below contributed directly and generously to the shaping and content of this book. Many are quoted throughout.

Myriam Altounji: Counselor, Pasadena City College, Pasadena, Calif.

Heather M. Arena: Teacher of English, Exeter Township Senior High School, Exeter, Penn.

Gretchen Bajorek: Literacy Coordinator, Edsel Ford High School, Dearborn, Mich.

Dianna Behl: New Tech Director/ Assistant Principal, Pinckney Community High School; Pinckney Community Schools, Instructional Coach, Pinckney, Mich.

Scott Buchler: Principal, Northwest High School, Jackson, Mich.

Arlene Buchman: Coordinator of Professional Development 6-12, Souderton Area School District, Souderton, Penn.

Krista Carey: Reading Specialist, Abington High School, Abington, Penn.

Scott M. Casebolt: Principal, Edsel Ford High School, Dearborn, Mich.

Angela Church: As cited: Teacher of Grade 9 U.S. History, Berkley High School, Berkley, Mich. Currently: Reading Apprenticeship and Instructional Coach, Berkley High School.

Ann Coe: Assistant Principal, Holt High School, Holt, Mich.

Kay Cole: Teacher of English and Teacher Coach, Berkley High School, Berkley, Mich.

Amanda Corcoran: Instructor of English, American River College, Sacramento, Calif.

Anna Corral: Principal, Anaheim High School, Anaheim, Calif.

Jackie Counts: District English Curriculum Specialist, Anaheim Union High School District, Anaheim, Calif.

Rob Cushman: Teacher of Biology, Wyomissing Area Junior/Senior High School, Wyomissing, Penn.

Scott Davie: As cited: Principal, Titusville High School, Titusville, Penn. Currently: School Counselor, Talawanda High School, Oxford, Ohio.

Julie Deppner: As cited: Principal, Chelsea High School, Chelsea, Mich. Currently: Assistant Superintendent, Chelsea School District.

Melissa Devlin: As cited: Teacher of Reading and English and Literacy Coach, Wyomissing Area Junior/ Senior High School, Wyomissing, Penn. Currently: Director of Curriculum, Instruction, and Literacy, Antietam School District, Reading, Penn.; and Pennsylvania State Coordinator, Strategic Literacy Initiative.

David Donohue: As cited: Professor of Education, Mills College, Oakland, Calif. Currently: Senior Director of the Leo T. McCarthy Center for Public Service and the Common Good and Professor of Education, University of San Francisco.

Catherine England: Faculty, Adult Basic Education, Everett Community College, Everett, Wash.

Kevin English: Teacher, Wayne-Westland Community School District, Wayne, Mich.

Moninda Eslick: Academic Facilitator, Francis Bradley Middle School, Huntersville, N.C.

Tess Ferrara: As cited: Teacher of English and Teacher Coach, Berkley High School, Berkley, Mich. Currently: Literacy Consultant.

Ann Foster: Instructor of English, Santa Rosa Junior College, Santa Rosa, Calif.

Tracy Francis: As cited: Teacher of Science and Teacher Coach, Berkley High School, Berkley, Mich. Currently: Educational Consultant.

Shawn Frederking: Instructor of English, Yuba College, Yuba City, Calif.

Charlene Frontiera: Dean of Mathematics and Science, College of San Mateo, San Mateo, Calif.

Randall Gawel: Principal, Berkley High School, Berkley, Mich.

Janet Ghio: Consultant, Strategic Literacy Initiative, WestEd, Oakland, Calif.

Jake Gilboy: Social Studies Department Head, Abington High School, Abington, Penn.

Emily Gonzalez: Professor in the Natural Science Department, Northern Essex Community College, Lawrence, Mass.

Rebecca Graf: Director of Humanities, Charlotte-Mecklenberg Schools, Charlotte, N.C.

Debbie Harman: Director of Student Learning, Brown County Schools, Nashville, Ind.

Lilit Haroyan: Associate Professor of Physics and Astronomy, East Los Angeles College, Montery, Calif.

Joan Herman: Instructor of English, Lower Columbia College, Longview, Wash.

Katie Hern: English Instructor, Chabot College, Oakland, Calif.; and California Acceleration Project Co-Founder.

Cindy Hicks: Emerita Instructor of English, Chabot College, Oakland, Calif.

Nika Hogan: Associate Professor of English, Pasadena City College, Pasadena, Calif.; Community College National Coordinator, Strategic Literacy Initiative; Reading Apprenticeship Project Director, 3CSN.

Tiffany Ingle: Instructor of English as a Second Language, Pasadena City College and Glendale Community College, Pasadena and Glendale, Calif.

Sara K. Jones: Teacher of Social Studies, Titusville High School, Titusville, Penn.

Vicki Jones: Director of Language Arts Services, Abington School District, Abington, Penn.

Amy Keith-Wardlow: Literacy Coordinator, Fordson High School, Dearborn, Mich.

Charles Kolbusz: Assistant Principal, West Senior High School, Traverse City, Mich.

Lisa Krebs: Teacher of English, Dixon High School, Dixon, Calif.

Becky Leist: Administrator, Concord Academy-Boyne, Boyne City, Mich.

Michele Lesmeister: Faculty, Basic Studies Department, Renton Technical College, Renton, Wash.

Mary Ann Liberati: Consultant, Strategic Literacy Initiative, WestEd, Oakland, Calif.

Laurie Lintner: Literacy Coordinator, Dearborn High School, Dearborn, Mich.

Theresa Martin: Professor of Biology, College of San Mateo, San Mateo, Calif.

Walter Masuda: Dean of Arts, Humanities, and Education, Yuba College, Yuba City, Calif.

Michael Matsuda: Superintendent, Anaheim Union High School District, Anaheim, Calif.

Beth May: Instructional Coach, Avon High School, Avon, Ind.

Andy McCutcheon: As cited: Instructor of English, College of the Canyons, Santa Clarita, Calif. Currently: Interim Dean, School of Humanities, College of the Canyons.

Ryan McMahon: Principal, Milan High School, Milan, Mich.

Cindy Miceli: Teacher of Science, Anaheim High School, Anaheim, Calif.

Allyson Morcom: Teacher of World Studies, Abington High School, Abington, Penn.

Catherine Morrison: Literacy Coordinator for Middle Schools, Dearborn Public Schools, Dearborn, Mich.

Youssef Mosallam: Principal, Fordson High School, Dearborn, Mich.

Barbara Moss: Teacher of Biology, Abington High School, Abington, Penn.

Kathleen Motoike: Instructor of English, Santa Monica College, Santa Monica, Calif.

Naomi Norman: Interim Assistant Superintendent, Achievement and Student Services, Washtenaw ISD and Livingston ESA, Mich.

Chris Padgett: Professor of History, American River College, Sacramento, Calif.

David Pfaff: Principal, Eastern Hancock High School, Charlottesville, Ind.

Daniel S. Pittaway: Student Success Coordinator, Coastline Community College, Westminster, Calif.

Dawn Putnam: Teacher of English, Chelsea High School, Chelsea, Mich.

Julia Raddatz: Principal, Manistee High School and K–12 Curriculum/Testing Director, Manistee, Mich.

Shane Ramey: Professor of Biology, College of the Canyons, Santa Clarita, Calif.

Harley Ramsey: Principal, Otto-Eldred Junior-Senior High School, Duke Center, Penn.

Curtis Refior: Consultant, Strategic Literacy Initiative, WestEd, Oakland, Calif.

Allyson Robinson: As cited: Assistant Principal, Harrison High School, Farmington Hills, Mich. Currently: Principal, Power Upper Elementary School, Farmington Hills, Mich.

Kellie Rodkey: Assistant Principal, Avon High School, Avon, Ind.

Wayne Roedel: Superintendent, Fowlerville Community Schools, Fowlerville, Mich.

Marcia Rogers: Instructor of English, Orange Coast College, Costa Mesa, Calif.

Shelagh Rose: Associate Professor of English as a Second Language and First Year Pathways Faculty Lead, Pasadena City College, Pasadena, Calif.

Alicia Ross: Teacher of History, Blue Ridge High School, New Milford, Penn.

Adina Rubenstein: Teacher of Science and Teacher Coach, Berkley High School, Berkley, Mich.

Janet Rummel: Chief Academic Officer, Goodwill Education Initiatives, Indianapolis, Ind.

Abdiel Salazar: Teacher of Grade 6, Freemont Elementary School, Stockton, Calif.

Patricia Schade: Professor of Academic Preparation, Northern Essex Community College, Lawrence, Mass.

Melody Schneider: Fulltime Faculty of High School Completion Department and Faculty Development Coordinator, Edmonds Community College, Lynnwood, Wash.

Lauren Servais: Instructor of English, Santa Rosa Community College, Santa Rosa, Calif.

David Simancek: Principal, Swartz Creek Academy, Swartz Creek, Mich.

Kristine Simons: As cited: Principal, Covert High School, Covert, Mich. Currently: Assistant Superintendent, Curriculum and Instruction, Benton Harbor Area Schools, Benton Harbor, Mich.

Debbie Swanson: Reading Apprenticeship Teacher Leader, Willow Run 6–8 Intermediate Learning Center, Willow Run, Mich.

Jennifer Taylor-Mendoza: Dean of Academic Support and Learning Technologies, College of San Mateo, San Mateo, Calif.

Eric Turman: Principal, Reading High School, Reading, Penn.

Ricci Ulrich: Principal, Buchanan High School, Clovis, Calif.

Samuel A. Varano, Jr.: Principal, Souderton Area High School, Souderton, Penn.

Julia Vicente: Superintendent, Wyomissing Area School District, Wyomissing, Penn.

Shelley Warkentin: English Language Arts and Literacy K–12 Consultant, Manitoba Ministry of Education and Advanced Learning, Manitoba, Canada.

Kay Winter: Literacy Coach and English Department Chair, Anderson High School, Anderson, Ind.

Lori Wojtowicz: Teacher of English, Huron High School, Ann Arbor, Mich., retired.

Douglas Womelsdorf: As cited: Teacher of Science, Pleasant Valley High School, Pleasant Valley, Penn. Currently: Science Curriculum Specialist, Northeastern Educational Intermediate Unit (PA IU19).

Notes

1. Four randomized controlled trials of Reading Apprenticeship have found statistically significant mediating impacts of Reading Apprenticeship teacher professional development on student achievement:

   Fancsali, C., Abe, Y., Pyatigorsky, M., Ortiz, L., Chan, V., Saltares, E., Toby, M., Schellinger, A., & Jaciw, A. P. (2015). *The impact of the Reading Apprenticeship Improving Secondary Education (RAISE) project on academic literacy in high school: A report of a randomized experiment in Pennsylvania and California schools.* (Empirical Edcuation Rep.No. Empirical_RAISE-7019-FR1-OO.2). Palo Alto, CA: Empirical Education Inc.

   Greenleaf, C., Hanson, T., Herman, J., Litman, C., Rosen, R., Schneider, S., & Silver, D. (2011). *A study of the efficacy of Reading Apprenticeship professional development for high school history and science teaching and learning.* Final report to Institute for Education Sciences, National Center for Education Research, Teacher Quality/Reading and Writing, Grant # R305M050031.

   Greenleaf, C., Litman, C., Hanson, T., Rosen, R., Boscardin, C. K., Herman, J., Schneider, S., with Madden, S., & Jones, B. (2011). Integrating literacy and science in biology: Teaching and learning impacts of Reading Apprenticeship professional development. *American Educational Research Journal, 48,* 647–717.

   Somers, M.-A., Corrin, W., Sepanik, S., Salinger, T., Levin, J., & Zmach, C., with Wong, E. (2010). *The enhanced reading opportunities study final report: The impact of supplemental literacy courses for struggling ninth-grade readers* (NCEE #2010-4021). Washington, DC: National Center for Education Evaluation and Regional Assistance, Institute of Education Sciences, U.S. Department of Education.

2. *Reading for Understanding* Chapter 2: The Reading Apprenticeship Framework is a free download available from the Reading Apprenticeship website: http://readingapprenticeship.org/wp-content/uploads/2014/01/RFU-Ch-2-Excerpt.pdf

Leading for Literacy

CHAPTER ONE

How to Start?

We want reading to be woven into the fabric of what is happening on our campus, to put reading into every conversation about student success, whether it is equity, first-year experience, basic skills, even accreditation—and to connect those conversations and initiatives.

—Chris Padgett, American River College history instructor

DISCIPLINARY READING—the reading that middle school, high school, and college teachers assign day after day in class after class—is foundational to students' success. For anyone in doubt, new academic standards and workforce expectations make the demand for academic literacy emphatically clear. What is less clear is how to support students to achieve that literacy-based, future-oriented success.

For many if not most administrators, teachers, students, and parents, these new expectations may require a paradigm shift in understanding how learning happens best. This shift includes new ways of thinking about the relationship of literacy to subject area content, students' and teachers' roles in learning, and, most important, students' potential for critical thinking and disciplinary reasoning. Change of this depth cannot spread beyond a few classrooms and is not sustainable without system-level support.

The Reading Apprenticeship Framework,[1] developed to promote students' engaged academic literacy, has a solid history of catalyzing this kind of transformative change—for individuals and within institutions.

Taking Up Transformational Change

Reading Apprenticeship makes a difference in the way people teach and the way kids learn, but it's not something you can say, "We're doing this tomorrow," and have it be done tomorrow. It takes time and energy, and some patience and commitment from all parties involved.

—Randy Gawel, Berkley High School principal

To implement and scale up meaningful change in classrooms, teachers must deeply understand and own the goals and principles of such change. Many interventions focus on structural or cultural change in school climate or governance as the way to improve student outcomes. Other interventions focus on improving students' engagement and achievement by changing what happens in the classroom. Reading Apprenticeship is in this second category, with a focus on transforming classroom interactions between teachers and students, between students and their peers, and between students and texts of all types.

As an intervention with an explicit focus on changing classroom practice, Reading Apprenticeship takes a strengths-based approach to how both teachers and students learn. Reading Apprenticeship first shows teachers how to make visible the "invisible" knowledge they already have of how to read with rich comprehension in their own content areas. This process then enables teachers to help students become aware of their own thinking processes, giving them confidence and skills to solve comprehension problems and to read more deeply.

To take the risks involved in trying out new ways of teaching, teachers need significant support from their schools and districts. Such support includes new *structures*, such as dedicated literacy teams and communities of practice, and more *time* to engage in high-quality professional learning, professional collaboration, and problem solving with colleagues. These challenging professional activities also require *political cover* on the part of site and district administrators to protect teams and their time from challenges that may arise in the community or at higher levels in the system.

Successful education reform includes the awareness that each school, district, and college campus is particular and resists cookie-cutter replication of even the most rigorously proven interventions. A context-sensitive approach to Reading Apprenticeship implementation calls for a balance of flexibility and fidelity. Teachers and systems require the flexibility to make Reading Apprenticeship their own. At the same time, for interventions to be effective, integrity to the core principles is crucial. We have seen and heard about too many "toxic mutations" of Reading Apprenticeship not to urge educators to keep the key elements of Reading Apprenticeship—the Framework, an inquiry stance, and a strengths-based approach—front and center. Without these core principles, implementation cannot achieve the powerful change that is required to improve learning for a large number of students.

In this chapter, we offer examples to suggest how educators in secondary schools and on college campuses can start to extend Reading Apprenticeship into the broader system in which they work. Familiar questions surface:

- How can teachers, convinced from their own experience of the effectiveness of Reading Apprenticeship, create opportunities for *genuine* buy-in from other teachers and administrators?

- Are there ways administrators can initiate classroom change without the well-known pitfalls of top-down implementation?

- How can leadership teams turn external mandates into positive steps to meet their own goals for change?

- How can schools incorporate Reading Apprenticeship without adding to reform overload?

As we take up these questions, it is with the understanding that the avenues for introducing Reading Apprenticeship are different at the secondary and college levels. Each institutional structure creates different opportunities for instructional leadership and supports professional learning in parallel but different ways.

Leading Change at the Middle and High School Level

> Reading Apprenticeship can't be seen as an extra program, it can't be seen as a one-off. It has to be embedded into professional development and revisited.
> —Janet Rummel, Chief Academic Officer for
> Goodwill Education Initiatives, Excel Centers[2]

Reading Apprenticeship sometimes spreads from one or two teachers at a middle or high school who have discovered Reading Apprenticeship on their own and are sharing it informally with colleagues. More commonly administrators concerned about students' academic literacy hear about Reading Apprenticeship through professional connections and make the decision to bring it to their faculty, often as an experiment for a few teachers to try but sometimes with top-down expectations for wider implementation.

Whether the initial energy to address student literacy comes from teachers or administrators, for that energy to grow, others in the system need to see evidence that local classrooms are changing and students are benefiting. So, for example, teachers who have felt frustrated with their ability to support their students' disciplinary literacy but then experience success using Reading Apprenticeship approaches need opportunities to share with colleagues what they and their students are learning.

If schools already have professional learning structures in place, such as professional learning communities or department teams, these can be a base for bringing attention to disciplinary literacy and strengthening what it means to collaborate for the benefit of students. And if Reading Apprenticeship arrives at a school or district as more of an expectation than an invitation, increased support for teacher learning and shared administrative and faculty responsibility can create safe space for taking on the challenge of transforming educational practice.

Building Excitement from Teacher to Teacher

Secondary school administrators who have shepherded Reading Apprenticeship implementation cite teacher-to-teacher excitement as the bottom line for success. They find that the enthusiasm of teachers whose students are benefiting from Reading Apprenticeship is highly contagious.

When Randy Gawel was a relatively new principal at Berkley High School, he received an announcement that a team from his school could participate at no cost in a literacy professional development study.[3] He asked two teachers for their opinions of the offer. The teachers were impressed, so he forwarded the announcement to the entire staff. Those two teachers and three others replied that they were interested in spending a week of their summer vacation learning about Reading Apprenticeship and getting ready to try it out in their classes.

Randy remembers the energy those five teachers brought to the beginning-of-the-year staff meeting when he asked faculty members to describe what they were looking forward to: "Every one of those Reading Apprenticeship teachers independently said—and these were great teachers—'I'm looking forward to implementing Reading Apprenticeship in my classroom, and it's going to change the way I teach, and it's going to change it for the better.'"

Over the following school year the five teachers worked as a team to implement Reading Apprenticeship in their own classes. They deliberately avoided trying to train staff. Instead, with the support of their principal, they shared with their colleagues what they were experiencing and what they were excited about.

At Chelsea High School, it was also the principal, Julie Deppner, now Chelsea district assistant superintendent, who learned about Reading Apprenticeship through her administrative network. But again, it was well-regarded teachers who primed the pump for what Julie calls "a huge cultural shift at the school." (See Close-Up 1.1, Priming the Pump at Chelsea High School.)

CLOSE-UP 1.1

Priming the Pump at Chelsea High School

At Chelsea High School in Chelsea, Michigan, it took only two teachers to prime the pump for what principal Julie Deppner calls "a huge culture shift."

> I certainly had to pick the right people to start off in the Reading Apprenticeship model, teachers who were excited about it and well respected by their peers—and then trust them. They took ownership of Reading Apprenticeship, and we embraced it after hearing them talk about what they were doing in their classrooms.

The two teachers who became the Reading Apprenticeship pioneers supported one another in the ups and downs of trying a new teaching approach. Their principal encouraged them to share what was happening in their classes with the staff. When Reading Apprenticeship professional development was made available to more staff, a combi-nation of concrete results and peer pressure turned the tide. Julie describes the teacher-to-teacher nature of scaling up Reading Apprenticeship at the school:

> We had two teachers from the math department that went to the training because they just wanted to be better teachers. They said, "If this can have an impact on what I'm doing in my classroom, I want to go." They came back excited, and they sold it to others in the department.
>
> Teachers saw it was great for kids. If you hadn't gone to the training, you felt like you were missing out. You wouldn't know what they were talking about in the teacher's lounge. Reading Apprenticeship has changed the way our teachers teach and the way they think about learning.

As Sam Varrano, principal of Souderton High School, points out, when pioneer teachers have the opportunity to share their Reading Apprenticeship experiences with the rest of the staff, a persuasive appraisal will include the challenges as well as the benefits of learning new practices:

> We looked for teachers we knew would embrace it, our very best lunatic-type people, and who would promote it when they were being successful and honestly share their setbacks so we could get better.

By offering these pioneer teachers' experiences to other staff, and making it clear the administration held them in high regard, Sam was able to convince a strategically important second group of teachers—whose peers would recognize them as typically more reluctant to try new things—to give Reading Apprenticeship a chance. "Once you get those people on board and they're talking highly of it," he says, "there's no stopping that momentum."

Building on Existing School Culture and Structures

Increasingly, secondary schools support teacher learning with structures such as professional learning communities and literacy teams. Reading Apprenticeship's inquiry model of professional development can be an organic way to animate this kind of faculty collaboration.

The Reading Apprenticeship teacher leaders at Berkley High School are quick to credit the school's history of collaboration as an important factor in their evolution as a team—and in their colleagues' openness to the Reading Apprenticeship literacy teams they have nurtured. Teacher leader Angie Church tracks the school's move toward collaboration from her vantage point of sixteen years on the staff:

> Over the course of those years we moved from a school of all teachers who taught in isolation to a building in which teachers talked to each other about what they were doing in their classrooms. We had content professional teams throughout our building. It seems super simple, but that's huge. Because we were immersed in it, we might not have noticed how big that was.

Buchanan High School is another school where professional learning communities (PLCs) long predated Reading Apprenticeship. At the same time, however, Buchanan's principal, Ricci Ulrich, worried that the PLCs had lost some of their edge as learning communities. The Reading Apprenticeship model of teacher inquiry, she says, has brought new life and meaning to the school's PLCs:

> We've always had a very collaborative staff. Since its inception Buchanan has had teacher time to work together built into the school day. But over a number of years, it was a lot of informational meetings and department meetings, but not working in teams or establishing a set of common goals or really going after an instructional model with something that tells us the kids are having success.
>
> Now when teachers are meeting as PLCs, it's a much different conversation. I believe Reading Apprenticeship helped us establish goals and become diagnostic. The focus is on what the kids are doing, very specifically tied to literacy. That's a big culture shift for us. This is very authentic, very different, and ties back to the adults having a higher level conversation about what we can do instructionally so students have more success.

Top-Down Change as a Positive Path?

Although many stories of successful Reading Apprenticeship implementation initially involve small numbers of teachers or faculty, there are also cases at the secondary level in which administrators have successfully introduced Reading

Apprenticeship and still managed to avoid faculty skepticism or resistance that sometimes typifies mandated professional learning initiatives.

David Pffaf, principal of Eastern Hancock Middle School and High School in rural Charlottesville, Indiana, heard about a high school grant-funded Reading Apprenticeship professional development opportunity from an acquaintance at the Indiana Department of Education and decided to investigate. Convinced that the Reading Apprenticeship program addressed the needs of his school's students, he worked to persuade his staff, laying out students' reading competence as the school's overriding academic responsibility:

> There's just nothing our kids are going to do when they leave here where reading is not going to be an essential, foundational skill. So what is there that we can do that would be more valuable to our kids than to give them this tool, this ability to read something that is not easy to read? I can't think of a job we have that's more important.

Eastern Hancock is a small high school, with only thirty-two teachers. None of them escaped David's vision for advancing the school's literacy culture, and he included himself as a learner along with his teachers:

> If the principal doesn't believe this is really, really important, then don't bother. The principal has to be fully in. The principal can't send some teachers off and then be done with it.

In another small school district, the superintendent and the principal of the combined junior–senior high school took steps to initiate a focus on literacy after interviews with local employers and nearby colleges and universities led them to understand that improved academic literacy was the most important service they could bring to their community. They found Reading Apprenticeship as a place to start. To signal district commitment, principal Harley Ramsey participated with faculty members in Reading Apprenticeship professional development and further prepared to lead the effort by taking a Reading Apprenticeship course designed specifically for principals. (See Close-Up 1.2, Leading from Community Needs.)

When principals, district leaders, or a team of teacher leaders and others can communicate a strong vision and provide teachers with time and support to learn about and try out Reading Apprenticeship for themselves, a top-down approach can lead to positive results. The only way this can work, however, is if supports are in place to help teachers grow into new practices that involve deep changes in their professional identify, their ways of relating to students, and sometimes in their conception of their discipline.

CLOSE-UP 1.2

Leading from Community Needs

At Pennsylvania's small Otto-Eldred School District, administrators were concerned that the teaching and learning there had stagnated. In a community with intergenerational poverty and high unemployment, they wanted to be sure their graduates would be prepared to meet the demands of local employers and higher education. Superintendent Matt Splain and high school principal Harley Ramsey met with leaders from regional industries and colleges to find out what they wanted from incoming employees and students. What they found out, Harley says, led the district to a tight focus on literacy. "We asked a few very basic questions: What are you looking for—what types of education, what types of skills? We took all that information and synthesized it. The areas of need boiled down to content area literacy."

Working backward from this community input, the district administrators asked themselves what they needed to provide from an experiential and curriculum standpoint to make sure that students would be truly college and career ready. "That's when we started looking at adjusting our curriculum, adjusting our pathways," says Harley. "That's when I first started looking at Reading Apprenticeship."

Harley echoes a point that other school leaders have made when using Reading Apprenticeship for deep school-wide change.

You can't approach it as, "We are going to be doing Reading Apprenticeship." It has to be literacy, and then the model that you're using is the Reading Apprenticeship model. Initiatives come and go, but literacy has to stand.

Once teachers understand, "Okay, this is our objective, this is our duty, this is where we're going from a literacy perspective," then they'll see, "Oh, Reading Apprenticeship fits that perfectly. Why wouldn't we use it?"

One of the advantages of a top-down approach to such innovations is the opportunity to build systems of support that include in-depth professional learning, curriculum, coaching and feedback, and explicit articulation with teacher evaluation.

Two examples of Reading Apprenticeship implementations that have been designed for large-scale rollout and comprehensive support are described in Chapter Seven. These models, from Canada's Manitoba Province (see "Building Capacity System-wide: A Canadian Case Study") and the 18,000-teacher Charlotte-Mecklenburg Schools (see "Building Momentum for a District-wide Rollout"), generously invest institutional resources in the service of deep, iterative teacher learning.

Opportunities for Scale-Up at the Community College Level

Our campus is a place now where more faculty who aren't in the reading department are willing to concede that their students need help.

—Amanda Corcoran, American River College English instructor

Compared with their colleagues in secondary schools, college faculty members enjoy considerable instructional autonomy, and they have many more opportunities for initiating instructional change within and beyond their classroom walls. Interest in Reading Apprenticeship on a college campus typically begins with one or two entrepreneurial instructors willing to engage others and then leverage initial interest across departments or into campus-wide programs.

Originally, Reading Apprenticeship found its way onto college campuses as a way to address the literacy needs of underprepared students. Its use has spread from remedial applications into a wide range of subject area departments. Many instructors are starting to see that their own disciplinary ways of reading can be a powerful resource for apprenticing students. Additionally, colleges' attention to student engagement and a focus in recent years on growth mindsets and productive persistence has helped faculty see how the Reading Apprenticeship Framework's attention to the social and personal dimensions of classroom life and metacognitive conversation connect to goals they and their colleagues have for their students.

Reading Apprenticeship is also becoming more common in campus-wide programs like new-faculty seminars and student first-year experience courses that depend on a design partnership between faculty and college administrators.

Statewide networks for the scale-up of Reading Apprenticeship on college campuses are also emerging. As described in Chapter Seven, this work is supported by a vibrant California network (see "Communities of Practice: An Educator-Led, State-Supported Network") and another that is building momentum in Washington. (See "Building a Statewide Network from a Spark.")

Inviting Colleagues to Take a Look

Many college faculty are keenly aware of how little they have been prepared to apply learning theory and effective instructional practices to the disciplinary expertise they have developed. Concerns about students' needs for literacy support are particularly vexing.

Biology instructor Shane Ramey's experience is representative of what college faculty are increasingly recognizing as a new responsibility to their students. Shane teaches honors molecular and cellular biology at College of the Canyons. He was uneasy about whether his advanced students were understanding the course content:

> I asked my students to raise their hands if they had read either—or both—of the two chapters we were scheduled to cover during the day's lecture. I was disappointed, but not surprised, that not a single student raised a hand.

At American River College, a campus-wide survey asked instructors to take a look at their students as readers. The survey is designed to create a portrait of students' expectations, preparation, and the background they bring to courses where faculty assign academic reading. Instructor Chris Padgett, co-director of the campus Reading Apprenticeship Project, says the reading survey, developed with the college reading and research divisions, is useful because it offers a fairly quick, efficient portrait of the state of reading on campus. "With any luck," Chris says, "it will have an effect on the ways folks think about reading here and its place in the overall goal of student success."

Inviting faculty members to take a look at their students' reading needs is a first step. What happens next often has a persistent individual involved. That was certainly the case at Northern Essex Community College where Trish Schade first brought attention to Reading Apprenticeship and nurtured an increasingly supportive campus-wide response. (See Close-Up 1.3, Starting with a Group of One.)

CLOSE-UP 1.3

Starting with a Group of One

About a decade ago, Trish Schade was one of the very first college instructors to take a look at how Reading Apprenticeship might provide disciplinary support for student literacy. She was a member of a small inquiry group of California instructors trying out Reading Apprenticeship in their college classes. When she later moved across the country—from California's Merced Community College to Northern Essex Community College in Massachusetts—she was eager to share Reading Apprenticeship with her new colleagues, but no one had heard of it. Trish needed ways to get their attention.

One way she built interest in Reading Apprenticeship was through paired courses she taught with other faculty. In her classes, students were learning Reading Apprenticeship routines. Before long, Trish says, her faculty partners were noticing and asking her about her teaching: "What are you doing to get the students so engaged?"

Trish also decided to start a Reading Apprenticeship inquiry group. She wasn't sure who would show up, so she invited professional tutors, lab coordinators, and librarians as well as faculty across disciplines. The group that assembled monthly was small but persistent. They tried out Reading Apprenticeship strategies, presented to others, and slowly grew in numbers and confidence.

Now, the Reading Apprenticeship inquiry group has developed into the college-supported Transitions to Academic Success Initiative, and Reading Apprenticeship approaches have become integral to the first-year seminar at Northern Essex. The college administration, pleased with the team's contribution to student literacy, asked the group to bring their focus on academic literacy to the most rigorous classes on campus—gateway courses in the academic disciplines. For example, Emily Gonzalez, who now co-chairs the Transitions team with Trish, has been instrumental in spreading interest in Reading Apprenticeship to members of her science department.

Starting with a group of one, Trish and then Emily and others who saw the promise of Reading Apprenticeship built a grassroots movement to make academic literacy a campus-wide mission.

Making Use of Campus Structures for Professional Learning

When campus interest in Reading Apprenticeship develops, instructors who take the initiative to introduce Reading Apprenticeship to others may first have gotten up a little steam simply by inviting faculty members to visit a class where they are trying out Reading Apprenticeship approaches.

More formally, enthusiastic teachers can use college structures for professional learning, as Trish Schade did with a campus FIG[4] at Northern Essex Community College.

Paid "flexible" (flex) learning days are another professional learning structure available for interesting others in Reading Apprenticeship. For example, at American River College, instructor Amanda Corcoran, who is now a co-leader of the Reading Apprenticeship Project at the college, first found out about Reading Apprenticeship in a three-hour flex presentation:

> I understood that my students needed additional literacy support and
> I couldn't quite figure out what it was. So I went to a Reading
> Apprenticeship flex presentation and what they said about how students
> needed to be apprenticed—even though I'm not a reading teacher—
> it made perfect sense to me.

Amanda is now a veteran of the three-hour flex structure, introducing Reading Apprenticeship as a regular offering on campus professional learning days.

Communities of practice are another structure community college faculty and staff have embraced for building Reading Apprenticeship expertise and advocacy. These can be self-supporting on a campus or organized across campuses. (See Chapter Seven for more about communities of practice.)

On some campuses, it is administrators rather than faculty members who set the course for increased attention to disciplinary literacy, providing material and political support. When this happens, the pace of scale-up can really accelerate. At Renton Technical College, for example, fully 80 percent of the faculty has participated in college-underwritten Reading Apprenticeship professional development. A forward-thinking college president and a small team of faculty and staff made it happen. (See Close-Up 1.4, Galvanizing a Campus Around Reading.)

Integrating Support for Reading Apprenticeship Across Campus Programs

In community college, beyond Reading Apprenticeship's central role in subject area teaching, it can also play an important part in strengthening student services. Programs designed to provide special support for student success, such

CLOSE-UP 1.4

Galvanizing a Campus Around Reading

Renton Technical College is attractive to many students who prefer not to read. Students typically think of themselves as hands-on learners. They enroll to train for jobs like veterinary assistant, phlebotomy technician, or welder—jobs, they perhaps assume, where reading is not a feature.

Back in 2008, however, when Renton got focused on reading, college president Steve Hanson and other campus leaders were concerned that students' reading inexperience was keeping too many of them from completing their coursework or attaining career gateway certificates and degrees.

As a first step in the campus plan to home in on reading, the college underwrote the participation of three instructors and a librarian in an intensive week of leadership training in Reading Apprenticeship. The four came back excited, with a vision of what they could change in their own classrooms and how they could support colleagues.

After a successful year piloting what they had learned, they were convinced that their experiences would translate into faculty interest in a shared literacy agenda. Instructor Michele Lesmeister, for example, had collected data that her Adult Basic Education students were completing their requirements in two-thirds to one-half the time of students nationally. Students' persistence in her classes soared from 51 to 89 percent.

The college paid for four more faculty members to attend Reading Apprenticeship training, and Michele and her colleagues sent out newsletters,

sponsored faculty meetings, and modeled in classrooms. "Let us know," they encouraged colleagues, "how you want us to help." Librarian Debbie Crumb collected a robust library of Reading Apprenticeship books and articles, tip sheets, and videos.

After three years, with the demand for Reading Apprenticeship professional development increasing, Michele collaborated with staff at the Strategic Literacy Initiative at WestEd to develop Reading Apprenticeship 101, a six-week, thirty-hour online course specifically for community college instructors.[5]

Michele taught the first, pilot section to a sold-out contingent of Renton faculty who learned about and tried out Reading Apprenticeship routines and then exchanged reflections with their colleagues. At the end of six weeks, she reported:

> I have been here twenty years and I have never seen this campus pulled together on one topic like Reading Apprenticeship has done. People right now are changing curriculum like you can't believe.

With *reading* as the catalyst, dynamic teacher leaders, an engaged administration, and an open-minded faculty are moving their campus toward an increasingly ambitious culture of learning. Eighty percent of faculty has Reading Apprenticeship training, and this two-year college has just launched its first four-year bachelor's degree program, in applied science.

as tutoring, summer bridge, and first-year experience courses, have found that the Reading Apprenticeship Framework is a natural fit. When colleges can integrate a coherent strengths-based approach to student learning—across subject areas and support services—students' academic experience makes sense.

Pasadena City College is one campus where academics and support services share a Reading Apprenticeship foundation. For a description of how Pasadena students benefit, see Chapter Seven, "Infiltrating a Campus, One Program After Another."

Using External Pressures to Move Toward Local Goals

> We're being pushed politically to do something about student success, so why not use that process to push for an instructional program that genuinely works.
> —Chris Padgett, American River College history instructor

External pressures for change frequently result in quick-fix, surface-level approaches. In some situations, however, leadership teams of faculty and administrators are able to use external pressures to create opportunities, and sometimes to secure funding, for deeper improvements that align with their goals. Finding ways to match these pressures with the goals of a school, a district, or a campus takes skill and vision.

From Data Discussions to Deeper Reading

In many secondary schools, high-stakes test scores drive schools' search for improvement opportunities. Similarly, community colleges are increasingly pressured by state requirements—as well as their own goals—to improve student persistence and completion rates. Looking at student data is a concrete way to begin a discussion about needed improvement.

Beyond Reading Scores

At Titusville High School, administrators were unhappy with students' low reading scores on the Pennsylvania Keystone Exams. Their first thought was to ask the English department to step up. It didn't take much discussion with staff, however, to recognize that students needed subject-specific reading skills to access content in all their courses. Principal Scott Davie has seen an initial focus on test scores evolve into an appreciation for how literacy transforms subject area learning:

> Standardized tests don't always drive the bus, but they are an obvious fit
> for discussion. Students were not doing well on the state reading exam.
> The need to become better teachers of reading motivated us to jump on
> board with Reading Apprenticeship, but we continue to be on board
> because as students' reading skills improve, you can take things further
> with the content. You can go deeper, you can get that evidence drawn
> out, and you can have more enjoyable class discussions as a result of your
> kids' ability to do that.

Beyond Defensiveness

A different discussion about data was taking place at Manistee High School. Principal Julia Raddatz says that when more and more students began struggling to meet grade-level expectations, the staff acknowledged that, although they were teaching the same way they always had, their students weren't learning. "Instead of defending our teaching, we said, 'Let's really look at what our kids need, and, as a teacher, what do I do?'"

For Julia and her teachers, the key was recognizing the role of disciplinary literacy in student thinking:

> Before Reading Apprenticeship, I don't think our science teachers would
> have thought of themselves as literacy specialists. And that's what
> changed everything. Our teachers, especially content level teachers, now
> understand how literacy instruction enhances content instruction. You
> really can't have a great biology classroom until your kids learn how to
> read biology and have the independence of their own thinking in biology.

Focusing on Student Engagement

Savvy educators dealing with external pressures to improve test scores know that if test scores are the problem, student engagement is going to be key to any solution with staying power. The Reading Apprenticeship Framework's focus on the social and personal dimensions, and emphasis on metacognitive conversation, means that issues of engagement, motivation, and developing academic dispositions are always an important driver in successful implementation.

As next described, in two schools where SSR Plus[6] caught fire (the Reading Apprenticeship program that puts a metacognitive spin on sustained silent reading), test scores rose along with students' reading pleasure. In a college English class for first-generation students, students being apprenticed into the expectations of college reading learned that engaging metacognitively with text can be a kick.

The Kids Are in the Library Like You Can't Believe

For almost a decade, about half of students at Reading High School, in Reading, Pennsylvania, had failed to graduate, in no small part because of poor reading skills. Students' passing rate on the state's Keystone literature exam, for example, ranged between 30 and 40 percent. When a new principal, Eric Turman, arrived, test scores and graduation rates were at the top of his agenda.

He moved students to teachers whom he thought would best be able to help them. The passing rate on the literature test moved from 37 percent to 54 percent. The following year, he further refined teaching assignments. Four of his English teachers had recently begun Reading Apprenticeship professional development. Those teachers took on the six hundred eleventh graders least likely to pass the literature test.

Nine months later, Reading High School beat the state average, with 61 percent of students passing the exam. Eric credits his teachers, Reading Apprenticeship, and the Reading Apprenticeship SSR Plus program (see Close-Up 1.5, SSR Plus: We're Going to Read for Two Minutes), with turning nonreaders into readers:

> We went from 37 percent to 61 percent in two years with those teachers.
> My librarian emailed me, "You're not going to believe this. The number
> of books the eleventh graders are checking out is off the charts. These
> kids are in the library and checking out books at a rate I've never seen."

Eric's vision for his school is one of a Reading Apprenticeship *building*—a place where attention to literacy is embedded in the school culture. "Having

CLOSE-UP 1.5

SSR Plus: We're Going to Read for Two Minutes

If Reading Apprenticeship's model for sustained silent *choice* reading takes time every day out of subject area instruction, how can that improve students' subject area performance?

Nicole Dysart and Sindy Goodhart are coteachers of those eleventh graders at Reading High School who are most in need of help to pass the Pennsylvania-required literature test. "At our Reading Apprenticeship training," Nicole says, "we saw how we could turn this community of nonreaders into readers, without them even realizing it."

Their students use the same curriculum and read the same literature as the other eleventh graders. The difference is the amount of reading their students do *in class*. "We read pretty much the entire time," Sindy says. "We start with SSR. I've seen SSR before, where it's just, 'Read for twenty minutes.' We didn't do that."

As Nicole explains, "We started small. I would say to the class, 'We're going to read for two minutes.' Initially, they would say, 'That's so long!' We'd read, and I'd call time. They'd be, 'It's done?' They were astounded that was two minutes. As we progressed, they wanted more. 'Well, can't we read for five? Can't we read for ten?' It actually increased our students' vocabulary and reading stamina exponentially.

"And since we teach literature skills such as theme or characterization," Nicole continues, "with the metacognitive logs, we could say, 'Today when you're reading your SSR book, you're going to focus on characterization. Tell me how this character changed and why.' Then we would shift into the piece of literature we had for the curriculum that day, and I'd say, 'Just like in your metacognitive log, we're going to focus on characterization.' It was an easy transition from one thing they were really invested and interested in to something that—not so much. But they know about characterization, because they just did it in their metacognitive logs. That helped a lot to build their confidence in their reading and in their skills."

When it came time for Nicole and Sindy's students to take the literature exam, students themselves recognized how much Reading Apprenticeship helped them. As Sindy recalls, "They kept asking before the test, 'Can we write on the [test] books, can we Talk to the Text?' I said, 'Absolutely. Please do. Circle things that are confusing to you, go back to them. Identify words that you're unsure of, then use the context.' I said, 'Mark those books up!' When they came back from the test, they were so excited, 'Oh my god, I used Talking to the Text, and I did this, and I did that.' It was such a moment for me, 'Okay, I think we're on the right track here.'"

seen the success we had with Reading Apprenticeship in literature classes, bringing it into science and history is a no-brainer," he says. "Hopefully, in the next three to five years we'll be a Reading Apprenticeship building. We could really be talking about something special."

Turning a Stigma into Success

In Michigan, when a high school has been rated in the state's bottom 5 percent, based on a number of metrics, it is listed as a Priority school, and sanctions apply. At Edsel Ford High School in Dearborn, when the Priority rating hit, principal Scott Casebolt had been at the helm for only a year.

The Priority rating mandated an extra hour of instruction, Monday through Thursday, for the vast majority of Edsel Ford students. On Fridays, teachers stayed late for an hour of professional development.

Out of a school population of 1,400, about 1,100 students were assigned to a Language Arts Plus, Math Plus, or Science Plus intervention class that kept them in school that extra hour four days a week. "Plus" was the key in each course, and it refers to SSR Plus—the Reading Apprenticeship approach to SSR that invites students to read for pleasure within a metacognitive framework. Scott has special enthusiasm for the role of the intervention classes:

> We knew the kids needed to read, and we knew that they needed to have that metacognitive piece. They are all reading for 20 minutes a day, even in Math Plus. We're linking that to a huge part of our success.
>
> Kids had lost interest in reading going back to second, third, and fourth grade because they lost access to high-interest materials. They lost the enjoyment piece, and we brought it back with the SSR. It's carried over to the academic piece.

With a combination of grant funds and funds related to the Priority rating, close to 75 percent of the faculty were able to participate in Reading Apprenticeship professional development, including extra time for teachers to meet and collaborate—time that Scott and the teachers see as crucial. Now when Scott does classroom walk-throughs, he sees the payoff for this kind of focus. "I think we've truly established a culture for learning," he says. "The classroom environment you see is supportive. You see the Reading Apprenticeship routines, you see the metacognitive piece, the tie-in with the Common Core. You can ask the kids what they're doing and they know. There's just a tremendous transformation in the classrooms."

Scott and the Edsel Ford staff and students were successful in exiting Priority status in a single year. In the state's Top to Bottom ranking, they jumped from the 1st percentile to the 29th percentile. Students proficient in reading improved from 49 percent to 59 percent. The school's improvement plan and funding are still in place for another year at least, which means continued intervention classes. Scott anticipates that students' experience of success and growth will continue as well:

> They're starting to have success in their classes, they're performing better on tests, and they see the improvement. Apparently, that success is helping motivate them.

Apprenticing College Students to Ask, "Why Does This Matter?"

Lauren Servais, who teaches English at Santa Rosa Junior College and coordinates the campus Puente program,[7] was initially drawn to Reading Apprenticeship because it reminded her of the many important ways she herself had been apprenticed as a first-generation student. Now when she meets with faculty members in a faculty interest group or facilitates Reading Apprenticeship workshops for colleagues, she makes a point to connect her experience learning how to be a college student with the Reading Apprenticeship Framework:

> There are so many things about being in college—how do I really apprentice them into college? What I'm trying to do is have students engage text and wonder about the things we're reading. I want them fired up: "What does this mean for me? What does this mean in the time when it was written? Is it still relevant? How does it connect to my life and the experiences of my classmates?" I want them to see that reading can be this very active, engaged thing, "What are we doing here? Why does this matter?"

Turning Reform Overload into Reform Coherence

> Connect the dots: Reading Apprenticeship, Danielson, Common Core. I try to help staff to understand that these are all pieces that fit. Everything we're doing is based on literacy in the content areas.
>
> —Harley Ramsey, Otto-Eldred Junior-Senior High School principal

When schools and colleges are bombarded with improvement initiatives, large and small, how can leaders help teachers make sense of them? How can they amplify the power of Reading Apprenticeship in concert with other institutional priorities? The ability of leaders to promote coherent visions and help colleagues see how Reading Apprenticeship connects to other reforms, potential resources, and existing structures is a key element of success.

Some schools and colleges see the opportunity to introduce Reading Apprenticeship under the umbrella of school improvement plans or when it can complement other high-priority local reforms, such as college and career readiness standards, teacher evaluation frameworks, or a college effort to "accelerate" students through remedial courses.

Reframing Competing Demands

When state, national, and local reform priorities seem to collide and overwhelm staff, the Reading Apprenticeship Framework can be used as an opportunity to clarify areas of overlap and reframe competing demands as complementary.

In Pennsylvania, for example, teachers deal with Pennsylvania Core standards for curriculum, they have the Danielson Framework for Teaching for teacher evaluation, and they must track evidence of growth on Student Learning Opportunities (SLOs). Otto-Eldred High School principal Harley Ramsey makes a point of working with teachers to show them how these initiatives fit together and strengthen the school's overriding focus on literacy in the content areas.

> I've been very purposeful and specific with teachers. If you look at the Reading Apprenticeship and the Pennsylvania version of the Common Core, they are strongly convergent in content literacy. If you take a look at Danielson, it's all about creating persistent, independent learners. The focus is on the student, a student-centered classroom, which is really what Reading Apprenticeship is. If an SLO's not literacy-based, well, why? Literacy should be threaded through everything we're doing.
>
> Now we're starting to understand the connections. "Oh, it's not a big deal because it's already part of what we're doing. This is just how we represent it, or how we assess it, or how we're evaluated on it." It just makes sense.
>
> In post-observation conferences, I will ask, "Okay, you did x, y, z literacy activity in class today. Where does it fall [in the Danielson framework]?" Then we start a side conversation, "Okay, what if you did this, where does that fall?" So they're always drawing the conclusion themselves, "Yeah, if I do this I'm pushing 'distinguished' in most of these categories."

For schools that use Charlotte Danielson's Framework for Teaching along with Reading Apprenticeship, a crosswalk tool helps teachers find the commonalities between these two powerful systems. Many teachers have been introduced to the simple tool in Chapter Six, Team Tool 6.17, Mapping Reading Apprenticeship onto the Danielson Framework, for constructing their own understanding of the complementary nature of Reading Apprenticeship and the Danielson framework.

The Common Core State Standards and other new college and career readiness standards are a major new focus for secondary schools in many states.

At California's Anaheim Union High School District, administrators saw the value of Reading Apprenticeship for supporting teachers' implementation of the Common Core standards and the special value of Reading Apprenticeship's metacognitive routines for the district's plurality of English learners.

District superintendent Mike Matsuda had been head of district professional development when he learned that the district's high schools were eligible to participate in grant-funded Reading Apprenticeship professional development. He jumped on it. "I was in the position to really bring this forward," he says. "I framed it as a support for the training for Common Core, especially for history and science. That's how we got started."

District leaders also recognized the opportunity as one that would benefit the district's large population of English learners. Jackie Counts, Anaheim's English curriculum specialist, says, "What Reading Apprenticeship was offering—metacognitive strategies that students are taught very purposefully and that become part of their repertoire—are strategies that they can pull out when they need to. All students need that but English learners need it in a very structured, mindful way."

Seven high schools signed on and volunteer teachers began the professional development. Mike, who was monitoring teachers' evaluation of the program at the time, was impressed with the quality of the professional development itself and the "value-added" collaboration that was structured for teachers in the monthly professional learning community meetings. "Teachers felt the training was quite transformational," he reports. "That's a pretty powerful statement in terms of teachers taking ownership. A big piece is turning around attitudes about whether kids can access more complex texts."

Rethinking School Improvement Plans

Secondary schools all have school improvement plans (SIPs). When administrators and teachers share a desired focus on creating a culture of literacy in their school, the SIP is a logical place to make that commitment concrete and keep track of how they are doing. Close-Up 1.6, Accounting for Reading Apprenticeship in a School Improvement Plan, describes how the staff at one Michigan school made this work.

Accelerating Remediation on College Campuses

Many college campuses have found that the Reading Apprenticeship Framework helps faculties coalesce around a unifying approach for achieving their equity goals. This might begin with changing instruction to accelerate underprepared

CLOSE-UP 1.6

Accounting for Reading Apprenticeship in a School Improvement Plan

When the Dearborn, Michigan, school district chose Reading Apprenticeship as the district's secondary school literacy initiative, Youssef Mosallam had been principal of the 2,400-student Fordson High School for one year. A believer in the power of the school improvement plan to shape school change, Youssef, and his staff, had already decided to build the school improvement plan around three initiatives—the SIOP sheltered instruction model (English learners make up 56 percent of the school population), Habits of Mind, and 6+1 Writing Traits—and stick to them. Now, given the new district priority, Fordson would have to add Reading Apprenticeship to their SIP. Youssef was concerned:

> The fear of every staff is, "This is a new fad. We'll do it for a couple of years and it will go away." As a new principal in a building so large, that had so much of a need, the last thing we wanted was to push forward on something and then pull it away later.

Meanwhile, Fordson's full-time literacy coordinator, Amy Keith-Wardlow, had participated in Reading Apprenticeship professional development along with a small group of volunteer faculty members. Youssef attended parts of the professional development as well. Given the district's emphasis on a Reading Apprenticeship approach, and Fordson's existing commitments to other initiatives,

they were encouraged that Reading Apprenticeship would be a good fit.

Amy signed on for more intensive training to lead Reading Apprenticeship professional development at her school. She could see the relationships between the pre-existing SIP priorities and Reading Apprenticeship, and it was going to be her responsibility to manage Fordson's professional development so that teachers did too.

Although the school improvement plan drives Fordson teacher evaluations, it does not do so in a vacuum. As Youssef explains, the professional development *process* is key:

> We aren't only going in and working with teachers and saying, "These are the areas we want you to improve on." We have those conversations, but every teacher has multiple layers of support. On a regular basis we have teachers visiting other teachers' classrooms, usually Reading Apprenticeship model classrooms, to observe. The teachers use an observation protocol, and then have a conversation with peers who were also in the observation. Amy is involved in that conversation, and that allows for, "Okay, I'm going to try that tomorrow." Then you see the emails going back and forth: "Amy, I'm going to do this tomorrow 4th hour. Can you come and observe?" There's the constant reinforcement.

students' path through non-credit-bearing remedial reading courses, but also include changes to instruction in credit-bearing courses that better support all students to meet rigorous academic demands.

Recent research on the promise of accelerating community college students' movement through remedial math and reading and writing sequences, and through non-credit-bearing ELL courses has prompted a growing development of alternative, accelerated courses. These courses have the potential to move students more quickly into credit-bearing courses.

When a campus decides to take on acceleration for its pre-college-level or basic skills courses, curriculum has to change, and so does instruction. Katie Hern, a leader of the acceleration movement nationally and co-founder and director of the California Acceleration Project (CAP), has long been aware of the synergy between the work of acceleration to redesign remediation and the affordances of Reading Apprenticeship to support literacy instruction in an accelerated environment:

> Once a college steps forward to do the kind of curricular redesign that is no longer pushing students through three semesters of non-credit-bearing remedial courses, it calls upon you to teach differently. You can't spend a whole semester doing grammar workbook exercises. You've got to get students in there with challenging texts and you have to be able to support them to be successful with those texts. That's where faculty are reporting that Reading Apprenticeship is a really great complement to the structural and pedagogical work they're doing with CAP. Reading Apprenticeship enhances their confidence and their toolkit around supporting students to be successful with challenging reading.

■ ■ ■

Bringing Reading Apprenticeship into any educational institution is a significant commitment. The Reading Apprenticeship Framework is designed to guide deep transformations of teaching and learning. Without sustained focus, such transformations become glimpsed opportunities that simply slip away.

The diverse community of Reading Apprenticeship schools and colleges suggests many ways to envision a culture of literacy and begin a process of implementation with staying power. Whether advocating as a single teacher or responding to an administrator eager to have everyone on board, there are a range of ways to make the case for using Reading Apprenticeship to meet local goals for students' engaged academic literacy.

In Chapter Two, we learn how administrators and teacher leaders have shared leadership roles in developing a culture of literacy with a Reading Apprenticeship foundation.

Notes

1. This approach to teaching is described briefly in the preface of this book and is the subject of an earlier book, *Reading for Understanding: How Reading Apprenticeship Improves Disciplinary Learning in Secondary and College Classrooms*, by Ruth Schoenbach, Cynthia Greenleaf, and Lynn Murphy, and published by Jossey-Bass in 2012. Also see Appendix A, a graphic representation of the Reading Apprenticeship Framework.

2. Excel Centers make up a network of fourteen charter schools in Indiana, Texas, and Tennessee—sponsored by Goodwill Industries—with a mission of bringing basic secondary education to adult learners, many of whom have been out of school and out of a job for years. Intensive professional development supports the teachers who support these students.

3. Reading Apprenticeship Improving Secondary Education (RAISE) was a five-year, federally funded study of Reading Apprenticeship implementation and scale-up.

4. The acronym FIG refers to faculty interest (or inquiry) group and is sometimes expanded to include staff as well as in SFIG.

5. This online course is now widely available to college faculty members. See more about it on the Reading Apprenticeship website: http://readingapprenticeship.org/professional-development/college/faculty-101-course

6. SSR Plus combines students' sustained silent reading of self-selected books with metacognitive logs and conversation. Students read for enjoyment and write and talk about their reading responses and processes (not about plot summaries). Chapter Six in *Reading for Understanding* describes the Reading Apprenticeship SSR Plus program in detail.

7. Puente community college programs are designed to improve the college completion rates of underrepresented students, typically those who are the first generation in their families to attend college.

CHAPTER TWO

Partnering for Leadership

In Wyomissing, Reading Apprenticeship really started with a group of ten teachers who sat around a table with me, and we had an open dialogue: 'Is this something you want to do?' I gave them my word that if it was, I would support them.

—Julia Vicente, Wyomissing Area School District superintendent

WITH AN ambitious initiative like Reading Apprenticeship, where the goal is to create a school-wide or campus-wide culture of literacy, where the roles and expectations of teachers, administrators, and students will be fundamentally altered, leadership must come from administrators and teachers alike. In the Wyomissing district, for example, the partnership between the superintendent and a team of teachers began with an agreement to go forward. That was the easy part. What the decision implied was that people around the table were also agreeing to share responsibility for what would come next.

In this chapter, we describe the different, complementary, and necessary roles of administrators and teacher leaders who partner in the implementation and support of Reading Apprenticeship, understanding that this will look quite different at the secondary and post-secondary levels, as well as from campus to campus. We draw heavily on the experiences and advice offered by those who have walked the walk. Their contexts are various, and so, we find, are their emphases about how to be effective. In each role, however, certain responsibilities come with the territory.

How Administrators Contribute

If we're going to ask our teachers to be engaged in something, and we are telling them it's worthwhile, then it should be worth our while to be engaged in it as well. Being in the trenches with your teachers goes a long way to making sure that something is going to be sustained.

—Scott Davie, Titusville High School principal

The impetus for introducing Reading Apprenticeship—especially at the secondary school level—often comes from an administrator, who may encourage a few volunteers to give Reading Apprenticeship a try or may promote his or her own enthusiasm for Reading Apprenticeship more broadly to a faculty. At the community college level, administrators may more typically respond to faculty interest than prompt it. In either case, however, administrators must understand the heavy lifting involved in shifting a school or campus culture, and value what the Reading Apprenticeship model can accomplish.

Administrators support a Reading Apprenticeship effort by being knowledgeable about what Reading Apprenticeship is and is not, and actively engaging with teachers to make it work. Because time for professional learning and ongoing collaboration is a huge factor in the successful implementation of Reading Apprenticeship, administrators also find, fund, and protect such time. Finally, administrators must be strong and reliable advocates—with staff, students, parents, and boards of education—for the sustained focus necessary to build the culture of literacy that Reading Apprenticeship models and informs.

Being Knowledgeable and Engaged

Being knowledgeable about Reading Apprenticeship and being engaged with the work teachers are undertaking include purposefully learning about the instructional implications of the Reading Apprenticeship Framework—whether independently, along with faculty, or in workshops that include other administrators. Supportive administrators also regularly visit classrooms where teachers and students are *doing* Reading Apprenticeship, attend meetings of a school's literacy team, and even model Reading Apprenticeship approaches in the design of staff meetings.

Learning Along with Faculty

What can happen when a single college administrator and a handful of faculty share a vision for change? At the College of San Mateo, they all attended an intensive seminar about Reading Apprenticeship and they followed up with collaborations to enlist faculty and administration interest. It went something like this:

Biology professor Theresa Martin had been inspired to learn about Reading Apprenticeship as a way to address equity issues in her science, technology, engineering, and math (STEM) classes. At a math and science division meeting, she announced an upcoming Reading Apprenticeship seminar and encouraged colleagues to enroll along with her. Around the same time, she also steered the division dean, Charlene Frontiera, to a state-wide leadership institute where Reading Apprenticeship was on the agenda as one of several ways to catalyze campus change. What Charlene learned about Reading Apprenticeship at the leadership institute prompted her to check back with Theresa: Could she join the faculty group attending the Reading Apprenticeship seminar?

Dean Fronteria's decision to learn about Reading Apprenticeship alongside her faculty meant she could understand what they were trying to accomplish, and she could provide "cover" for them as they took the pedagogical risks of trying out Reading Apprenticeship in their classrooms. Charlene's administrative support gave the Reading Apprenticeship team permission to innovate.

This partnership of one dean and a small team of faculty powered an explosion of interest in Reading Apprenticeship at CSM. In just eighteen months, sixty-eight faculty members and thirty student tutors were involved in Reading Apprenticeship professional development, Reading Apprenticeship was incorporated into the campus bridge program for first-time college students, the academic senate declared Reading Apprenticeship its highest institutional priority, and the campus planning and budget committee was presented with a well-received proposal for institutionalizing Reading Apprenticeship. (See Close-Up 2.2, Campus Institutionalization Budget Proposal, for more detail.)

At the secondary school level, administrators often learn about Reading Apprenticeship along with their faculty. They may feel their own earlier preparation was light on literacy or the constructivist pedagogy undergirding Reading Apprenticeship, or they may want to strongly signal support for the effort their teachers are making. In Kellie Rodkey's case, as assistant principal of Avon High School, it was a little of both. "Going through the training with the teachers did take a huge chunk out of my time," she says, "but it helped me immensely on my own buy-in. And when the teachers see an administrator there with them, side by side, that's huge."

Participating in Literacy Teams

One surefire way for administrators to recognize teachers' efforts and learn along with them is by attending team meetings. Teachers report that monthly team meetings are the most important way they have for deepening their understanding and practice of Reading Apprenticeship. Administrators support those team meetings by making the time for teachers to attend, but also by participating in the meetings, whether simply as observers or more actively.

From the perspective of teacher leader Sara Jones, the benefit of administrators' involvement with the Titusville High School literacy team extends back into the classroom:

> We find that having administrators there and understanding what the
> activities are and how we do them, and even what some of the challenges
> are, encourages them to come and see what we're doing. And when they
> come into our class, we feel less intimidated because they've heard our
> discussion. They're really curious to see how things are going, versus
> coming in to be critical or check off their checklist.

As a new principal at Anaheim High School, where Reading Apprenticeship was already under way, team meetings were an opportunity for Anna Corral to learn from her teachers. "Everyone's trying this together," she says. "I make sure they know that I'm there to hear from them. If I ask questions, it's because I want to learn."

Networking to Learn More

Administrators can also learn about Reading Apprenticeship through professional development tailored specifically for them. David Simancek, principal of a small alternative high school in the Swartz Creek district, found the peer exchange was especially valuable in the online course for administrators he took. "I learned so much," he says, "in talking to other people about how to create a Reading Apprenticeship vision and to build a supportive program." That same kind of exchange can be fostered directly, of course, by visiting or communicating with other districts where Reading Apprenticeship is going on. "Network with anyone you can," David advises.

Observing in Classrooms

Secondary school administrators are frequently in classrooms to observe teachers—often as part of formal teacher evaluations. In contrast, administrators' informal visits to classrooms where teachers are trying out Reading Apprenticeship are not evaluative. They signal support for teachers' efforts and build administrators' knowledge about how Reading Apprenticeship changes learning and instruction.

Classroom visits by Harrison High School assistant principal Allyson Robinson had this reciprocal benefit for Allyson and her teachers. In the online Reading Apprenticeship course for administrators, these kind of non-evaluative classroom visits were regular workplace-embedded learning assignments. Allyson was invested in observing what she was learning about in her course. What she saw firsthand not only deepened her understanding of Reading Apprenticeship, but it also enabled her to increase her support for her teachers' efforts:

> It was helpful to me, after reading *about* Reading Apprenticeship, to understand as an observer what it really looks like—seeing it in action.
>
> After I saw one lesson and the teacher and I were talking about it, I asked, "Well, what has been a biggest challenge for you in using Reading Apprenticeship?" He said it had been frustrating to remove himself from the center of the class and to turn over a lot of the control to the students. "Frustrating," he said, "but in a good way, because I could see how much better my class was running, how much better the results were."

He said, "Before Reading Apprenticeship training, if a kid asked me a question, I'd probably give them the answer—here's how you figure this out. Now, I question *them*: Well, what are the variables here? Which formula would we use? Why would you use that formula?"

I had observed him doing that, thoughtfully questioning until the group or the student got to the answer. So that's been nice to see. He really has changed his entire approach.

Administrators may not realize how much teachers value their visits. Teachers make a big investment in learning how to implement Reading Apprenticeship. They appreciate having administrators recognize how much they are doing—and what they are accomplishing.

Leading by Example

When administrators understand the Reading Apprenticeship Framework and the strategies teachers can use to implement it, a logical next step is to incorporate that knowledge into staff meetings and other faculty learning opportunities—modeling and reinforcing the instructional practices teachers are learning.

As Milan High School principal Ryan McMann learned about Reading Apprenticeship, he became convinced that staff meetings and in-house professional development were a powerful opportunity to model Reading Apprenticeship practices, including conscious attention to the social and personal dimensions of the Framework. "Now," he says, "Reading Apprenticeship is something I'm using as opposed to just something I'm telling teachers to use."

At Yuba College, where Walter Masuda is the dean of Arts, Humanities and Education, he and faculty member Shawn Frederking collaborate on developing and facilitating Reading Apprenticeship workshops and faculty interest groups. These invitations reach only a portion of the faculty, however. Walter and Shawn saw that the college's commitment to redesigning its basic skills reading and composition courses was an opportunity to model the usefulness of Reading Apprenticeship more widely as it relates to access and equity issues. "We have to address achievement gaps," Walter says, "and Reading Apprenticeship can be part of that." He remembers Shawn joking that maybe the way to get people to do Reading Apprenticeship would be to put it in the new reading and composition course outlines. Walter took her seriously. "That's exactly what we're doing," he says. "We feel it is that important."

Finding and Protecting Resources

Most school and college leaders agree that finding and funding the time for teachers to learn about Reading Apprenticeship and collaborate in its ongoing practice takes careful planning and even a bit of creativity. Funds for teacher leader release time or instructional coaching are also seen as necessary components for successful implementation by leaders in many schools. Finally, while Reading Apprenticeship does not require investment in particular instructional materials or textbooks, it does depend on students having access to a range of subject area books and reading materials, and some additional supplies to support text-based inquiry like sticky notes and lots of poster paper.

Making Time for Teacher Professional Learning

Time is money in any school budget, and Reading Apprenticeship takes time. Sometimes it is time (and money) for formal Reading Apprenticeship–certified professional development. Often it is time and leadership support so that teams can meet regularly to maintain a focus on improving their implementation of Reading Apprenticeship.

Naomi Norman, who helped lead the fourteen-district scale-up of Reading Apprenticeship in Michigan's Washtenaw and Livingston counties, found that giving teachers time for collaboration was essential:

> Teachers told us that the teacher-to-teacher accountability is why they were able to go as far as they went with the work and why they stuck with it. Someone was counting on them to bring in student work, to bring in their lesson plan, to tell how it went.
>
> The power of teacher-to-teacher collaboration is probably the only way we can get full-scale instructional change. I don't think it's doable without that. So I would say pay attention to that and attend to it in any way you can.

At Abington Senior Heights High School, the Reading Apprenticeship team convinced administrators that they needed time set aside for regular monthly meetings, and the district came up with coverage. Vicki Jones, the district's director of language arts services, explains that the coverage wasn't a slam dunk, but that the team's impressive dedication to improving their Reading Apprenticeship practice won administrative support year after year:

> One of the things that came out loud and clear from our Reading Apprenticeship teacher leaders was this desperate need to have meetings. I spoke with their principal, and, I have to be honest, there was a little hesitation. She had built a schedule a couple of years prior so teachers who had common content area courses had a common planning time, and it was not utilized. So the next year they didn't keep that going. Then right after that year, here was the Reading Apprenticeship team's request.
>
> But the meetings were scheduled for them and they got coverage. They are a true professional learning community when so many are forced. It's organic. If you want to keep that, it's hard not to let them know there's really somebody in their corner.

The administration at Pasadena City College supports a four-day professional development institute for faculty and staff who want to teach the campus first-year experience seminar, called College 1. Reading Apprenticeship routines and approaches are foundational in the College 1 professional development institute as well as in the seminar for students. Funding for College 1 has been systematically institutionalized in the campus budget, even as the cost of it has increased along with the number of students and instructors participating. For a fuller picture of how College 1 and Reading Apprenticeship have impacted the campus, see the section "Infiltrating a Campus, One Program After Another" in Chapter Seven.

Budgeting for Instructional Support

At the secondary level, instructional support for Reading Apprenticeship commonly includes some combination of the assignment of school or district personnel to mentor or coach teachers, funding for external WestEd coaches, or release time for teacher leaders to work with literacy teams.

At Edsel Ford High School, where about 75 percent of the faculty participated together in a year of Reading Apprenticeship professional development, principal Scott Casebolt applauds the district for providing the resources to support his teachers' transition from an initial learning year to a follow-up year focused on deepening practice. In this second year, faculty members regularly engaged in Reading Apprenticeship planning conferences with the lead Reading Apprenticeship teacher, the school's ELA coach-coordinator, or a department head. In addition, an external Reading Apprenticeship coach worked with the ELA coach-coordinator as well as with teachers. "Our goal," Scott says, "was for teachers to get classroom support a couple of times per week."

Support at the district level in Chelsea, Michigan, has included administrator time learning about Reading Apprenticeship as well as substantial funding for teacher professional development and teacher leader release time. In terms of students' reading growth, the results seem to justify the district's investment. (See Close-Up 2.1, Chelsea District Takes Charge.)

Community college budgets do not typically fund faculty development to the degree found in middle and high school budgets. But proactive and creative faculty and administrative leaders have found ways to link college initiatives with support for Reading Apprenticeship work.

Instructional support at the community college level may include institutional funding for Reading Apprenticeship presentations to faculty, for FIG leaders and participants, for external professional learning in Reading Apprenticeship institutes and courses, and for reassigned time for faculty leaders to organize the effort.

CLOSE-UP 2.1

Chelsea District Takes Charge

Since 2006, Michigan's Chelsea School District has trained over 90 percent of its core content and special education teachers, grades 5–12, in Reading Apprenticeship. The superintendent and building administrators participated in the professional development along with their teachers and became strong and steady supporters of the work. Recognizing the importance of teacher meetings and teacher leaders, they increased the amount of teacher leader release time in step with the increasing number of teachers being prepared to implement Reading Apprenticeship. Starting from a single release period per month, which quickly increased to a half-day per month, the now full-time position provides Reading Apprenticeship–based literacy support for all teachers in the district.

The effectiveness of this sustained model of teacher learning is reflected in students' scores on the Degrees of Reading Power assessment. On the DRP test, in which 1 DRP unit of growth per year is the norm, Chelsea students gained 3 DRP units in the first year of testing and 5.5 units on the most recent test. Special education students have shown even more dramatic growth.

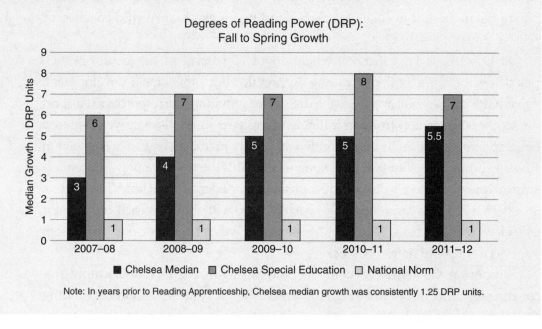

Degrees of Reading Power (DRP):
Fall to Spring Growth

Note: In years prior to Reading Apprenticeship, Chelsea median growth was consistently 1.25 DRP units.

At the College of San Mateo, where the campus planning and budget committee invited a proposal for institutionalizing Reading Apprenticeship, the proposal also included a half-time coordinator position, funding for data collection and analysis, and travel expenses for conference presentations. The line items, shown in Close-Up 2.2, Campus Institutionalization Budget Proposal, can be an instructive example for other campuses to consider.

On community college campuses, although deciding whether to appropriate funds for Reading Apprenticeship often requires sign-off by administrators, faculty are frequently in charge of programs with designated funding streams that can be tapped to support Reading Apprenticeship activities. Many Reading Apprenticeship faculty leaders know to ferret out such programs and make the

CLOSE-UP 2.2

Campus Institutionalization Budget Proposal

Following an 18-month rollout of Reading Apprenticeship at the College of San Mateo, the campus Leadership Group for Reading Apprenticeship, the Learning Center, and the Center for the Scholarship of Teaching and Learning—with the support of the Academic Senate—were invited to present a proposal for institutionalizing Reading Apprenticeship at the college. The proposed budget totaled just over $110,000 for the first year, with about a third of the total to cover a halftime coordinator position. Although this position was not funded, a high level of professional learning and dissemination was funded under a somewhat reduced budget.

Staff Time

Reassigned time for faculty coordinator	Four FLCs (76 hours)
Program service coordinator	50% with benefits

Reading Apprenticeship Professional Learning Opportunities

Leadership community of practice	Three participants per year
Three-day summer institute	Four participants per year
STEM seminar	One per year
Online class	Ten participants per year

Data Collection and Analysis

Data collection and analysis on MARSI

General data collection and analysis

External evaluator

Conferences

Registration/travel/food/lodging

Miscellaneous

CSM workshop presentations	Two per year, four faculty each
FIG leaders	Three leaders, two semesters each
New FIG participants	Fifteen per year
Materials and supplies	Books and general supplies
Marketing	Stickers, posters, banners
Food	Workshop food and drinks

case that a Reading Apprenticeship approach can advance a specific program's goals. For example, federal Title V grants available for improving the retention and preparedness of students attending Hispanic-serving institutions can support Reading Apprenticeship professional development. Equity and basic skills efforts and grants for improving access to the STEM pipeline are potential sources of funding. In California, funding from the Chancellor's Office through 3CSN (California Community Colleges Success Network) underwrites activities of the statewide Reading Apprenticeship Project and individual campus Reading Apprenticeship initiatives. (See Chapter Seven, the section "Communities of Practice: An Educator-Led, State-Supported Network.")

Campus-funded new faculty, summer bridge, first-year experience, and tutoring programs often have a strong Reading Apprenticeship component. College campuses may also have professional development and research funds that can be applied to Reading Apprenticeship activities. Close-Up 2.3, Finding Resources in Community College Budgets, is a quick look at where a number of Reading Apprenticeship campus initiatives have found financial allies and support.

Stocking the Shelves

Although Reading Apprenticeship does not require the purchase of particular curricula, technology, or instructional materials, there are a few resources that must be budgeted for. In often-impoverished secondary schools, providing ample school and classroom libraries to support students' extended reading is a first order of business. Given a selection of books representing a wide variety of genres, topics related to students' interests and cultural experiences, and a broad range of difficulty levels, students are more receptive to reading than teachers or others at the school may anticipate.

Many schools seek to supplement their often limited budgets for school and classroom libraries. Local bookstores can help by sponsoring book fairs that benefit the school library. Book drives that solicit gently used books are another way to augment school and classroom libraries and increase the selection of books available to students.

Other budgetary considerations include providing students with consumable paperbacks or photocopies of reading materials that they can mark up with Talking to the Text comments and queries. In Indiana, students are charged a textbook rental fee for most courses. In Brown County Schools, the district carefully considers the types of instructional materials the fee will cover. Debbie Harman, the district's director of student learning, explains that with Reading Apprenticeship in mind, some of those course fees can be allocated for

CLOSE-UP 2.3

Finding Resources in Community College Budgets

As these examples demonstrate, community colleges fund Reading Apprenticeship efforts in ways both large and small. Sometimes they use campus professional development funds, sometimes they apply streams of state or federal grant monies, and sometimes they assign or reassign staff time.

Grant Monies

"Equity money from the state Chancellor's Office came to the college, and the Basic Skills coordinator, who had attended some of our Reading Apprenticeship workshops, asked us to find as many faculty as possible to take the Reading Apprenticeship 101 course. Basic Skills monies funded their registration, and that growing cohort is helping to build and sustain Reading Apprenticeship at ARC."

—Amanda Corcoran, American River College

"We have a STEM focus and were fortunate to receive some support from the state Reading Apprenticeship Community College STEM Network grant.* That's been an opportunity to give our STEM faculty some more Reading Apprenticeship training and coaching."

—Jennifer Taylor-Mendoza, College of San Mateo

Reassigned Staff Time for Leadership Activities

"One of the first things we did was to get a unit and a half of release time for our core team to keep working on Reading Apprenticeship as a collective initiative for the campus."

—Theresa Martin, College of San Mateo

"We have a rigorous, robust, overworked research division, so the trick for us was to make the case that the student reading survey [to demonstrate campus-wide need for increased attention to student reading] was worthy of their resources and time. It is competitive to get these resources, but people were aware of the Reading Apprenticeship work Amanda and I had been doing, we had established the rationale for doing this next step, and we had built relationships and followed through on our projects. So when we came to ask for support, we found ourselves near the front of the line because most of the groundwork had already been done."

—Chris Padgett, American River College

Campus Professional Development Funds

"I secured money from our Faculty Fund for Advanced Study to send ten faculty members to a three-day Reading Apprenticeship summer institute, and I applied for a 3CSN** scholarship to supply the rest of the money. That group then created a FIG the following year."

—Ann Foster, Santa Rosa Junior College

"Reading Apprenticeship is completely embedded and scaffolded in our College 1 professional development. We also redesigned our year-long new faculty seminar to embed Reading Apprenticeship metacognitive routines."

—Shelagh Rose, Pasadena City College

*This three-year grant is funded by the Leona M. and Harry B. Helmsley Charitable Trust.
**3CSN, the California Community Colleges Success Network, is funded by the California Community Colleges Chancellor's Office to promote selected professional development programs statewide; Reading Apprenticeship is one of these.

supplementary texts that students can annotate. "It doesn't have to cost any extra money," she says. "It's just a different use of the money you already collect."

Advocating

Secondary school administrators have many audiences to convince of the importance of creating a school-wide culture of literacy—staff members, the central office, the school board, and parents, for example. And they find a variety of ways to reach them, both directly and indirectly.

Bringing Staff on Board

As discussed in Chapter One, many administrators must protect teachers from initiative overload. Getting the message across that Reading Apprenticeship represents systemic change, not just the *soup du jour*, can be important reassurance for sometimes dubious teachers. Administrators who help staff members see how Reading Apprenticeship fits with other core initiatives can not only cut down on staff resistance but also amplify the effectiveness of all initiatives when teachers understand how they work in concert.

At Harrison High School, according to assistant principal Allyson Robinson, Reading Apprenticeship is framed as a tool that supports teachers in their other ongoing initiatives:

> We've had a few new things in the past couple of years in our district, including our teacher evaluation process and formative assessment. So rather than saying, "Oh, and also here's Reading Apprenticeship," we're trying to say, "Here are some ways you can support your formative assessment practices, your teaching practices." We're presenting it as an enhancement to what we're already doing.

Administrators at Harrison High School also create opportunities for teachers to make their own associations between Reading Apprenticeship and the district's instructional goals by exposing staff to Reading Apprenticeship with instructional rounds. Allyson says that when teachers walk into a science classroom, for example, and see a science teacher teach science literacy, "They recognize the shift in the mode of instruction. It's like, 'Wow, what a change.'"

Communicating District-Wide and Campus-Wide

Secondary school administrators often find themselves spreading the word about Reading Apprenticeship to other district administrators. Northwest High School principal Scott Buchler lobbied both his district office and the principal of the feeder middle school with the message that getting middle school students on board with Reading Apprenticeship would result in a seamless and more dramatic literacy boost at the high school level.

At the community college level, administrators have the opportunity to promote cohesive support for Reading Apprenticeship across the different divisions and student services on a campus. Jennifer Taylor-Mendoza is dean of Academic Support and Learning Technologies at the College of San Mateo, where she learned about Reading Apprenticeship from biology professor Theresa Martin. The campus learning center had just started a new tutoring program and Theresa and Jennifer brainstormed ways to incorporate Reading Apprenticeship. As a result of this early partnership, Jennifer has become a campus champion of Reading Apprenticeship, explaining its promise to other administrators, the board of trustees, and faculty and peer tutors working with students in the campus labs and learning centers. "We're so busy in education," she reflects, "I have to take time and sit down and speak with people about Reading Apprenticeship. Why do we want to do this? What are our goals as an institution for our students to be successful? Really getting buy-in—for me that has been so important."

Reaching Parents

The role of secondary school administrators to advocate for Reading Apprenticeship with parents falls into two categories: proactively letting parents in on what Reading Apprenticeship will mean for their children, and having teachers' backs when parents misunderstand.

At Otto-Eldred Junior Senior High School, principal Harley Ramsey knows his remote, rural community. He knows that most parents have had short, very traditional school careers and do not expect their children's school experience to be much different. If their teenagers come home complaining that teachers are expecting much more reading and new levels of engagement and effort, he wants parents to know why.

Reading Apprenticeship was introduced at Otto-Eldred as a response to what area business and university leaders told Harley and Superintendent Matthew Splain they wanted from high school graduates. Harley passed the message along to parents at a school event designed to bring them into the conversation, with free spaghetti dinner the headliner.

In a community of 4,200, the spaghetti dinner drew a crowd of five hundred. Among the things parents learned was that Reading Apprenticeship was intended to help all their children be successful—those going directly into the workforce, or into the military, or to technical college, or to four-year college and beyond. "Once parents realized that I wasn't pushing a four-year liberal arts school on everybody," says Harley, "then I was able to get across why we're doing certain things—Reading Apprenticeship, literacy routines, communication." Beginning with the spaghetti dinner, Harley and his staff were able to engage parents. "We really started to break down those barriers, especially in a community of people that generally did not have a good experience in school.

We are totally into the fact that literacy has to be the foundation of what we do, and parent engagement is a key part of that."

For the Otto-Eldred spaghetti dinner recipe, see Close-Up 2.4, Winning Parents' Stomachs, Hearts, and Minds.

At Blue Ridge High School, principal Matthew Nebzydoski sometimes finds that it is the parents of high-achieving college-bound students who need help

---

CLOSE-UP 2.4

Winning Parents' Stomachs, Hearts, and Minds

In a small rural community, how do you get 500 people into a school building to learn about a new approach to literacy? Otto-Eldred Junior Senior High School principal Harley Ramsey decided to feed them. Spaghetti.

As Harley explains, in a district with two overriding concerns—literacy and community outreach—it's not surprising that such a spaghetti dinner would be organized by a staff member whose position covers literacy coaching, literacy data management, *and* community outreach.

We all understood that community involvement was absolutely critical. We just started brainstorming: How can we get parents involved? We figured out a spaghetti dinner would be the best way to get parents in the building. We were pretty confident that if we could get parents in the door we could truly and authentically engage them and use those opportunities to teach them what we're doing and why.

We advertised through Facebook, flyers home, the newspaper—we used a whole range of broadcast and phone messages.

We had local organizations come as well, the YMCA, Birth to Three, Pre-K for the IU [the regional Intermediate Unit]. That way the parents could access services while they were here. They could understand that if I need x,y,z, this is who I go to, from birth all the way up through adult literacy.

When the families came in, they got a punch card, and they used that punch card to access different sites all throughout the building. Each place they went they got punched, and after they reached so many sites, they could put their punch card in the drawing for books and technology. The PTO donated five Kindles. We gave away two hundred books. Peer Helpers, Varsity Club, National Honor Society, Library Club, all those student organizations gave money.

Some of the biggest feedback we got was that the school and classrooms simply looked different than what the parents were used to seeing. Students' work was posted, there was a lot of writing on the work, like Talking to the Text. Word Walls—they weren't used to seeing those, or Evidence/ Interpretation charts.

They got to play with the iPads and see how we use them for instructional purposes, same with laptops, even down to our woodshop where they got to do "make and take." And, of course, while they're there, they're seeing the drafting and drawing programs and some of the very high-order thinking students are doing in shop. Our goal was to give the parents a comprehensive view of what we do in the school, to educate and engage.

The relationship building was huge. The teachers, the superintendent, and I did everything as far as cooking and serving at the tables. And then the teachers were throughout the building either assisting or demonstrating—serving in some way.

It was extremely positive. We all agreed the spaghetti dinner has to be an annual event. [And so it has.]

understanding the value of Reading Apprenticeship. Alicia Ross, who teaches both AP history and AP economics, appreciates the support she gets from her principal when parents want to know who changed the rules on their A students:

> That first marking period can be tough if you don't have the support of your administrators. When parents call—and they will when you do this new thing—it's really important for an administrator to understand what's happening in the classroom. Especially some of the honors kids don't want the rules of the game to change: "I always got A's, leave me alone. Just tell me what's on the test, and I'll be fine."
>
> Matt supported us when parents and students pushed back. He made the connection between how the kids are doing, their level of engagement, and Reading Apprenticeship. That is really huge.

As Alicia says, her principal understood Reading Apprenticeship. He had attended professional development with his teachers, he stops by classes and observes, and he talks to students about it. So he was comfortable explaining it to parents and able to defuse their anxiety about this more interactive and independent way to learn.

How Teacher Leaders Contribute

> Why take on this leadership role? One of my driving motivations is that the Reading Apprenticeship Framework makes me, in my profession, more valuable than I ever was. I've always known the importance of teachers. But I feel that we are now doing things that are helping kids in ways they've not been helped before.
> —Angie Church, Berkley High School teacher leader

In schools and on college campuses, Reading Apprenticeship teacher leaders—teachers who are willing to take a next step in their professional responsibilities but often do not have an official leadership or coaching role—share a deep commitment to fostering an engaged culture of literacy. In their role as teacher leaders in secondary schools or as campus coaches or leaders of communities of practice in community colleges, they take primary responsibility for the professional collaboration and continued learning of a team of their peers. Many of them are also invested in the spread of Reading Apprenticeship practices beyond their immediate team. In these roles, their leadership shines through in the inquiry stance they model and in the relationships they build within their team, with other faculty members, and with their administration.

Pulling a Team Together

At the community college level, pulling a team together can mean, first of all, finding people to be on your team. Even if it's only one!

Chris Padgett, who first got interested in Reading Apprenticeship through the online course for community college faculty (Reading Apprenticeship 101), recalls his determination to find a Reading Apprenticeship partner at American River College. "I assumed that if I could find someone to share my enthusiasm for Reading Apprenticeship and participate in the organizing of campus efforts, having a partner would make all the difference." Amanda Corcoran, a professor of English, expressed an interest in Reading Apprenticeship, and Chris followed up. As a team of two, they began to offer professional learning opportunities through which faculty receive professional development credit.

To add dedicated members to a team, Chris, at American River College, and Theresa Martin, at the College of San Mateo, have the same recommendation: Start locally. For Chris, this means sometimes lurking in the hallways of the history department to connect with colleagues. Similarly, Theresa found her strongest Reading Apprenticeship allies in the hallway that connects the CSM biology department. "For me," Theresa says, "the single most important piece was having that critical mass of support from my department. There are three of us in biology that started it, and because we have offices right next to each other, we could just talk about it in the hallways."

Teacher leaders at the secondary level operate in a somewhat less entrepreneurial context, one in which they have limited control. For example, they are not in charge of whether their fellow team members are volunteers or volunteered. In addition, as at most college campuses they do not control whether meeting time is covered in teachers' contracts, or how policy or budgetary shifts may propel or derail their efforts.

Yet their efforts are equally important in pulling together a professional team with a shared focus on supporting an inquiry into reading, instructional practice, and metacognitive conversation. At Souderton High School, after an intensive week of Reading Apprenticeship professional development, team leader Arlene Buchman recognized how different from their current practice Reading Apprenticeship was going to be for everyone and, likewise, how important the team would be. "When professional development takes you out of the box, it's a little bit scary," Arlene explains. "I wanted to do everything I could to support our team because, basically, we were pioneers. So it was really important that we stay together and help each other, support each other."

Understanding the Potential Roles of Teams and Team Membership
At school sites and on college campuses, literacy teams and Reading Apprenticeship–focused FIGs serve their members as a source of ongoing learning and support. Team members try on the Reading Apprenticeship

Framework and routines—within the team and in their classrooms—and together discuss and troubleshoot their experiences.

They may also use team meetings to read and discuss professional articles that prompt reflection about Reading Apprenticeship–aligned teaching and learning. When teachers are learning about Reading Apprenticeship in concert with other initiatives, team meetings can be a time to map and bring coherence to ways these initiatives may dovetail or amplify each other.

In doing this work, the team takes an inquiry stance toward their professional learning, recognizing the strengths they contribute to the team individually and together.

Theresa Martin describes the Reading Apprenticeship FIG meetings at the College of San Mateo in terms of mutual support. "In the beginning," she recalls, "we were encouraging each other to get free of that lecture mode, to move away from content delivery to really tackle the content in conjunction with students." Later meetings turned to problem solving. In one group meeting, several members raised a problem: they felt they were still having trouble surfacing their active reading strategies. To address this, the whole group decided to practice the Think Aloud routine, analyzing texts together to look at what kinds of reading strategies they could model for their students and that students could then appropriate.

Finding Your Leadership Identity

There are many ways teachers come to the role of teacher leader, and as many ways to fulfill the role as there are teacher leaders and teams. These processes are typically quite different in secondary versus college situations.

In some secondary schools, teacher leaders are selected by administrators, in others they are volunteers. They may have leadership experience as department heads or literacy coaches, or they may be relatively new teachers with fresh energy and enthusiasm. Or they may be teachers who emerge as leaders, finding their feet during the ongoing process of contributing to a Reading Apprenticeship community.

Many teacher leaders' biggest concern is whether they will be accepted by team members. Depending on their experience and status on the faculty, leadership may come more or less easily.

In a middle school or high school context, when administrators have selected the team's teacher leader, other team members may feel a pang of jealousy: "Why did she get picked?" Some team members may even express resentment that a peer is in a position that may seem to have more power or status.

Sara Jones was asked by her principal to lead the Reading Apprenticeship team at Titusville High School. As a social studies teacher who had just moved from the local middle school to the high school, she was concerned that team members might resent her, on a couple of counts—they had much more experience at the high school level, and the English people also had more experience with reading. Sara was transparent with her team members. As she recalls, "I was upfront that I recognized I was in a new role, all the way around—new classroom, new building, new administrators. Also, I was clear that I knew they didn't have time to waste, and that even though I wasn't sure what the meetings would look like, they would be meaningful."

As it turned out, Sara's colleagues appreciated her willingness to take on the role of teacher leader, but she admits to early nervousness "organizing" her peers. Their forbearance gave her a chance to settle into her role.

When Heather Arena was asked to be teacher leader of the Exeter High School Reading Apprenticeship team, she still felt a little junior professionally. She had some misgivings about whether she could represent her team effectively with administrators and actually get her peers to work together. "In the role of teacher leader," she reflects, "I had to learn how to advocate—for myself, for my team, for my students—what everyone needed. I also had to learn how to coordinate things with my peers. There's a balance of leading but not overstepping those boundaries."

At Berkley High School, where across several years Reading Apprenticeship has become the school's implicit instructional framework, the five teacher leaders—who facilitate on-site Reading Apprenticeship professional development as well as literacy team meetings—do sometimes become objects of teachers' frustration with the challenging work of learning new ways of teaching and of moving out of their comfort zone:

> There have been people who were bluntly negative with us because, to them, we represent this struggle of adjusting how they view their content area, their craft, and their role as a teacher. This is a massive shift that they're engaging. So they'll challenge us, hard, sometimes.
>
> We had to learn how to step back and recognize the times when a teacher's frustration—with us—was because we represented the discomfort they were facing. At those times, it was valuable to have other teacher leaders who could help us summon this less personal perspective.

Making Room for All Team Members

On any team, members will naturally have different levels of skill and enthusiasm for implementing Reading Apprenticeship as well as different degrees of comfort in sharing their experiences. Teacher leaders negotiate these differences in pulling a team together.

By maintaining an inquiry stance in the team meetings, teacher leaders lower the risk for everyone—of trying something new and of talking openly about what happened. As a new teacher leader, one of Cindy Miceli's strategies for encouraging risk taking is to model it. At Anaheim High School, her students sometimes serve as guinea pigs for the whole team:

> I think I'm more willing to take risks in my class because I just want to be able to share with the team, "Here's what I did." So, I guess I feel motivated to be more—daring? Or willing to try strategies that I'm not comfortable with, just to be that example to my team and say, "Hey, I tried it. I stunk at it or it was really great, and what do you think we should do differently, or how did you guys do it?" Then it kind of opens up discussion more.

Experienced Berkley High School teacher leader Angie Church finds that her empathy for teachers' risk taking is genuinely reassuring to them. She makes time informally, outside of team meetings, to encourage teachers who may need a little extra attention to unload confusions or questions:

> I know for myself, when I was trying to really transform my classroom, there were so many things I was questioning—am I even doing this the right way? So one of the things that I've tried to do within our building is to have those informal conversations, "What's going well? What are you struggling with? What questions do you have?" I think by using that inquiry stance, I've built relationships with people I probably wouldn't have otherwise. It's a form of support for people as they're trying to find their way.

Nika Hogan, a Reading Apprenticeship leader at Pasadena City College, expands on the importance of recognizing colleagues as learners with their own particular path. In her experience, even resistance or dissent can signal potential shifts, and deep learning, especially if the learning community remains open to differences:

> Those hard moments when a colleague feels seriously out of step with the group can be a gift to the community if it becomes an opportunity to show that there is space for dissent. We really don't know what is going to happen next for any one learner. It's unproductive to judge where people "should" be or what they should get out of something. That's not how learning works. I think our job is to sustain engagement in real inquiry and let people show up as themselves. We're trying to generate new knowledge. For that, we need authentic participation, and for that, we need to honor all kinds of perspectives.

Basic Considerations for Successful Team Meetings

The particulars of team meetings, such as when they happen, whether they are covered in teachers' contracts, or whether stipends are available, affect a team's culture and have a lot to do with a team's success. Teacher leaders do not set these conditions, but they do have to work with them. Regular communication with team members is one of the ways teacher leaders set a positive tone for collaboration, regardless of factors outside of their control.

In many instances, Reading Apprenticeship teachers volunteer their time for getting together; in others professional development time, staff meeting time, or departmental time is allocated for team meetings. In schools where teachers meet after school, paid time and volunteer time often merge. Teacher leader Rob Cushman finds that at Wyomissing High School, where meetings start at the final bell, they sometimes run into the dinner bell. "We've had meetings," Rob says, "where people just stayed and continued conversations well after the meeting was officially over."

At Anaheim High School, for two years running the team scheduled their own meetings. According to teacher leader Cindy Miceli (and many other teacher leaders), finding a good time for everyone is a challenge. "With our school," Cindy says, "there's not a great time for twelve teachers to meet together, so it is hard to get everybody on the same page. We've got people that teach zero period, so before school doesn't work. We have teachers that are coaches after school. We have two separate lunches."

Anaheim principal, Anna Corral, recognizes the importance of having coordinated time for Reading Apprenticeship team meetings. "Next year," she promises, "we want to schedule team meetings up front, give dates in advance, and tell people, 'Clear your calendar.'"

In Close-Up 2.5, Representative Team Meetings, typical meeting time is shown to range from a maximum of 40 minutes a week to a minimum of 30 minutes a month. Meetings are built into late start and early release times, before and after school, and even during school.

Another aspect of scheduling team meetings is *where* they happen. Typically, teams meet in the school, perhaps in the library or a team member's classroom. The Berkley team of teacher leaders meets on Saturday mornings, at one of their homes. Blue Ridge High School teacher leader Alicia Ross thinks that to build a feeling of collaboration, it's important that team members meet in one another's classrooms, in rotation.

Teacher leaders also have a few suggestions about keeping lines of team communication open, both to remind people of upcoming meetings and to build collegiality. Rob Cushman and the two other Wyomissing teacher leaders are consistent in helping their team members prepare for meetings. They send an email about one week before a meeting reminding team members what they may need to bring—student work or lesson plans, an article—and to think about something that will lead into the individual thinking time that begins each meeting. Sara Jones emails team members a draft agenda for the next meeting about a week after the most recent one and asks for feedback, which she incorporates. When the agenda is final, she sends it out to team members and copies the school administrators.

CLOSE-UP 2.5

Representative Secondary School Team Meetings

Team meetings range from thirty to ninety minutes and are typically held once a month. Some schools pay teachers for the time, while in other instances teachers voluntarily meet on their own time.

School/Spokesperson	Meeting Frequency	Meeting Time	Time Paid or Not
Souderton Area High School, Souderton, PA "The administration was fabulous in acknowledging the extra work teachers were putting in." —Arlene Buchman, teacher leader	Monthly	After school/ Sixty minutes	Not paid
Titusville High School, Titusville, PA "Our teachers are making the time to have these discussions, to keep things moving. They're not asking me to turn the master schedule upside down." —Scott Davie, principal	Monthly	Before school/ Thirty minutes	Not paid
Wayne Memorial High School, Wayne, MI "Every Tuesday afternoon is a scheduled departmental PLC meeting. The principal has allowed us one Tuesday a month for Reading Apprenticeship." —Kevin English, teacher leader	Monthly	After school/ Sixty minutes	Not paid
Anaheim High School, Anaheim, CA "At the beginning of the year, when there was more confusion and less confidence, it went longer because each teacher wanted to take their time and say, 'Am I doing it right?' 'What about this?'" —Cindy Miceli, teacher leader	Monthly	After school/ Forty minutes	Paid
Anderson High School, Anderson, IN "Before this year, our meetings were after school, and not everybody could come. But teachers agree the monthly meetings have been the front lines. So this year we have worked them into our school day." —Kay Winter, literacy coach	Monthly	Early release/ Forty-five minutes	Paid
Avon High School, Avon, IN "Our school day for teachers starts at 7:15, but the students don't start until 8 o'clock. So, we have about half an hour." —Beth May, instructional coach	Monthly	Before school/ Thirty minutes	Paid
Berkley High School, Berkley, MI "Teachers have told us that having our administration support their time out of the classroom for meetings has placed added value on the time." —Tracy Francis, teacher leader	Monthly	5th period Sixty-one minutes	Paid
West Senior High School, Traverse City, MI "Different groups PLC together. The Critical Friends Group wanted to work together on Reading Apprenticeship." —Charles Kolbusz, assistant principal	Six meetings	After school/ Ninety minutes	Paid

Alicia Ross believes in lots of informal communication with team members—in the hallways and lunch room—as well as on email and the team's Edmodo page, where team members post things like Reading Apprenticeship–related articles or something they are trying with students.

Managing the Elements of Team Meetings

What do teacher leaders need to know about running team meetings? Here are suggestions from experienced teacher leaders: Team members must first of all find the meetings worth their time. Agendas must telegraph a structure that reflects the Reading Apprenticeship Framework, and, especially for new teams, protocols lighten the burden of including everyone and moving along. When possible, food, too, is good!

Respecting Everyone's Time

Teacher leaders have all been in plenty of school meetings, some more valuable than others. They bring lessons about what to emulate or avoid to their own Reading Apprenticeship team meetings.

Sara Jones has only thirty minutes for meetings with the Titusville High School team. There is no time to waste, and the tone of the meetings is an important marker of what the team values:

> We're busy. So you don't want to come in without a plan, without an agenda. We talk about what the kids *can* do. And even with the challenges, we focus on how do you make that better. Our meetings do not devolve into complaints. We've never had to say, "Let's not have negative comments." That's the culture of our school, and it really works for the team as well.
>
> Even if it's thirty minutes a month, at 7:00 in the morning when everybody's tired, it is so valuable to have that sounding board, that support to work through the challenges, and to recognize how many students you're impacting in your entire building.

Alicia Ross also works with a thirty-minute meeting time frame, and describes her planning as "pretty metacognitive" about how to focus: "What's going to help you do your job better and how are you going to help the kids more." She is equally clear about what to avoid: "Complaint or gossip sessions—that's toxic!"

Using Agendas and Protocols

Teacher leaders find that even the simplest of agendas communicate respect for team members' time and that protocols are immensely helpful in guiding teams' inquiries. Some leaders explicitly recommend that these materials be provided in hard copy for each team member. Berkley High School teacher leader Kay Cole explains how the Berkley team leaders came to this idea:

> Each meeting we always started with a quick written reflection on how we have used Reading Apprenticeship over the previous month and what challenges or successes we want to bring to the team. At first, we just had people write on a piece of notebook paper. Then, sort of as a signal of the importance of this reflection, we typed up the prompts and made photocopies that people could write on.

With this slight adjustment, Kay says, teachers wrote more and the responses became fuller.

In a similarly small but significant move, the teacher leaders at Wyomissing High School have made it a point to print three-hole-punched meeting handouts that team members can write on and save. The handout is an organizer that begins with individual reflection, moves on to describe the group activities or protocols, and concludes with reflection on how an individual might take a concrete next step as a result of the day's meeting.

Teacher leaders build into their agendas a variety of protocols, such as those for looking at student work, sharing successes and challenges, or planning Reading Apprenticeship–rich lessons. (Chapter Six includes a range of detailed protocols.) Teacher leader Kevin English sees the protocols as a coherent piece with the Reading Apprenticeship Framework and an important tool for staying intentional:

> I'm really seeing the rewards of turning back to the same thing over and over again. Going back to the same four [Framework] dimensions, going back to student work, going back to struggles and successes, going back to this idea that our kids should be reading in their content areas. They have to learn how to read as historians or scientists. To read as writers. To go back to those ideas again and again and again just really helps us stay focused on what we're doing in our classroom and whether or not we're being intentional with our practices.

Food Is Good!

Breaking bread together—or even doughnuts—has a long history of building bonds. Teacher leaders mention food as a meeting staple with considerable regularity:

> —We do coffee, and juice, and doughnuts from 7:30 to 8:30.
> —To establish loyalty, feeding people is good.
> —Whoever facilitates brings food. So if there's food in the meeting, that makes it even better.
> —Reward the small victories. Any little thing we celebrated, we had food.
> —I think food could be underestimated.

Cultivating Relationships Beyond the Team

Reading Apprenticeship teacher leaders represent the team and the team's hard work beyond the confines of the team itself. They often serve as ambassadors to other colleagues, to administrators, and to a range of staff members whose interest helps to support a wider culture of literacy.

Learning to Talk Clearly About Reading Apprenticeship

When the principal of Blue Ridge High School started sending other teachers to observe in her classroom, Alicia Ross realized that she needed to better understand how to talk about the Reading Apprenticeship Framework that informed what they were seeing:

> People who didn't get the Reading Apprenticeship training are often coming to me. I'm having to talk about it more, so I think it's deepening my understanding of the Framework and metacognitive conversation. When people ask you questions, then you are thinking again about what you do. They'll ask you a question about a strategy, and you need to get across that this is about more than disjointed strategies.

Informing the Larger School Improvement Conversation

At Wayne Memorial High School, teacher leader Kevin English sensed that an emerging school-wide focus on discrete literacy strategies rather than the more holistic approach of Reading Apprenticeship made it important for his team to be explicit about what they are gaining from their experiences with the Reading Apprenticeship Framework as an alternative.

> We have two kinds of literacy movements in our building right now. There's a larger building-wide literacy initiative, it's being called, where they're really focusing on strategies—people bring ideas to a team put together by the principal, and the committee decides, "Let's develop this idea and present it to the staff."
>
> Then completely separate from that is the Reading Apprenticeship team that's focusing on changing the framework of their classrooms.
>
> It's been interesting because there are a few of us who straddle both groups. So we've been able to talk to the principal's team more about routines and frameworks that lead to greater reading or better reading, and to say, "This shift takes time, especially based on what we're seeing."

The exchange of information has been helpful. As Kevin explains, when the principal's team gave the Reading Apprenticeship team an opening to facilitate the school-wide professional development, they chose to focus on formative assessment, to highlight the more fundamental, less discrete-strategy-based way they are approaching literacy.

Making Common Cause with Reading Departments

In colleges with designated reading departments, Reading Apprenticeship can sometimes appear to be a threat to the expertise and dedication—or even the jobs—of these specialized faculty members. On the other hand, making common cause on behalf of students' literacy development benefits everyone.

At American River College, co-coordinators of the Reading Apprenticeship Project, Chris Padgett and Amanda Cocoran, were determined that Reading Apprenticeship be understood as a complement to the work of the college reading department, not as competition. As Chris says, the partnership that developed with the reading department was not immediate:

> In the beginning, a few of the reading department folks were curious, but also a bit guarded. Even if Reading Apprenticeship was not a replacement for the reading department, would it perhaps reduce the need for reading? But we were saying, "Absolutely not."

Chris and Amanda came up with the metaphor of their campus reading initiative as a three-legged stool. Two legs directly support students. The first leg is the reading department courses that students can take. The second leg is a support service run by the reading department where students can go for help with assigned reading in non-reading courses. The third leg supports faculty—so they can better support students. It takes the form of Reading Apprenticeship professional learning to help teachers of non-reading courses engage their students in reading course texts and in participating fully in the courses they are teaching.

Reaching Out to Administrators

In high schools and middle schools, administrators are sometimes members of the Reading Apprenticeship team or will at least drop in on team meetings. If not, the team leader has an important responsibility and challenge to keep them in the loop and rooting for the team. The more administrators know about what happens in the team meetings and what teachers are discovering and working on, the more the team *belongs* to the administrator when support is needed. Some teacher leaders have informal ways to invite administrators into the workings of the team. Others set regular meetings to update them and enlist their help and support. Whenever possible, inviting administrators to observe informally in classrooms where Reading Apprenticeship routines are embedded can be a powerful way to build understanding, appreciation, and support for the unique challenges and benefits of implementing Reading Apprenticeship school-wide.

On community college campuses, it can be important for teacher leaders to understand the prerogatives of various administrators and something about how budgets work. On campuses that stress shared governance, it helps to know where the connections are between faculty, staff, and administration in terms of decision making and budget allocation. Many faculty leaders of Reading

Apprenticeship efforts point out those deans are an invaluable base of support, for getting started and for making broader connections.

■ ■ ■

In all of their roles supporting Reading Apprenticeship—whether as advocates, petitioners, facilitators, or learners—Reading Apprenticeship leaders understand that inquiry—enacted through metacognitive conversation—is at the heart of Reading Apprenticeship professional learning, not only student learning. Chapter Three explains the role of inquiry in Reading Apprenticeship professional learning and why it matters.

The Role of Inquiry in Reading Apprenticeship Professional Learning

I am no expert here, except in the way all of my colleagues are experts in their own lives and experiences. We are going to share practice, try things out and reflect together, and do it over time. I'm calling the meetings, but I believe that the leadership will come from us all.

—Melody Schneider, Edmonds Community College teacher leader

THE READING Apprenticeship approach to professional learning, just like the Reading Apprenticeship Framework, is a product of collaborative research and development over time. Many teacher partners of different subject areas and grade levels helped us conceptualize our approach. Even more have participated in testing and refining it. Finally, numerous research studies, including randomized controlled studies, attest to the effectiveness of Reading Apprenticeship professional development for teachers and their students.

At its core, the Reading Apprenticeship approach to professional learning is a series of inquiries. These are designed to build teachers' understanding of the myriad internal activities they personally engage in to comprehend complex texts, their knowledge of the features of text that may present challenges to the inexperienced reader, their recognition and appreciation of the specific literacy practices of their disciplines, their ability to articulate the formerly tacit mental moves they rely upon when faced with comprehension problems, and their confidence in their capacity to support students in becoming stronger readers and learners in the disciplines. Inquiries also support teachers in understanding the ways social environments have shaped their own literacy capacities and identities over time and, by extension, play weighty roles in their students' relationships to reading, writing, and learning in school. In addition, by understanding and using Reading Apprenticeship tools and approaches, teachers are able to learn from their students in the very process of teaching—through ongoing formative assessment, inquiry, and reflection.

Clearly, this kind of teaching is a highly complex endeavor, involving thinking, planning, decision making, and assessment of students in the dynamic flow of classroom instruction. Teachers carry out instructional actions that bring new ideas in education to life, shape students' opportunities to learn, evaluate students' performance and capabilities, and orchestrate students' interactions with one another and class materials, including texts.[1] To orchestrate such complexity moment by moment, teachers need access to professional learning that recognizes and informs their professional capacity and judgment related both to what they teach and how students acquire specific content knowledge and skills, including literacy practices.[2]

We have found that by engaging teachers in a variety of inquiries into their own and their students' reading practices, we can assist teachers in constructing richer and more complex theories of reading, in seeing their students' capacities to read and learn in new and more generous ways, and in drawing on and developing their own resources and knowledge as teachers of reading *in their discipline.* Importantly, we have seen teachers transform their classrooms into places where students develop new identities as capable academic readers.

In this chapter we present a case for an inquiry-based approach to teacher learning that is strategically designed to transform teachers' classroom practices by building key teaching capacities and a deeply experiential knowledge of reading. In designing inquiries for professional learning, our goal is to build *generative* knowledge for teachers—knowledge that enables them to create, or *generate,* from their deep understanding of reading, informed and helpful instructional responses to students' reading and thinking in the academic disciplines.[3] The methods we recommend in these pages both draw from and contribute to the knowledge base in the field about best practices in professional development. They start with an active, inquiry stance toward teaching and learning and literacy itself.

Why Inquiry?

Our approach to teacher professional learning grew from our own observations and authentic questions. Students often profess to have completed assigned readings, yet say they do not understand the text. Students stumble over words when they read aloud in class. Teachers often feel they must summarize assigned texts for students if the class is to have a meaningful discussion of academic ideas. Why, we wondered, do students seem to have such difficulty reading the texts assigned in their classes? As is so often the case, one question led to another: How do students approach the reading? What do they actually do when they read? And what do we really mean by *reading*? What are we expecting to see in student performance? Finally, we pondered, Come to think of it, what do *we* do when we read texts like these?

Pursuing answers to such questions led to the development of the Reading Apprenticeship Framework, based on case study research with students, surveys of the field, and current understandings of language and learning. But this pursuit turned out to have another important benefit: teachers who engaged in these inquiries into their own and their students' reading processes learned a great deal about the nature of literacy, about the complexities of academic texts, about themselves as readers, about the discipline-specific nature of their own literacy practices, and about their students as literacy learners. They replaced long-held misconceptions about reading as a simple skill with the recognition that reading is a complex endeavor. These teachers came to see that despite their students' inexperience doing highly sophisticated academic work, these same students *could* do this level of work when given the right support.

By exploring reading and thinking processes that support their own and student reading, by experiencing specific pedagogies that facilitate their own work with complex texts and tasks, and then by trying these pedagogies out in their classroom instruction, teachers came to see both the utility and limits of these moves and strategies for their students. They exercised new professional judgment and developed confidence in their own capacity to make instructional decisions, try new strategies, and solve problems as needed to address implementation challenges.

This wasn't a surprise. After all, a great deal has been written about the value of teacher action research for renewing instructional practice and teacher effectiveness.[4] Leaders in teacher education have long promoted an inquiry stance toward teaching, with teachers learning in and from practice by documenting and reflecting on their work and the responses of their students.[5] We share these values but also know that teachers have many demands on their time and attention. Pursuing one's own questions about instruction can lead to great insights, but the path may necessarily meander. In reality, very few teachers have the luxury of generating their own research projects, given the press of their many responsibilities. Yet we believe all teachers, indeed all learners, can benefit from opportunities to reflect and inquire.

By definition, inquiry cannot be passive. It is an active, intentional process animated by questions and observations. The inquirer actively engages in constructing new understandings by building theories, finding patterns, and making meaning. Inquiry experiences are therefore potentially transformative in their impact on knowledge and practices. And so, we wondered, Could we distill what we had learned and experienced about effective inquiries to make teacher learning opportunities as focused and efficient as possible yet still retain the active, inquiry experience of exploring and asking authentic questions in the company of others, similarly engaged?

Inevitably, professional development provides a model of instruction, and often a poor one, with delivery of specific strategies and information taking center stage.[6] With this in mind, we designed inquiries to embed the pedagogies we hoped teachers would enact in their classrooms (especially regarding grouping, integrated strategy instruction, inquiry practices, and discussion protocols). Engaging in inquiries would therefore provide teachers with an experiential knowledge base of literacy routines and strategies, as well as a set of tools that would support them to implement these practices. Over time, such ongoing inquiry would develop teachers' adaptive expertise, allowing them to solve problems and implement routines flexibly.[7] This experiential, instructional tool kit, situated in ongoing inquiry activities and explorations, would meet teachers' needs for concrete and practical solutions to the everyday problem of students' limited comprehension of course texts. The collaborative inquiry, by its nature, would invite teachers to reflect on and critique particular instructional techniques and to adapt them to teaching and their own students.[8]

Targeting Key Teacher Learning Goals

We set out to design inquiries that could focus teacher learning in areas we had found were key to strengthening literacy instruction in the academic disciplines. We were aware of several ways teachers commonly misconstrue literacy and how to foster it; these were ripe for exploration.

First, from long experience we knew that many secondary and post-secondary teachers view reading as a basic skill, one that students should have mastered before arriving in their classrooms. When faced with students who are ill prepared to tackle the complexity of texts and tasks required in their subject area classes, these teachers often conclude that it must be someone else's job to catch them up.

Second, because teachers are frequently very familiar with the texts they teach from, they may have "expert blind spots" that prevent them from seeing the complexities and stumbling blocks these texts present to learners. Failing to appreciate the difficulty that disciplinary texts and tasks may present to inexperienced students is one reason teachers find it perplexing when their students do not comprehend what seems perfectly plain to them.

Third, many teachers who themselves wield specific knowledge and interpretive practices in the reading of texts in their disciplines remain unaware of their uniquely disciplinary practices and knowledge. They may hold expectations of skillful performance that are shaped by the values of their discipline yet hold these expectations unaware. When students miss the mark, these teachers may describe students' failings as a lack of critical thinking skills or an absence of interpretive facility when, in fact, these students merely lack experience with disciplinary practices and texts.

Fourth, some concerned teachers readily recognize the difficulties their specialized texts pose for students who are unprepared for them—the prior knowledge expected by authors but which their students are unlikely to share, the vocabulary their students have not acquired, the concepts their students will find foreign. These teachers often believe texts present only barriers rather than opportunities for learning. Thus, they avoid the text as much as possible, finding other means to deliver content to students. Even teachers of literature may feel pressed to find other ways to introduce their students to disciplinary texts—by reading aloud, playing recordings, or even showing feature films based on works of the canon. Unless students somehow already have acquired the vocabulary, concepts, and knowledge expected by an author, teachers may believe reading will have little value. Yet they themselves have often read in order to learn something they did not know; indeed, a fundamental purpose for writing is to share with others new ideas, emerging knowledge, novel insights, and compelling understandings.

Finally, having rarely seen their students exhibit facility with complex texts or keen insights into text meaning, many teachers from across the academic spectrum harbor perhaps secret beliefs that their students are simply not up to the academic tasks increasingly seen as necessary for college and careers. They almost never see their students in arenas outside their classrooms, where a fuller representation of students' skill, knowledge, experience, and talent may be on offer. They may naturally mistake students' inexperience for inability. Without a vision of their students' promise, they perhaps reduce their expectations of what students may accomplish and therefore reduce the challenge and academic rigor of their courses.

This is the set of understandable but nevertheless unproductive conceptions that many teachers hold and that we have designed potent professional learning inquiries to address.

Building Teachers' Generative Knowledge of Literacy

To dispel a view of reading as a simple skill, teachers need to experience reading as an active, problem-solving process. By reading complex texts with others and surfacing how they are making sense of these texts, teachers begin to develop a sense of the many mental moves involved in reading, including the work they and others do to manage their own engagement with texts. By hearing their colleagues work to construct meaning with texts, they see how it is that many alternate understandings are sensible. Guided inquiries into new genres and forms of text lead teachers to attend to the knowledge demands of texts as well as to novel text features that convey meaning.

Similarly, by having challenging experiences in which they themselves learn from text, building knowledge intentionally about words, content, and genres with which they were previously inexperienced, teachers come to reassess the role texts may play in learning. And by contrasting their approaches to texts and tasks to those held by teachers of other disciplines, teachers begin to see the uniquely disciplinary aspects of their literacies and to value the contributions they are uniquely positioned to make to their students' learning.

An example of one such inquiry we have used with teachers who do not themselves teach biology is a phylogenetic investigation involving finch photos, guided by a set of disciplinary questions: What are the physical characteristics of each bird? Which birds might be most closely related? What makes you think so? What questions do you have? We support teachers to explore these questions by engaging in metacognitive reading and discourse routines that they can then implement in their classrooms. (See Team Tool 3.1, A Phylogenetic Investigation for Not-Biology Teachers, for a description of the inquiry.)

Engaging in metacognitive conversation about their reading and reasoning processes prepares teachers to hold such conversations in their own classrooms. They experience the wonder of many other minds at work, see how specific inquiry prompts support readers to dig into their mental processes, and come to recognize how this kind of inquiry drives engagement and learning for those who participate in it.

In designing such inquiries into the reading process, we draw on understandings about literacy and on studies of teacher professional development, our own and those of others. Unpacking what is required to accomplish tasks like complex reading comprehension, constructing an algebraic proof, or composing an essay builds an experiential understanding of what is hard for learners in carrying out such tasks. The National Writing Project, Cognitively Guided Instruction, and many other successful professional development enterprises build knowledge for teaching by engaging teachers in carrying out valued tasks and simultaneously analyzing what is necessary to know and be able to do to accomplish these tasks.[9] Similarly, Graves (1989) invited teachers to know their own literacies through inquiries into their own reading processes.[10] To capture the reading processes we engage in, however tacitly, we ask: What are we doing to make sense of this text? How are we going about it? What do we do when the text isn't making sense to us? How do we solve comprehension problems?

TEAM TOOL 3.1

A Phylogenetic Investigation for Not-Biology Teachers

PURPOSE

By discovering unique "literacies" of an unfamiliar discipline, teachers recognize and value the contributions they are uniquely positioned to make to students' learning in their particular discipline. This sample is for not-biology teachers. Similar model lessons about unfamiliar content, with texts at a challenge level for teachers, can be designed in any content with a similar result. Teachers are always able to identify new vocabulary and concepts that they worked out through metacognitive conversation with partners and small groups, as well as new ideas and information they acquired in the process.

SAMPLE PROCEDURE

- List for the whole group a set of guiding questions:
  - What are the physical characteristics of each bird?
  - Which birds might be most closely related?
  - What makes you think so?
  - What questions do you have?
- Distribute to partners photographs of a set of different finches and direct them to the guiding questions. While one partner makes observations, problem solves, and thinks aloud, the other partner listens and records what the first partner is saying.
- In groups of four, after pairs share their most interesting observations, reflections, questions, and conclusions, the group discusses their ideas about which finches might be most closely related.
- Together group members construct a claim and support it with evidence from the photographs.
- Finally, groups design a whiteboard explanation to share with other groups explaining their hypothesis about relationships between the finches, including a schematic representation of how the group thinks the finches are related, observations and evidence that support their claim, relevant background knowledge, connections and interpretations that could be researched and substantiated, questions, research limitations and unresolved issues, and a proposal for additional research.
- Participants follow this hypothesis construction by conducting similar collaborative inquiries as they read and discuss a set of challenging, original-source texts (Darwin's field studies of the Galapagos finches), using Think Aloud and small group protocols identical to those engaged in with the finch photos.
- Groups return to their whiteboard explanations to revise their work based on new understandings from their reading.
- Reflecting on this process, participants identify any new ideas or learning they experienced from reading the varied texts (photographs and field notes), and how the process of learning was supported by pair and small group metacognitive conversations.

TEAM TOOL 3.2

What May an Arrow Mean?

Science diagrams, such as the one depicted here, are a rich resource for teachers' inquiry into the perhaps surprising puzzles their own texts may present inexperienced readers.

SAMPLE TEXT

Consider the following diagram from a data portal associated with the U.S. Department of Energy. Although an extensive text caption (not shown) accompanies the diagram, focusing on the diagram alone can generate insights into the varieties of texts and ways of signaling meaning used in academic materials.

Photosynthesis Production of Hydrogen from Water

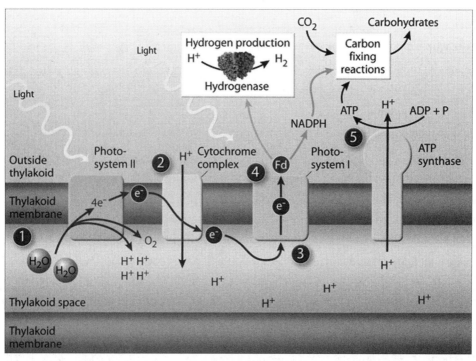

Source: Office of Biological and Environmental Research of the U.S. Department of Energy Office of Science. Download the diagram from https://public.ornl.gov/site/gallery/detail.cfm?id=152&topic=&citation=9&general=&restsection=

In designing inquiries into text structures and features, we draw on work in text and discourse analysis.[11] For example, in the discipline of literary interpretation, Rabinowitz (1987) describes how readers construct understandings of literature by recognizing and using the signposts authors design into their writings—applying rules of notice, rules of signification, and rules

"Photosynthesis Production of Hydrogen from Water" is depicted with several different types of arrows:

- An undulating series of arrows curves through rectangles labeled "Photosystem II," "Cytochrome complex," and "Photosystem I"

- A set of wavy lines labeled "Light" head toward the microscopic parts of the "Thylakoid membrane" on the inside of a leaf

- Arced lines labeled "Hydrogen production" and "ATP synthase" associated with molecules appear at steps 4 and 5

- Straight lines strike boldly down, and up, at numbered steps 2, 3, and 5, associated with H+

- Additional curving lines connect the action within the thylakoid to boxes labeled "Hydrogen production" and "Carbon fixing reactions"

Nowhere in the diagram are the meanings of these differently shaped lines explained. In this science diagram, arrows and order and shape convey meaning and rely on conventional understandings for their communicative power. But what if a reader is highly inexperienced with such texts and does not share these conventions?

When we have engaged teachers in exploring what an arrow may mean with diagrams such as this one, even naïve science readers are able to identify the different arrow types and, together with colleagues, come up with plausible meanings.

Such inquiries open teachers' eyes to the hidden-from-view, coded messages their own texts can hold.

of configuration to the interpretation of a literary text.[12] By extension, authors of historical texts, scientific explanations, and the like leave conventional signposts throughout their writings in order to guide readers' interpretation. Steeped in their discipline and its aims, they write assuming that others share social purposes and understandings about the nature of their texts. Scientists, for instance, are engaged in explaining phenomena in the world, using the best evidence available to them, oftentimes evidence they themselves generate through experimentation.[13] Understanding science texts to be evidence-based arguments for particular explanations helps readers engage with and interpret them.

Just as language practices are socially and culturally shaped and may not be shared across people—resulting, perhaps, in miscommunication and misinterpretation—readers who do not share the interpretive practices and conventions relied upon by writers may have difficulty understanding authorial intent. In surfacing what we know about the signposts and conventions and genres of texts in our disciplines, we ask: What do we know? How do we know it? What in the text are we using to build our understanding? What do we know about texts like this? How they are constructed? How do they work? What are they for? For example, Team Tool 3.2, What May an Arrow Mean, describes an inquiry into the conventions of reading a science diagram— conventions that may elude readers who are inexperienced with this specialized text.

Building Teachers' Insight into Student Learning and Assets

To dispel a view of students as incapable of complex academic reading tasks, teachers need opportunities to explore and theorize about student performance, in the company of others. In our professional development work, we often use videotapes of classroom lessons, small group conversations, and even individual students' reading and thinking aloud to provide windows into student reading processes. Often these snapshots of student performance are designed to present moments in which students struggle, juxtaposed with moments of astonishing clarity and insight. What do we notice about students' thinking and talk about reading? What does the talk among students in this small group reveal about how students are making sense of the text?

Student work products can serve a similar purpose for inquiry once teachers have themselves examined the texts and tasks and can appreciate the complexity of the work students were tackling. For example: What can we learn when students have been asked to read and annotate a text? What do we notice about their thinking from these annotations? What strategies do we see students using to make sense of the reading? What understandings of scientific or literary or historical or mathematical reasoning do these samples demonstrate? What resources do students bring to their reading of this text? What strategies, knowledge, or dispositions do they yet need to acquire?

In a collegial dialogue driven by evidence and interpretation protocols, when multiple perspectives about students' work products are being considered, teachers have an opportunity to notice what resources and assets students draw on to carry out assigned work, as well as to notice ways students yet need to develop. Exploring student work for evidence of student thinking helps teachers see students as theory builders and pattern finders. They begin to notice the assets students bring to their work, rather than merely seeing the gaps and deficits in their performances.

Building Teachers' Insight into Instruction

Our work with teachers aims at helping them develop a collaborative classroom environment in which metacognitive conversations about reading experiences can become routine and students have extensive opportunities to read with the support of the teacher and their peers. In such classrooms, instructional techniques for explicitly teaching comprehension strategies can accelerate students' development of valuable conceptions about and approaches to reading. Yet for teachers to make effective use of instructional techniques, they need opportunities to try them out, to assess how they work to support reading and learning, and to smooth out any kinks in their use. They need to see instruction itself as a process of inquiry.

To promote teachers' effective use of particular instructional strategies, we engage them in using specific strategic approaches as they read together from complex fiction and nonfiction materials. Encountering various approaches to instruction while working in groups to comprehend a piece from *Scientific American* or *The Atlantic,* for example, gives teachers an opportunity to assess for themselves how these strategies work to support the group's learning. Teachers learn these strategic approaches in the very context they will need to help students apply them—while working collaboratively with other readers to construct meaning with texts. In doing so, teachers deepen their knowledge about the nuances of strategy choice and use.

For example, teachers may have been told that frontloading vocabulary that will come up in texts reduces barriers to subject area learning. When they explored reading and learning processes with challenging science texts themselves, one group of science teachers realized that many of the vocabulary words they needed to learn were, in fact, scientific concepts. In this instance, frontloading strategies for vocabulary learning did not help them gain needed knowledge *ahead* of their reading. Instead, they noticed that their concept knowledge deepened as they read, especially if they were invited to keep track of how their ideas about a concept were changing. Rather than frontloading conceptual vocabulary, these teachers designed ways of assisting their students to monitor conceptual change while reading, to support their science learning.

Similarly, Raphael's QAR strategy[14] is often promoted as a comprehension strategy for use with challenging texts. When teachers work together to use the strategy, they discover that categorizing a question as one of Raphael's question types—"right there," "pulling it together," "text and me," or "on my own" —can be slippery (and not always salient).

Working through these issues as they read together allows teachers to stumble on and think through problems that emerge in the practice of strategy instruction. Instead of using instructional strategies as all-purpose recipes, teachers explore using them for their own purposes. They gain confidence as well as firsthand knowledge of the processes involved. As teachers gain experience with these strategies, we encourage them to exercise their professional judgment about how well particular strategies serve their instructional ends.

Teachers may respond to this invitation by adapting question frames to focus on key ways of thinking in particular disciplines or by selecting particular strategies for their utility in helping students acquire particular thinking habits. For example, visualizing structures, processes, and interactions is important to learning in many branches of science. So focusing students' attention on creating mental images, drawing structures or processes, or walking through an interaction between objects can pay off handsomely when carried out with science reading. Similarly, helping students to ask discipline-based questions—for instance, "Is there a pattern here?" when they explore a math problem or graph, or "From whose perspective is this written?" when they explore a history text or artifact—may help students into discipline-based ways of thinking better.

As teachers practice using particular instructional strategies to support their own reading in professional development sessions, we invite them to adaptively integrate these strategies into their subject area instruction. Ultimately, these invitations to inquire into the nature of reading and reading processes, into students' thinking and theory-making, and into specific instructional and disciplinary approaches help teachers begin to approach their own teaching as inquiry.

By engaging in repeated inquiries of this type, with different texts, tasks, disciplines, and levels of complexity, teachers build a deeply experiential knowledge base about literacy. Carrying out such inquiries in a professional community helps teachers articulate and build a language for describing largely internal states and aspects of language and texts they have not necessarily given name to. In addition, carrying out collaborative inquiry offers teachers ongoing practice in metacognitive conversation. They *rehearse*, in the company of colleagues, precisely the kind of conversations they will need to hold in their classrooms, with students, to apprentice students in disciplinary literacies.[15]

Equally important, as teachers learn to notice what student learning looks like and sounds like[16] through examining and theorizing about student work and work products, they will begin to listen differently to their students in class during discussions and small group work, to see students differently when they grade and score their work, to draw on the knowledge and experiences evident in classroom metacognitive conversation, and to value the process as well as the product of learning.[17]

Cycles of implementation, reflection, and refinement of instruction occur as teachers try out new approaches in the classroom and return to discuss their experience with their colleagues and to engage in additional inquiries and learning experiences. As teachers create metacognitive conversations in their own classrooms, they bring their work back to professional development sessions to share. They reflect on how things are going in their classrooms, use evidence from their classrooms to gauge the quality of student reading and thinking, and anticipate their next instructional steps. Teaching begins to resemble a cycle of inquiry as teachers innovate, reflect, and refine their practices. This type of long-term, recursive inquiry enables teachers to continue to learn in and from their own teaching practice.

Building Professional Capacity to Advance Student Literacy

Advancing the academic literacy of all students as envisioned in new standards for college and career readiness requires effective methods of building teacher capacity through ongoing teacher professional learning. Much of the professional development traditionally offered for literacy in the subject areas focuses on specific instructional methods for teaching comprehension strategies, rather than on building teachers' understanding of literacy practices, processes, and learning. Yet we know from a long history of research in reading that reading comprehension strategies are rarely taught in subject area classes, even when teachers are trained to use these strategies.[18] Furthermore, even when teachers do try to implement literacy strategies, they often struggle to "balance" content and strategy instruction. For many others, a culture of whole class direct instruction means that engaging students themselves in the active processing of text and learning is an unnatural act.[19]

We have charted a different course by focusing on collaborative, metacognitive inquiry as a means for learning—for teachers and for their students. The mode of instruction that characterizes Reading Apprenticeship requires teachers to responsively navigate interactions between learners, texts, tasks, and content. We take to heart Ball and Cohen's formulation of instructional capacity:[20]

> Instructional capacity is partly a function of what teachers know *students* are capable of doing and what teachers know *they* are professionally capable of doing with students. . . . Every student and curriculum is a bundle of possibilities, and teachers whose perceptions have been more finely honed to see those possibilities, and who know more about how to take advantage of them, will be more effective.

How then to transform more traditional forms of instruction in which teachers convey and test students' retention of information into active, inquiry-based, apprenticeship learning opportunities? The inquiry designs for teacher learning and collegial teamwork that we describe in this book aim to build teachers' capacity to engage with students in collaborative meaning making and problem solving *during ongoing instruction with course readings.*[21] They are designed to foster teachers' *adaptive expertise,*[22] honing teachers' perceptions of the possibilities in the texts and in their students, and building teacher capacity to surface and model effective ways to address comprehension problems that arise as the varied learners in the classroom interact with course materials. When professional learning fosters and supports inquiry, teachers take an inquiry stance to their own teaching, learning from ongoing practice how best to perfect their craft.

Our studies of inquiry-based professional development for secondary and post-secondary teachers demonstrate that with the support of well-designed inquiry activities, teachers make profound changes in their teaching practice. (See Appendix B for a summary of this research.) These changes, in turn, provide powerful new learning opportunities to students that make a difference in student achievement. Through this kind of generative professional learning, teachers learn to closely and critically read both their curriculum materials and their students' performances to inform their professional judgment and instructional actions. They develop the means by which to weigh competing ideas about literacy and classroom methodologies. They are able to move beyond the eddying currents of debate and mandate to take warranted action in the classroom. They become designers as well as implementers, informed professionals rather than mere conduits for other people's designs and agendas. Educating all students to their highest potential rests on this kind of professionalism.

■ ■ ■

Ensuring that a culture of literacy has a reasonable chance to take hold, structures are needed that embed ongoing collegial inquiry into workplace practices. Such structures for teacher collaboration and discourse are best established with attention to the social and personal dimensions of the Reading Apprenticeship Framework. Chapter Four describes what goes into setting the social and personal foundations for the risk taking inherent in professional inquiry.

Notes

1. Ball, D. L., & Cohen, D. K. (1996). Reform by the book: What is—or might be—the role of curriculum materials in teacher learning and instructional reform? *Educational Researcher, 25*(9), 6–8, 14.

   Coburn, C. E. (2003). Rethinking scale: Moving beyond numbers to deep and lasting change. *Educational researcher, 32*(6), 3–12.

Darling-Hammond, L., & Sykes, G. (1999). *Teaching as the learning profession: Handbook of policy and practice. Jossey-Bass Education Series.* San Francisco: Jossey-Bass.

Lin, X., Schwartz, D. L., & Hatano, G. (2005). Toward teachers' adaptive metacognition. *Educational Psychologist, 40,* 245–255.

Rose, M. (Winter, 2015). School reform fails the test. *The American Scholar.* Retrieved from https://theamericanscholar.org/school-reform-fails-the-test/#.VUqhKmbA3i8

Shulman, L. S. (1986). Those who understand: Knowledge growth in teaching. *Educational Researcher, 15,* 4–14.

Shulman, L. S. (1987). Knowledge and teaching: Foundations of the new reform. *Harvard Educational Review, 57,* 1–22.

2. Ball, D. L. (2000). Bridging practices: Intertwining content and pedagogy in teaching and learning to teach. *Journal of Teacher Education, 51,* 241–247.

Desimone, L., Smith, T. M., & Phillips, K. (2013). Linking student achievement growth to professional development participation and changes in instruction: A longitudinal study of elementary students and teachers in Title I schools. *Teachers College Record, 115*(5), 1–46.

Garet, M. S., Porter, A. C., Desimone, L., Birman, B. F., & Yoon, K. S. (2001). What makes professional development effective? Results from a national sample of teachers. *American Educational Research Journal, 38*(4), 915–945.

Guskey, T. R., & Yoon, K. S. (2009). What works in professional development? *Phi Delta Kappan, 90*(7), 495–500.

Lampert, M., Franke, M. L., Kazemi, E., Ghousseini, H., Turrou, A. C., Beasley, H., et al. (2013). Keeping it complex: Using rehearsals to support novice teacher learning of ambitious teaching. *Journal of Teacher Education, 64*(3), 226–243.

3. Darling-Hammond, L., & Bransford, J. (Eds.) (2005). *Preparing teachers for a changing world* (pp. 40–87). San Francisco: Jossey-Bass.

Franke, M. L., Carpenter, T. P., Levi, L., & Fennema, E. (2001). Capturing teachers' generative change: A follow-up study of professional development in mathematics. *American Educational Research Journal, 38*(3), 653–689.

Lai, M. K., McNaughton, S., Amituanai-Toloa, M., Turner, R., & Hsiao, S. (2009). Sustained acceleration of achievement in reading comprehension: The New Zealand experience. *Reading Research Quarterly, 44*(1), 30–56.

Penuel, W. R., Fishman, B. J., Yamaguchi, R., & Gallagher, L. P. (2007). What makes professional development effective? Strategies that foster curriculum implementation. *American Educational Research Journal, 44*(4), 921–958.

Rose, M. (Winter, 2015). School reform fails the test (see note 1).

Zhang, J., Hong, H. Y., Scardamalia, M., Teo, C. L., & Morley, E. A. (2011). Sustaining knowledge building as a principle-based innovation at an elementary school. *The Journal of the Learning Sciences, 20*(2), 262–307.

4. Altrichter, H., Feldman, A., Posch, P., & Somekh, B. (2013). *Teachers investigate their work: An introduction to action research across the professions.* New York: Routledge.

Cochran-Smith, M., & Lytle, S. L. (1999). The teacher research movement: A decade later. *Educational Researcher, 28*(7), 15–25.

McNiff, J. (2013). *Action research: Principles and practice*. New York: Routledge.

Somekh, B. (2010). The Collaborative Action Research Network: 30 years of agency in developing educational action research. *Educational Action Research, 18*(1), 103–121.

5. Anderson, G. L., & Herr, K. (2011). Scaling up "evidence-based" practices for teachers is a profitable but discredited paradigm. *Educational Researcher, 40*(6), 287–289.

Cochran-Smith, M., & S. Lytle (1996). Communities for teacher research: Fringe or forefront. In *Teacher learning: New policies, new practices*, M. McLaughlin & I. Oberman (Eds.), 92–112. New York: Teachers College Press.

Schon, D. A. (1983). *The reflective practitioner: How professionals think in action*. New York: Basic Books.

Stenhouse, L. (1981). What counts as research? *British Journal of Educational Studies, 29*(2), 103–14.

6. Anderson, G. L., & Herr, K. (2011). Scaling up "evidence-based" practices (see note 5).

Lefstein, A. (2008). Changing classroom practice through the English National Literacy Strategy: A micro-interactional perspective. *American Educational Research Journal, 45*(3), 701–737.

7. Bransford, J., Derry, S., Berliner, D., & Hammerness, K. (2005). Theories of learning and their role in teaching. In L. Darling-Hammond & J. Bransford (Eds.), *Preparing teachers for a changing world* (pp. 40–87). San Francisco: Jossey-Bass.

Lai, M. K., McNaughton, S., Amituanai-Toloa, M., Turner, R., & Hsiao, S. (2009). Sustained acceleration of achievement (see note 3).

Lampert, M., Franke, M. L., Kazemi, E., Ghousseini, H., Turrou, A. C., Beasley, H., et al. (2013). Keeping it complex (see note 2).

8. Gutiérrez, K. D., & Penuel, W. R. (2014). Relevance to practice as a criterion for rigor. *Educational Researcher, 43*(1), 19–23.

Penuel, W. R., Fishman, B. J., Haugan Cheng, B., & Sabelli, N. (2011). Organizing Research and Development at the Intersection of Learning, Implementation, and Design. *Educational Researcher, 40*(7), 331–337.

Penuel, W. R., Fishman, B. J., Yamaguchi, R., & Gallagher, L. P. (2007). What makes professional development effective? (see note 3).

9. Borko, H. (2004). Professional development and teacher learning: Mapping the terrain. *Educational Researcher, 33*(8), 3–15.

Franke, M. L., Carpenter, T. P., Levi, L., & Fennema, E. (2001). Capturing teachers' generative change (see note 3).

Lieberman, A., & Wood, D. R. (2002). The National Writing Project. *Educational Leadership, 59*(6), 40–43.

Stankevich, D. M. (Ed.). (2011). *Getting it in writing: Quests to become outstanding and effective writing teachers*. Charlotte, NC: Information Age Publishing.

10. Graves, D. H. (1989). *Discover your own literacy*. Portsmouth, NH: Heinemann.

11. Cazden, C. B. (1988). *Classroom discourse: The language of teaching and learning.* Portsmouth, NH: Heinemann.

    Cope, B., & Kalantzis, M. (1993). *The powers of literacy.* Pittsburgh: University of Pittsburgh Press.

    Courts, P. L. (1997). *Multicultural literacies: Dialect, discourse, and diversity.* New York: Peter Lang International Academic Publishers.

    Delpit, L. (1995). *Other peoples' children: Cultural conflict in the classroom.* New York: The New Press.

    Fang, Z., & Schleppegrell, M. J. (2010). Disciplinary literacies across content areas: Supporting secondary reading through functional language analysis. *Journal of Adolescent & Adult Literacy, 53*(7), 587–597.

    Goldman, S. R., & Rakestraw, J. A. (2000). Structural aspects of constructing meaning from text. In M. L. Kamil, P. Mosenthal, P. D. Pearson, & R. Barr (Eds.), *Handbook of reading research (Vol. 3,* pp. 311–335). Mahwah, NJ.: Erlbaum.

    Langer, J. A. (2011). *Envisioning knowledge: Building literacy in the academic disciplines.* New York: Teachers College Press.

    Pearson, P. D., & Camperell, K. (1994). Comprehension of text structures. In R. Ruddell, M. Ruddell, & H. Songer (Eds.), *Theoretical models and processes of reading* (pp. 448–468). Newark, DE: International Reading Association.

    Thier, M., & Daviss, B. (2002). *The new science literacy: Using language skills to help students learn science.* Plymouth, NH: Heinemann.

12. Rabinowitz, P. J. (1987). *Before reading: Narrative conventions and the politics of interpretation.* Ithaca, NY: Cornell University Press.

13. Cavagnetto, A. R. (2010). Argument to foster scientific literacy: A review of argument interventions in k–12 science contexts. *Review of Educational Research, 80*(3), 336–371.

    NGSS Lead States. (2013). *Next Generation Science Standards: For states, by states.* Washington, DC: The National Academies Press.

    Osborne, J. (2002). Science without literacy: A ship without a sail? *Cambridge Journal of Education, 32*(2), 203–218.

14. Raphael, T. (1982). Question-answering strategies for children. *Reading Teacher, 36*(2), pp. 186–191.

15. Lampert, M., Franke, M. L., Kazemi, E., Ghousseini, H., Turrou, A. C., Beasley, H., et al. (2013). Keeping it complex (see note 2).

    Lampert, M., Ghousseini, H., & Beasley, H. (2015). Positioning novice teachers as agents in learning teaching. In L. Resnick, C. Asterhan, & S. Clarke (Eds.), *Socializing intelligence through academic talk and dialogue.* Washington, DC: American Educational Research Association.

16. Sherin, M., & van Es, E. (2005). Using video to support teachers' ability to notice classroom interactions. *Journal of Technology and Teacher Education, 13*(3), 475–491.

    Sherin, M. G., & van Es, E. A. (2009). Effects of video club participation on teachers' professional vision. *Journal of Teacher Education, 60*(1), 20–37.

van Es, E. A., & Sherin, M. G. (2002). Learning to notice: Scaffolding new teachers' interpretations of classroom interactions. *Journal of Technology and Teacher Education, 10*(4), 571–596.

van Es, E. A., & Sherin, M. G. (2008). Mathematics teachers' "learning to notice" in the context of a video club. *Teaching and Teacher Education, 24,* 244–276.

17. Borko, H. (2004). Professional development and teacher learning (see note 9).

Desimone, L. M. (2009). Improving impact studies of teachers' professional development: Toward better conceptualizations and measures. *Educational Researcher, 38*(3), 181–199.

Garet, M. S., Porter, A. C., Desimone, L., Birman, B. F., & Yoon, K. S. (2001). What makes professional development effective? (see note 2).

Guskey, T. R., & Yoon, K. S. (2009). What works in professional development? (see note 2).

18. ACT, Inc. (2009). *ACT national curriculum survey 2009.* Iowa City, IA: Author.

Alvermann, D. E., & Moore, D. W. (1991). Secondary school reading. In R. Barr, M. L. Kamil, P. B. Mosenthal, & P. D. Pearson (Eds.), *Handbook of reading research* (Vol. 2., pp. 951–983). New York: Longman.

Duffy, G. G., Roehler, L. R., Meloth, M. S., Vavrus, L. G., Book, C., Putnam, J., & Wesselman, R. (1986). The relationship between explicit verbal explanations during reading skill instruction and student awareness and achievement: A study of reading teacher effects. *Reading Research Quarterly, 21*(3), 237–252.

Duke, N. (2000). 3.6 minutes per day: The scarcity of informational texts in first grade. *Reading Research Quarterly, 35*(2), 202–224.

Durkin, D. (1978). What classroom observations reveal about reading comprehension instruction. *Reading Research Quarterly,* 481–533.

Fielding, L. G., & Pearson, D. P. (1994). Reading comprehension: What works. *Educational Leadership, 51,* 62–68.

Ness, M. K. (2008). Supporting secondary readers: When teachers provide the "what," not the "how." *American Secondary Education, 37*(1), 80–95.

Richardson, V. (Ed.). (1994). *Teacher change and the staff development process.* New York: Teachers College Press.

Snow, C. (2002). *Reading for understanding: Toward an R&D program in reading comprehension.* Santa Monica, CA: RAND Corporation.

19. Reed, D. K. (2009). A synthesis of professional development on the implementation of literacy strategies for middle school content area teachers. *Research in Middle Level Education Online, 32*(10), 1–12.

20. Ball, D., & Cohen, D. (1999). Developing practice, developing practitioners: Toward a practice-based theory of professional education. In L. Darling-Hammond & D. Sykes (Eds.), *Teaching as the learning profession: Handbook of policy and practice* (pp. 7–9) San Francisco: Jossey-Bass.

21. Greenleaf, C., Brown, W., & Litman, C. (2004). Apprenticing urban youth to science literacy. In D. S. Strickland & D. E. Alvermann (Eds.), *Bridging the literacy achievement gap, grades 4–12* (pp. 200–226). New York: Teachers College Press.

Greenleaf, C., & Schoenbach, R. (2004). Building capacity for the responsive teaching of reading in the academic disciplines: Strategic inquiry designs for middle and high school teachers' professional development. In D. Strickland & M. Kamil (Eds.), *Improving reading achievement through professional development* (pp. 97–127). Norwood, MA: Christopher Gordon Publishers.

22. Bransford, J., Derry, S., Berliner, D., & Hammerness, K. (2005). Theories of learning and their role in teaching (see note 6).

Lai, M. K., McNaughton, S., Amituanai-Toloa, M., Turner, R., & Hsiao, S. (2009). Sustained acceleration of achievement (see note 3).

CHAPTER FOUR

Setting the Social and Personal Foundations for Inquiry

The teachers in our network made those connections about the Reading Apprenticeship Framework: the same things they were doing in the classroom for their kids—including building the social dimension, working on that personal dimension—they needed to do with each other, also.

—Naomi Norman, Interim Assistant Superintendent,
Achievement and Student Services, Washtenaw Intermediate
School District and Livingston Educational Service Agency, Michigan

IN A READING Apprenticeship team, professional learning community, or faculty inquiry group, just as in Reading Apprenticeship classrooms, the social and personal dimensions are a necessary foundation for the collaborative learning and risk taking that Reading Apprenticeship encourages.

One of the first challenges teachers encounter is to their understanding of the teacher's role—each of their individual roles in a Reading Apprenticeship classroom. As community college physics instructor Lilit Haroyan found, this is the kind of challenge when it helps to have a supportive team to see you through:

Are we really transmitters of the information or are we facilitators of the learners? Traditionally I would go to the board and do my stuff. I would look at the students and say, "You got it, right, guys?"

My identity as an instructor has changed. When we find our true identity in a classroom—what is our role—then according to that we can adjust. Adjustment is always hard, and time-consuming, and requires lots of effort. So it's very important to have a community around you that can support you with that.

In this brief chapter, we consider three routines that teams have found helpful as they begin to build their community and before they launch collaborative inquiries: (1) setting norms for how the team will work together, (2) sharing experiences via the Personal Reading History about the formation of their own reader identities, and (3) setting learning goals for themselves and their students. Doing these routines as a team is also a valuable way for everyone to rehearse doing them with students.

One item of business in anticipation of all the work teams will do together: When team members have a notebook or other way to store their meeting agendas and materials, they have a convenient way to review their progress, moments of discovery, and remaining questions. A team's norms and team members' Personal Reading Histories and learning goals would be logical first entries.

Setting Norms for Collaboration and Risk Taking

> — Be encouraging! Who doesn't like a little encouragement?
> — Know that we are here to learn from each other and there is no judgment. Everyone's experience and insights are appreciated.
> — I am going to be out in left field trying to figure out how to do this in a math classroom. So please don't assume everyone understands reading lingo.
> — Ask questions. Don't be afraid to reveal that you don't know something!
> — I agree with all of you on having a safe place to ask away.
>
> —Norms from a group of community college instructors
> in an online Reading Apprenticeship course

The generous and not atypical norms above were established by a cross-disciplinary group of community college teachers. Because teachers commonly experience students' sense of them as authorities—with *answers*—these norms create a safe space for teachers to be honest about their questions. The team-generated norms help members remain sensitive to the risktaking involved in making public a range of personal reading processes and instructional practices that are usually private. Setting norms for collaboration honors the social and personal dimensions of the team's learning community.

When teams focus on participating in inquiry rather than demonstrating expertise and establish collegial norms at the beginning of their work together, participants establish a foundation for a safe and productive learning community.

At Santa Rosa Junior College, instructor Ann Foster facilitates a Reading Apprenticeship community of practice for new faculty as part of their induction into the campus culture. Ann finds that setting and returning to norms encourages everyone's involvement in the well-being of the group:

> We are able to identify what are the things we need as learners, whether it's somebody listening, or everybody participating, or just something logistical like making sure we have lots of breaks, or making sure we have a chance to work with everybody. So it is the very first thing we do.

> Then I type those up and throughout the community of practice we
> build a PowerPoint—here are the norms we set last time, here's our
> feedback after the first meeting, and this is how I'm trying to incorporate
> the feedback today. So I'm always trying to include their voice and truly
> take on more of a facilitation role than a leadership role.

The Santa Rosa new-faculty groups prepare for setting norms by writing a quick reflection on a learning situation that supported them and why it did. Alternatively, some teams warm up to setting norms by surfacing their fears and hopes for the team's experience together. (See the norm-setting protocol, Team Tool 4.1.)

Even with participation norms in place, team members will have different degrees of comfort coming to the team for help. Sara Jones, teacher leader at Titusville High School, describes how her team made room for one member who was hesitant to share his teaching experiences with the group:

> It's a fine line you walk to support without being overbearing and to
> encourage people without making them feel bad about not doing what
> some other people are doing.
>
> We had somebody who had been trying some things in his class-
> room, not as often as a lot of people on the team, and some things were
> going well and some not, but he was leery to share that with the team.
>
> Then we had one meeting three-quarters of the way through our
> first year when he came to the meeting with something he had tried that
> didn't go very well. He shared the challenge and asked the team for
> advice and support. That was really important because it was the first
> time he was comfortable enough to trust the team, to say, "I tried this
> and it's not going as well as I had hoped. I'm not really sure what to do
> about it. Can you all help me figure that out?"
>
> To come in and say that—for somebody who was an observer up to
> then—I think that was such an important point for the team as well as
> the individual.

Teams may find as they go along that they want to add to their norms or change them. At Souderton High School, team leader Arlene Buchman recalls that the team decided to be more explicit about how they would listen to one another:

> We let the person speak completely. We never interrupted. It was
> important that people weren't jumping all over each other.

Some norms take the form of meeting agreements, more focused on logistics than participation: We will turn our cell phones off. The host will bring refreshments. We will meet the third Wednesday of every month. We will meet for one hour.

TEAM TOOL 4.1

Norm-Setting Protocol for Team Participation and Accountability

Norm setting can include making basic agreements about when, where, and for what number of minutes a team will meet. But often these agreements are already in place before a team sits down together to set their participation norms—*how* they will meet.

AFFIRMING YOUR TEAM'S PURPOSE

Participants in a team share the understanding that the group's purpose is to learn together through ongoing inquiry. Team members should expect to be interactive and collaborative; being explicit about what they value from one another supports that collaboration. The participation norms the group establishes together are those explicit expectations.

INDIVIDUAL THINK-WRITE WARM-UP

Explain that team members, including yourself, will respond in writing for the next two minutes to these two prompts.

- Fears: If this team turns out to be one of your worst professional learning experiences ever, what might be some of its characteristics?

- Hopes: If this team turns out to be one of your best professional learning experiences ever, what might be some of its characteristics?

CHART RESPONSES

Solicit fears and hopes from the team and have two team members record for all to see.

Facilitate a discussion about what agreements the team can make to decrease the likelihood of realizing team members' fears and increase the likelihood of achieving team members' hopes.

Have the recording team members edit the charts to reflect the agreements.

Check for consensus. Explain that these norms belong to the group and can be changed or added to at any time, by the group.

Make a final set of norms that can be reproduced for team members, on three-hole-punched paper, for example.

REVISIT NORMS ANY TIME

It may be that a particular team experience is the catalyst for revisiting norms. Or the team may decide simply to revisit their norms after a few meetings because they have a better sense of how they want to work together. If you or any other team member wants to revisit the team norms, try this simple writing prompt to set up a discussion:

- What norms would make this an optimal learning community for you?

*See also the discussion and protocol for class norm setting in *Reading for Understanding*, Chapter 3.

It was one of these meeting agreements that tested Heather Arena's leadership in the second year of the Exeter High School team's work together. One team member wanted to change the biggest norm of all—we will meet:

> Over the summer we had set our norms of when we would be meeting, who would be hosting, how long the meetings would run, and we uploaded those into our school calendar so everyone was aware of the meetings ahead of time. Mid-October, one team member emailed the rest of us that since we don't *have* to have these meetings, she would like to not have them at all, because she felt a little burned out.
>
> It does happen that we get meetings thrown at us as the year progresses, but it's not our goal to just drop off after the first year of Reading Apprenticeship. We had thought that our team meetings were very important and we wanted to continue them.
>
> I sent out an email to the team, and I thanked her for opening dialogue among the team so that we could discuss it and possibly revise our norms if we wanted to do that. I didn't want to ignore her or leave it on a back burner, but I did emphasize that we set our meetings ahead of time to try to avoid this predicament.
>
> Email dialogue opened up and some people did voice concern about the length of the meetings. We had hour-long meetings our first year and we had said we wanted to continue that our second year. So the compromise was to shorten the length of the meetings but not the number of meetings. We felt the monthly check-in was a very important boost to continue the Reading Apprenticeship work we were doing, and just to support one another.
>
> The compromise did work out, and she continued to come to meetings.

By inviting the team to reconsider their meeting agreements in the face of one member's unhappiness, Heather honored the team's collaborative norms and was able to keep the team together.

Sharing Personal Reading Histories

> Tom and I discussed how our reading experiences may not be that different from our students' and that we tend to think reading is an easy process for everyone else. Perhaps we could help more students if we took the mystery out of it and said, "Yes, it is hard."
> —High school principal sharing with other administrators in an online course

When team members share Personal Reading Histories, they make connections to one another and to the literacy lives of their students. They build understanding about how reading experiences (their own and others') profoundly affect individual lives and identities.

Within a team, exchanging reading histories is not only relevant to team members' work together, but it also contributes to developing and strengthening the social and personal dimensions on the team. For colleagues, just as for students, speaking honestly about one's own reading history can cross into painful territory, where norms of a safe community are crucial. Hearing from colleagues about how they were or were not supported to value reading or to read complex text, team members recognize the range of reading identities, attitudes, and beliefs represented on their team and often expand their sensibilities about the varied kinds of literacy expertise and barriers we all have. Close-Up 4.1, Personal Reading Histories: Building Team Community, samples a few of these reflections.

The Personal Reading History Protocol, Team Tool 4.2, is a two-part activity that structures personal reflection and sharing within the team. The protocol prompts teachers to recognize that negative experiences can be as important as positive ones in a reader's development, and, even in a group of educators who

---

CLOSE-UP 4.1

Personal Reading Histories: Building Team Community

When adults reflect on their own Personal Reading Histories, they can more easily see what any reader needs in the way of support and how commonly barriers get in the way.

As an undergraduate I was an avid reader of fiction, yet I struggled with textbooks and information, trying to remember what I read. I panicked when I started graduate school. Everyone on the East Coast seemed so much smarter than me. So it was helpful to remember some of these things when talking with Jennifer about my reading history. It made me empathize even more with my students in so many ways—struggling, being frustrated, thinking that everyone else knew what was going on.

—Kathleen Motoike, community college composition instructor

The first big thing that stands out to me in my history is that my mom was a reader, and she read all the time. I was in a supportive environment where I not only had someone modeling and encouraging me to read, but she also went out of her way to make sure I had books to read. I wonder if I hadn't had that growing up, if I would be the type of reader I am today. Whether reading comes easily to someone, or if it is difficult, you really do need a support system to become independent.

—Becky Leist, K-12 building principal

Creating my Personal Reading History in terms of "barriers and supports" really forced me consider just how certain events or influences played specific roles, both good and bad, in my evolution as a reader. Talking with Mark personalized the process and helped me to realize just how unique our own histories are. I felt a heightened sensitivity to the complex and individual histories our students each bring to the classroom.

—Andy McCutcheon, community college reading instructor

TEAM TOOL 4.2

Personal Reading History Protocol

Individually and then together, team members reflect on high and low moments in their reading histories and the implications for their work inquiring into their own reading and the reading of their students.

PURPOSE

The group understands that the Personal Reading History routine is an opportunity to reflect on how people develop reader identities and what hinders or helps in that development. By sharing their reader histories, team members will better understand the beliefs and attitudes about reading development they bring to their work together. The activity will also help team members rehearse what it might be like to bring the Personal Reading History into their classrooms.

INDIVIDUAL WRITING

Provide about ten minutes for team members to write individual responses to prompts about key moments or events in their development as readers:

- What reading experiences stand out for you? High points? Low points?

- Were there times when your reading experience or the materials you were reading made you feel like an insider? Like an outsider?

- What supported your literacy development? What discouraged it?

PARTNER SHARING

Explain that partners and then the whole group will share highlights from their journey to becoming adult readers and subject area teachers. Allow six minutes for partners to share. Provide these guidelines:

- Take turns describing some highlights of your reading histories. Let one person speak without interruption, then discuss. Reverse roles after three minutes.

- Discuss commonalities and surprises in your histories.

- What were some similarities in your barriers and supports?

- What were some surprises?

GROUP DISCUSSION

The whole group debriefs these reflective partnerships. As in debriefing the Personal Reading History in classrooms, it is important to make sure there is space made for participants to talk about reading barriers and not to assume that reading has been easy and supported for everyone on the team.

- What ideas do you have about the impact of reading experiences in people's lives?

- What ideas do you have about how reflecting and sharing our Personal Reading Histories may impact our work as a team?

- How might teachers and students benefit from doing Personal Reading Histories in class?

*See also the discussion and protocol for classroom investigation of Personal Reading History in Chapter Three of *Reading for Understanding*.

readily value reading, almost all will have had formative reading experiences when they felt like outsiders, flummoxed by complex texts in particular subject areas, as well as insiders, confident of working their way through other kinds of text.

Setting Learning Goals

> I love the teacher practice rubric because it gives me a great reality check and reminds me of the areas of Reading Apprenticeship that I want to work on and need to work on in the classroom.
>
> —Joan Herman, community college instructor

What do team members hope to gain personally and as a team from their time together? What do they hope to know and be able to do? What goals do they have for their students? Reading Apprenticeship can initially feel overwhelming to teachers until they discover for themselves the secret for success emphasized in *Reading for Understanding*: Start small and keep trying.

Two tools can help teachers focus on a manageable set of Reading Apprenticeship goals: the Reading Apprenticeship Teacher Practice Rubric and the Reading Apprenticeship Student Learning Goals (Appendix C). Once a teacher selects a set of goals to focus on, these goals can serve as a reference for teacher and student formative assessment. Teachers can also refer to the teacher and student goals as they plan lessons and observe in one another's classrooms.

Over time, selected goals may change as learning progresses and new areas of interest arise.

Using the Reading Apprenticeship Teacher Practice Rubric

Team Tool 4.3, Inquiry into Teacher Practice Goals, suggests a format that teams can use to select and share their individual goals, notice commonalities and differences, and consider how the team's work can support everyone.

Using the Reading Apprenticeship Student Learning Goals

Learning goals for students parallel the Reading Apprenticeship Framework and are designed to be shared with students as well as to inform teachers' goal setting and instructional planning. Teams can adapt Team Tool 4.3 to focus on one or two student learning goals they wish to support in particular, and to think about the support they could use from team members to move toward those teaching changes.

TEAM TOOL 4.3

Inquiry into Teacher Practice Goals

PURPOSE

When teachers invest their limited time in being part of a Reading Apprenticeship team, they have certain hopes and expectations for what they will learn and how the team will support their learning. By setting individual learning goals, teachers give shape to those hopes. By sharing those goals, they have a better chance of providing one another the support they may need.

PROCEDURE

In advance: Team members will each need a copy of the Reading Apprenticeship Teacher Practice Rubric (Appendix C).

- Team members individually read and Talk to the Text of the *main goals* in the rubric, not the subgoals.

- Individuals then choose *one goal* to read more closely. They Talk to the Text on the subgoals for that goal, including ideas about which of those many subgoals they would like to work on and what support they might need to do so.

- Partners share their notes about the goal and subgoals they chose, why they chose them, and the supports they would like.

- If time allows, team members share their goals with the whole group, noting similarities and differences and ways that team members hope to be supported.

Principles for Team Inquiry

When teams take time up front to acknowledge the social and personal dimensions of their work together, they set a foundation for their future shared learning. In anticipation of this work, we offer a set of principles based on our experience and the experience of colleagues on campuses across the country who have contributed to this approach to professional learning. (See Team Tool 4.4, Principles for Team Inquiry.) These principles, meant to evolve as they are used in local settings, support teachers' capacity to teach disciplinary reading in response to student thinking. They help teachers keep the goal of expanding students' abilities for disciplined, creative, and critical thinking in the forefront of their work.

TEAM TOOL 4.4

Principles for Team Inquiry

These four principles can help teams make effective use of their time together:

- Take one another's convictions (about the role of reading in your classroom, about students, about best ways to help students gain conceptual understanding in their discipline) as a starting point for inquiry and learning, rather than as a given.

- Engage one another in rigorous reading and metacognitive conversations about reading within and across academic disciplines.

- Practice multiple inquiry activities designed to build one another's capacities for high-quality, responsive teaching.

- Be conscious as a team of experiencing the same approaches promoted in the Reading Apprenticeship Framework for helping students to become engaged and strategic readers and learners.

■ ■ ■

Building on a foundation of the strong social and personal dimensions of collegial inquiry, Chapter Five introduces specific inquiries teams can make into their members' own reading processes, reading complex texts together as experts in some disciplines and novices in others. Chapter Six introduces team-based inquiries into Reading Apprenticeship instructional practices and students' literacy learning.

Exploring Reading as Colleagues

My experience with Reading Apprenticeship started a year ago when during a presentation we were asked to read a textual explanation of electrical current, accompanied by a diagram. We were told we would be asked questions after the reading. We read silently and later admitted we all struggled, but, nonetheless, we all "attacked" the complexity of the unfamiliar text. The questions asked in follow-up were not about the content we had read, but about the strategies we had used to create meaning. This activity was an epiphany for me. I have strategies I had never realized that I am continually employing when reading—and all of us in that room had them.
—Marcia Rogers, Orange Coast College English instructor

IT MAY BE that the most important work literacy team members can do together is to explore their own reading processes. The discoveries team members make about how *they* engage and wrestle with complex text—and the power of doing it collaboratively—have direct application to their work with students. By having their own experience of making their reading processes visible, teachers are able to build confidence in their ability to help students benefit from similar metacognitive, problem-solving approaches for understanding complex disciplinary text.

In this chapter, we describe a range of ways for teams to undertake the sometimes risky business of publicly engaging with challenging reading. Building on the norm setting described in Chapter Four for establishing a safe climate in which to share thinking, teams can productively engage in what we call Reading Process Analyses (RPAs), structures for exchanging tentative ideas, confusions, and interesting moments of clarity when working with complex text. Also described in this chapter, the Text and Task Analysis routine takes RPAs another step—into classroom practice—asking teachers to anticipate the challenges a text may present to students and to consider which RPAs might help. Finally, a brief discussion addresses how to choose texts for team inquiries that raise teachers' awareness of their own reading processes and disciplinary literacies.

In any apprenticeship relationship, success depends in large part on how well the mentor understands, articulates, and demonstrates his or her craft. Because proficient readers, teachers included, usually read in a fairly automatic fashion, a major focus of a team's work together should be to explore their own reading processes and to share what they are discovering—namely, that as successful readers in their own disciplines, they are their own best resources and guides in helping students learn how to engage with texts related to those disciplines.

By investigating their reading processes, teachers realize that in addition to a broad repertoire of comprehension strategies they can employ with difficult texts, they possess substantial knowledge about the *codes* of their respective disciplines. Teachers begin to see that by teaching these strategies and codes in the natural course of a subject area class, they are helping students develop independent access to the substance of the discipline.

Yet developing an explicit awareness of one's own reading process is more challenging, and rewarding, than might be expected. Teachers' investigation into their own reading begins a professional conversation that builds knowledge and insight into student learning and prepares teachers to engage students in metacognitive conversation about their own reading and thinking processes.

Metacognition at the Center

> This year we're trying to renorm everybody to this idea of metacognitive conversations really being the center.
> —Tiffany Ingle, Pasadena City College ESL and College 1 instructor

All Reading Apprenticeship practices have metacognitive conversation at their heart. It is true within the social and personal dimensions and it is perhaps never clearer than in the Reading Process Analyses described in this chapter. Yet we have been reminded that what may become clear over time can also be elusive when *everything* about Reading Apprenticeship is new and pulling for teachers' attention.

At Pasadena City College, where Tiffany Ingle has been part of a team designing Reading Apprenticeship–infused faculty institutes, metacognitive conversation was the implicit goal of the institute learning experiences, yet the team found they needed to be more explicit about what those conversations would look like and feel like and why they were important:

> We're being a lot more intentional with metacognitive conversation and why it's important. People need to experience the value of metacognition to build their own knowledge of pedagogy and to solve problems in their

own reading. We thought that would come out naturally, but it was hard for many of the professors. This year we took a step back and really delved deeply into that.

Cindy Hicks, who learned about Reading Apprenticeship over several years of participation in a cross-campus study group and in a faculty inquiry group at Chabot College, also found that a deep appreciation of metacognitive conversation came slowly. Now as a Reading Apprenticeship professional developer, Cindy cites her own understanding of metacognitive conversation as essential professional learning:

> The first two or three semesters that I was working on Reading Apprenticeship with my students, I saw increased engagement and retention right away. But not every student was engaged, and not every student succeeded or improved as I would have hoped. There was a lot of confusion at first, for students and myself too, about engaging in metacognitive conversation versus engaging in the classroom discussions that we normally engage students in.
>
> When I began to understand RPAs (Reading Process Analyses) and how they functioned to engage students in metacognitive conversation, then I saw real development. I pulled back so that I was using the same one or two RPAs regularly throughout the term. Later I began adding other activities, other RPAs to involve students in reflecting on their own process and to engage them with their own understanding. I began to see how to do that, what it means to really be student-centered.

As teams explore the many RPAs presented in this chapter, we echo Cindy's suggestion to choose one or two to practice regularly with students before moving on to others.

Suggestions for conducting any of these reading inquiries appear in Team Tool 5.1, Guidelines for Conducting Reading Inquiries.

Engaging in Reading Process Analysis

> Going through my own Reading Process Analysis was really powerful. It gave me real insight into how to talk to students about scaffolding their own learning. The most helpful thing about it was recognizing that there were times in my life when I really didn't understand what I read and I didn't know what to do, even though I'm a "good" reader.

Teachers may naturally feel they are supposed to *know* and *comprehend* what they read; however, upon meeting a complex text for the first time, virtually all readers must actually work at understanding its message and intricacy. Unveiling this *coming to understand* process, particularly in front of one's colleagues, can

> ## TEAM TOOL 5.1
>
> ## Guidelines for Conducting Reading Inquiries
>
> The following concrete suggestions can help teams organize inquiries into how they read—the reading processes they use, the confusions they encounter, and the role of collaboration in sorting them out.
>
> 1. Develop a clear set of goals and norms for your time together. Aim for a professional community that is safe and supportive, where it is "cool to be confused" by a hard text.
> 2. Continually ground your team's work by exploring your own processes of reading texts in and across your varied disciplines. *Use texts that are challenging for you as adults* so that you can make your problem-solving processes visible.
> 3. Protect time for inquiry into your own close reading processes. It will be natural to slip into teacher mode, thinking immediately about the implications of your reading processes for teaching students. Structure your time together with routines for inquiry, followed only near the end of your meeting time for reflection and exchange of ideas about implications for practice.
> 4. Establish the procedural routines and roles (such as facilitator or timekeeper) that will keep you on track with your own goals and norms. You might assign group members turns at being responsible for finding and providing complex texts for group inquiries.
> 5. Consider conducting reading inquiries within *and* across disciplines and organize to do so.

be uncomfortable. Admitting a lack of background information or knowledge, identifying where the struggles are coming up in a text, and simply finding words to describe the perhaps fleeting ideas and visual images that constitute thought is a strange experience for teachers.

Yet in our experience, the payoff for exploring reading processes with colleagues is worth the initial discomfort and uncertainty. For one thing, it is invigorating intellectual work to grapple with complex text, a process teachers often attack with authentic curiosity. For another, it is fascinating to hear how others think and reason. As one teacher said, laughing with surprise at a colleague's Think Aloud, "I just love your mind!" But most important, teachers gain new access to their own expertise and ways to make use of this expertise in mentoring students.

At Anderson High School, a member of the literacy team was able to use his experience inquiring into his own reading processes to help students understand that they had the capacity to take on difficult text. As team leader Kay Winter recounts, instead of telling students *about* the text, this teacher introduced them to the idea that they could *read* it:

> One teacher who has been teaching for thirty years in our corporation
> (district) said that he is a better, stronger teacher than ever because he is

now able to help the students understand the reading material instead of just glossing over it to get to the point of a lab or whatever it was that they were working on. He started out this year giving the students a college-level article about biology, and he modeled the first paragraph for them and then broke students up, and the students started going through and explaining it. At the end they'd had quite an interesting discussion, and all the students were kind of excited about it. Then he said, "That was a senior-level college text." The kids were amazed that they had read it, and understood it, and gotten through it. He started his school year that way, and that really made the kids understand, "Well, this is just a high school textbook. If I try, I'm going to be able to understand it," instead of just writing it off, "Man, this is a science textbook. I'm never going to understand it."

Our experience over the years has been that in collegial settings, teachers help each other overcome some of the natural awkwardness of trying to focus on their own reading processes. For any of us, sharing our thinking with others makes it possible to pay closer attention to things that might otherwise go unnoticed. Hearing another reader explain something he or she did to make sense of a text may well trigger a realization that we did something quite similar—or conversely, something quite different—even though we were not tuned into our strategy at the moment.

Through collegial inquiry into reading, team members learn or are reminded that just as a single proficient reader does not approach all texts in exactly the same way, different proficient readers will approach the same text in varied ways. Together, team members expand their repertoires of comprehension strategies and knowledge about how to read effectively within and across disciplines.

Most often, teachers work in disciplinary-specific groups to identify their reading moves. As knowledgeable readers in a subject area, they enact discipline-specific ways of reasoning with text or display knowledge about the purpose, structures, and intricacies of common types of texts in the discipline. They extend one another's appreciation for their discourse community—how disciplinary knowledge is communicated and understood.

For science teacher Douglas Womelsdorf, the inquiry he did with colleagues into the reading of science texts has been an evolving revelation that science content and science literacy are inseparable:

> Though my training is in science curriculum—and mainly the content involved—I must say I am really enjoying participating in the conversation about this line between science education and literacy that is slowly fading away for me. I now see the connection between the two and the need for both to work hand in hand. It is awesome to see as it develops. I might not be a literacy coach or have much training in academic literacy, but I sure now have an interest in the role it plays in teaching science.

Another science teacher, teacher leader Rob Cushman came to Reading Apprenticeship from a university education steeped in inquiry, yet he worried about how to translate that into his classroom practice. He found that the work he did with colleagues inquiring into their own disciplinary reading processes was the key:

> I felt like I didn't have that understanding of how you introduce and move students into an inquiry-based mentality. I think being able to approach reading in an inquiry-based way was a good scaffold for my classroom teaching as a whole, even in terms of the laboratory science we were doing.

The advantages of subject-specific literacy teams are many since teams can infuse their Reading Apprenticeship experience deeply into the workings of their particular academic departments. However, literacy teams need not be subject-specific. Many teams include teachers of varied disciplines. This is not a bad thing! Mixing teachers from different disciplines has interesting benefits. By exploring reading processes across disciplines, team members can make contrasting approaches, reasoning processes, and text features apparent in new ways and reveal to disciplinary insiders what may be hard for others outside their disciplines to understand. Cross-disciplinary reading inquiries can help teachers develop a better appreciation of their own knowledge and expertise and a clear set of purposes for undertaking Reading Apprenticeship in their subject areas.

Regardless of whether teams are disciplinary-specific or cross-disciplinary, the inquiries described in this chapter help all teams to engage in Reading Process Analyses. These begin with open-ended discoveries of what are often invisible reading processes, and then move along to focus on particular inquiries for more particular purposes, such as questioning a text or wondering about words. Finally, a few routines specifically help teachers plan lessons, anticipating the challenges students may face and how to scaffold their success.

All-Purpose Reading Process Analysis Routines

Reading Process Analysis routines can be used for many purposes, at first, perhaps, simply to acquaint readers with the various ways their reading processes ramble or focus. Teams will want to explore the open-ended nature of RPAs such as Capturing the Reading Process, Thinking Aloud, Talking to the Text, and Metacognitive Logs and Evidence/Interpretation note takers. Many teachers choose from these all-purpose RPAs when settling on one or two RPAs to first introduce and establish with their students.

Capturing the Reading Process

A useful starting place for professional exploration parallels the classroom activity of Capturing the Reading Process (see Chapter Four in *Reading for Understanding*), but with a complex and interesting text written for a knowledgeable adult readership. The various reading processes team members find themselves using to comprehend a challenging piece of text are "captured" for all to see on a list that demonstrates how varied the strategies are that readers bring to bear when making meaning from text. Team Tool 5.2, Capturing the Reading Process Inquiry, is a suggested protocol for facilitating a team's inquiry.

In Close-Up 5.1, Capturing the Reading Process Reflection, community college teacher leader Melody Schneider describes introducing colleagues at Edmonds Community College to their reading processes. As she says, it was

---

TEAM TOOL 5.2

Capturing the Reading Process Inquiry

PURPOSE

The purpose of this inquiry is not to build a comprehensive list so much as to make clear that different readers use both similar and different reading processes and can benefit from making them public to one another. (In classrooms, such lists are often used as the start of a Reading Strategies List for a particular text or for a more general "living list" of reading strategies that stays posted for reference, additions, and edits.)

When teams are cross-disciplinary, a popular variation of this inquiry is for team members to alternate hosting the inquiry with a text they select from their own discipline. The discipline "insider" who hosts refrains from sharing his or her reading processes until hearing from discipline "outsider" colleagues.

PROCEDURE

Team members read independently, then write for a few moments to capture or document any mental moves or affective responses they made during the reading. The team then compiles a Reading Strategies List with everyone's contributions and considers what insights they are gaining into the reading process.

- Set a time limit for team members to read a complex text to themselves for long enough to dig into it but not necessarily to finish the reading (seven to ten minutes). If the inquiry is being hosted by a disciplinary insider, the host briefly explains what kind of text it is.

(Continued)

- At the time limit, ask team members to respond in writing to these prompts about their reading process:
  - What did you do while you were reading to make sense of this text?
  - What got in the way of your reading?
  - Even if you weren't aware of it at the time, what comprehension problems did you solve while reading?
  - What if any problems remain?
- Following this individual documentation, lead the team in compiling and discussing a Reading Strategies List. Facilitate discussion that gets underneath team members' strategic reading moves. Probes like the following can help to highlight the complexities of close reading processes:
  - What is one thing you did to make sense of this text?
  - Where in the text did you do that?
  - What did it do for your understanding? How did it help?
- If the team has a discipline insider as host, that person shares what he or she noticed about the outsider group members' reading processes as well as how he or she approached the text as an insider. The host facilitates a discussion probing for commonalities and differences in reading strategies and experiences. Team members work to identify the particular schema demands of the text.
- Finally, facilitate reflection on classroom practice:
  - What implications can we draw from our experience in this inquiry for our students? For instruction?

"fascinating" for adults to think about their thinking with an unfamiliar text. And not always easy for them to put the content of the text to the side.

At Chabot College, one vivid experience of capturing the disciplinary nature of reading continues to reverberate for English instructor Katie Hern, who marveled at her out-of-discipline reading of a primary source document. Close-Up 5.2, Reading History with a Not Historian, describes what both she and her history colleague learned about disciplinary reading and apprenticing students to a disciplinary community.

To invite participation of colleagues with perhaps little experience talking about comprehension and reading processes, team leaders chart the authentic language team members use and only work toward more technical language for describing reading processes and strategies as examples surface naturally. Increasingly precise language will emerge over time.

Wonderful discoveries of uncharted mental processes have emerged from this kind of collegial conversation. One teacher realized that to comprehend

CLOSE-UP 5.1

Capturing the Reading Process Reflection

Community college faculty members are often new to thinking about their own reading processes. When Edmonds Community College instructor Melody Schneider convened a new faculty learning community devoted to Reading Apprenticeship, the first thing she did was announce a reading task: "Read this two and a half page text that you might use with students taking an acting class because they hoped to pursue acting as a career."

Group members read individually. Then Melody posted two questions and team members wrote responses:

- What did you do while you were reading to make sense of this text?

- Even if you weren't aware of it at the time, what comprehension problems did you solve while reading?

Melody explains what happened next:

This was fascinating. I took five pages of notes on the strategies they named and the issues and fixes they identified. Since nearly all were totally unfamiliar with the content of the text, it provided a great parallel for how our students often view text. Strategies ranged from rereading, to looking up words, to feeling lost or uninterested by the topic, to being completely engaged in some of the ideas.

The discussion was stimulating and led us to talk about how we work with text in our various classes. We discussed ways to introduce text to make unfamiliar ideas or references more accessible, we talked about how people read for different reasons—and because I did not give them any particular assignment or reason, they read in different ways. We talked about what we expect from our students when we teach and when we use reading, and we examined how we often do not set up assignments or work that help students reach those expectations.

One part that was interesting and somewhat challenging—some participants could not get beyond their reactions to and interpretations of the meaning of the text to talk about their own reading strategies. Even though the questions posted were only about strategies and fixes to comprehension issues, they couldn't go there. I thought a lot about that, how it is also difficult for our students to go to that place of awareness. Next time, I would be more explicit about strategies in the beginning.

the dense sentences in a Nabokov memoir, he was moving his body in time with the grammatical cadence of the work, struggling, as he said, "to find the music of it." Once he tuned his internal rhythm to the text, his comprehension flowed right alongside. Colleagues' genuine curiosity and encouragement help to reveal such gems of the human mind at work. At the same time, challenging material can also surface behaviors in a team of teachers that look more like those of struggling high school or college readers!

Two sample Reading Strategies Lists (see Close-Up 5.3) developed by different teams of teachers reading different types of texts reflect some of the many ways participants in such inquiries will approach an unfamiliar text.

When teams take up this inquiry, participants are likely to experience the need to set a purpose for their own reading or to motivate themselves to read

A cross-disciplinary Reading Apprenticeship faculty inquiry group at Chabot College had a routine at each meeting of reading a disciplinary text that one of them brought in as an example of what students might be reading in one of their courses.

As English instructor Katie Hern recalls, the purpose of this routine was "to surface unexamined disciplinary expertise and make that visible to each other."

Everyone in the group would read the text, but we don't necessarily have that disciplinary lens. I don't ever read a physics textbook. I'm not often reading primary historical sources either. A history colleague brought in a piece by a preacher in colonial America. It was about the importance of kindness from a man to a wife. I was getting my contemporary lens all triggered by the gendered language and had a reaction to the piece.

We used a protocol that allowed us to surface the kinds of questions that we asked, the kinds of comments that we made, responses that each of us had to the piece. The disciplinary person remained quiet and just listened to how her colleagues with graduate degrees, whom she respected, interpreted this text—and really did not interpret it in the way that she might. We don't share that disciplinary lens.

So it was really illuminating to see that it isn't just a problem of "My students can't read." It wasn't basic literacy. It was disci-

plinary literacy and the need to apprentice people to the ways of reading and thinking and questioning that you are an expert in, but you forgot how you learned to be.

When everybody went around and Jane (the historian) shared her response, she talked about the historical questions asked of primary sources, like a preacher's sermon. She was asking, "Why does he feel the need to deliver a sermon about a husband being kind to his wife?" What that tells her as an historian is that there was a problem of men abusing their wives in the community and he was trying to address that. I just remember my jaw dropping, that I had completely missed that the unstated historical force driving this sermon was this issue. It was part of her routine as an historian to ask a question like that.

She remembers back to me—an English teacher explicitly teaching the skills of critical reading, thinking, and writing in my classes—that my response to her was, "Oh, you want us to make an inference."

She sort of blinked and said, "Well, yes, I guess I do."

"Do you tell students that?"

She said no. So we both had this moment of realizing, "Oh, this is what we're learning. What do we need to make explicit for students to enable them to do the things we want them to do?" It was very, very powerful. A lot of light shone from that moment.

what may be a challenging text. They may also feel social pressure to finish the reading quickly or to demonstrate knowledge and understanding of the text. Great variety in the strategies and approaches different readers bring to this task will be in view. Hearing about others' reading approaches may stimulate team members to include these approaches in their own repertoires. They will also be able to see how different people's knowledge and experiences shape the

CLOSE-UP 5.3

Two Sample Reading Strategies Lists

The first list of reading strategies was developed by a cross-disciplinary group of teachers in response to their reading of an essay by Vladimir Nabokov, "Father's Butterflies." The essay is accompanied by illustrations, captions, and snatches from related letters and interviews.

Reading Strategies List: "Father's Butterflies" Essay

Annotate text—"leave tracks"

Look at images to make connections

Ask question: What was that about?

Chunk it to shorten—summarize beside each paragraph

Read it twice

Look for the gist

Reread for clarification

Set purpose for reading

Skip parentheticals to look for main idea

Reread parentheticals to enrich ideas

Utilize visuals

Preview text, identify roadblocks

Read title and subheadings

Be metacognitive about your own reading process to identify best strategy to use

Frequency of words in the text

Identify word meaning by using prefixes and suffixes

Set goal: push through

Negotiate (in mind) what's important to look at (e.g., captions, figures, visuals)

Look for vocabulary meanings in context

Skip difficult words (if they aren't essential)

Google it

Identify key vocabulary we need to know

Look for source, author to identify audience

Read sidebars to assist in finding meaning

Make connections to prior knowledge

Access schema

Break a word down into parts

Synthesize meaning of words

Context clues

Connections within text

Part of speech from context

This following list was developed by a smaller group of history teachers who read a collection of primary sources (e.g., family Bible, immigration papers, photographs, ticket stub) with the eyes of historians.

Reading Strategies List: Family Artifacts and Documents

Guess—do the best I can

Confirm hypothesis with research

Compare evidence

Connect evidence

Classify

Infer

Place in time/Periodization

Ask: What is the story here?

Ask: What is not here?

Ask: What is the evidence?

Ask: What is connection between the source and the evidence?

Predict—make hypothesis

Stance: There is always a story, a bigger story
    The story can always be revised in the light of new evidence

Corroborate evidence

Use all senses + objects + documents + places

Imagine

Put ourselves in others' shoes

Stance: patience, meticulous

meanings they derive from texts, and that meaning is in the interaction between individual readers and texts, not contained solely in the text itself.

These inquiries help teachers to make their thinking public—to identify and surface the resources they bring to various kinds of texts. It is useful for teachers to experience these reading inquiry activities multiple times with various kinds of texts. Doing so helps them build a fuller vision of the different reading processes and approaches a skilled reader has in his or her reading repertoire.

Inquiries such as these, which ask adult readers to defer their responses to and connections with a text's world of ideas and focus first on processes, can easily slip into a more natural discussion of content. In our experience, however, teachers gracefully accept reminders that the purpose of the inquiry is to experience and articulate how they, as proficient readers, make sense of text. At the same time, it is also valuable to reserve at least some time for team members to discuss the ideas in a text they have been reading together. Indeed, such discussions may yield further ideas about how teachers can link process-focused and content-focused reading discussions in their classrooms and can help them see how discussing the reading process spills over into content understanding for their students.

Harrison High School assistant principal Allyson Robinson was impressed when she observed the application of a Reading Strategies List in one of her team member's classes. In this instance, students were inquiring into how they could read science data:

> I was in one of our science teachers' room, and before they did a reading piece, he was having students in groups list out what strategies they can use to access and understand data—which, to be honest, is not something that we teach enough of. Each group had their little whiteboards, and they were writing down every strategy they could use if they came across a piece of data they didn't really understand, how they could interpret it.
>
> When they finished, the groups walked around looking at each other's strategies, and then the teacher called on a student in each group to really explain the group's strategies. Everybody added any strategies to their list they didn't have. The kids had great lists of strategies, and anyone in the group was able to explain what the strategies were and how they would work. To me, it just emphasized the idea of thoughtfulness, and being inquisitive, and being problem solvers.

When a team has had multiple experiences capturing their reading processes, it may be interesting for them to develop categories to describe similar types of moves readers engage in, according to the interests of the group. For example, a team might work to categorize individual responses into cognitive and affective areas of reading that individuals orchestrate as they read, or they might focus on the different kinds of prior knowledge they use to unlock a particular text.

Team Tool 5.3, Interacting Areas of Reading Inquiry, is a model teams can use or adapt when categorizing their reading processes, individually and as

TEAM TOOL 5.3

Interacting Areas of Reading Inquiry

PURPOSE

Team members surface the different kinds of resources they bring to the reading of a text. Their experience prepares them to support students in similar inquiries. (The categories in this model are a *sample* of how a team may want to focus their own inquiry.)

PROCEDURE

- Facilitate a discussion of the meaning of each of the categories team members will attend to in their reading process. In this sample, see the note taker categories of fluency, motivation, cognition, and knowledge.

- Ask everyone to read the selected text and then record their reading processes on the note taker.

- Facilitate a discussion of how individuals interacted with the text in the given categories and in any other ways.

  – How did the author's use of language affect your fluency while reading?

  – How did the author's use of language affect your motivation to read the piece?

  – What cognitive strategies did you use?

  – What schema or knowledge demands were placed on you as you read?

  – How else did you respond to the text as a reader?

- Facilitate a discussion of the implications of this inquiry for classroom practice.

Interacting Areas of Reading: Note Taker

Title:

Fluency (word recognition, decoding, sentence processing, style or rhythm of language)	Motivation (interest, purpose, engagement)	Cognition (strategic moves to support comprehension)	Knowledge (knowledge of content and the world, of texts, of language, of disciplinary discourse and practices)

Additional Notes

CLOSE-UP 5.4

Interacting Areas of Reading: History Textbook Example

A small interdisciplinary team of teachers individually read a moderately challenging history textbook excerpt and then charted some of their reading processes in several interacting areas of reading, including two categories of prior knowledge.

Title: "Totalitarianism Turned Hate into Genocide"

Fluency	Motivation	Cognition	Knowledge	
			Knowledge of Content and the World	Knowledge of Texts
I had to stop and reread some of the really complex sentences. I stopped cold at Solzhenitsyn's name because I know I can't pronounce (decode) it. I had to break up a word into its parts (take the root and suffix apart) to figure out what it really meant.	When I saw Solzhenitsyn's name, I had a sinking feeling. I never could get through his books. Truthfully, I wouldn't have read this if I wasn't in this situation, knowing I could draw on the social support of other readers. I only read this because I'm a "good" student and I was expected to.	I found myself arguing with the text, because I thought the Solzhenitsyn excerpt actually provided a counter-example to the author's position. I reread after I found I had blurred through a bunch of text. I realized I wasn't understanding what the author was getting at so I decided to read on a little.	Of course I was thinking of terrorism and all that's happening now. I had television and movie images in mind. Slavery Russia When I came to the phrase "paralyzed resistance," I consciously decided to think about my own experience and other knowledge I might have that would make sense of it.	I read the caption under the picture. It clued me in to what would be in the text. I looked for the publication date because I wanted to see what kind of slant it would probably take. I read all the titles and subtitles first.

a team. Close-Up 5.4, Interacting Areas of Reading: History Textbook Example, shows how one group of readers used the model with a textbook excerpt that included a passage from Alexsandr Solzhenitsyn's novel *The Gulag Archipelago*. They worked with the categories of *fluency, motivation, cognition,* and *knowledge.* In the category of *knowledge,* they focused on knowledge of texts and of content and the world; other options might include knowledge of language and knowledge of disciplinary discourse and practices—the particular ways members of a subject area community communicate and think.

Categorizing responses in the interactive areas of reading inquiry can make clear how readers simultaneously orchestrate many aspects of reading at once.

In the area of fluency, team members can explore how their prior reading experience influences their fluency in reading particular types of written discourse. Because teachers often assume that their students' reading fluency—particularly their pronunciation of novel words—is the source of their comprehension problems, intentionally drawing out teachers' own moments of dysfluency when reading a complex text can be particularly helpful. What is it about particular sentences or prose styles that cause us to trip up and restart a section of the text? What is fluency? Is reading fluency always a good thing? How does it support or interfere with comprehension? How does familiarity with particular discourses (e.g., in science, in history, in literature, in mathematics) interact with reading fluency? When are we more and less fluent?

Chemistry teacher Will Brown has worked through enough disciplinary reading to earn a doctorate in his field, and he knows that understanding complex science texts and reading fluently are rarely congruent, especially if fluency is understood to mean a relatively fast-paced, uninterrupted mental or oral rendering of a text:

> When I read science articles, it is like trying to move through dense thickets of ideas. I often get snagged by one bramble or another. I have to slow down and pick my way carefully.
>
> I am not concerned with fluency. In fact, if I do try to read quickly, it's likely that I will have only the barest sense, or no sense at all, of what I am reading. I have to work on it. New words are hard. Diagrams can be hard. Figuring out what each part or process is or what it contributes to the whole picture—these things take work.

In addition to considering the various ways fluency does or does not bear on comprehension, team members can explore the role of affect—the multiple positive and negative ways attitudes and beliefs about reading or a particular text impact motivation to read. For instance, they can recognize that a negative response to a text may either engage them more fully in their reading, as they take an argumentative stance toward the text, or disengage them altogether.

Team members also have the opportunity to explore the many ways that readers' prior knowledge influences their comprehension and meaning making. Differences in teachers' subject area can foreground team members' different expectations of the text structure and different disciplinary stances toward a text. A literature teacher may read a history text critical of the writing and voice of the piece, while a history teacher may read the same text aware of slant or bias and critical of the perspective taken, or even missing, in the text. Team members thus discover their own disciplinary lenses in contrast with those others apply to the same text.

By experiencing reading challenges firsthand, teachers will be able to communicate with authenticity to their students the key idea that until reading confusions are identified, they cannot be addressed. The motto adopted by many Reading Apprenticeship teachers, "It's cool to be confused," doesn't mean it's cool to stay confused, after all. It means knowing when you don't know and problem solving.

As part of her own literacy learning, high school English teacher Lisa Krebs remembers appreciatively the experience of being challenged by a text that was science, not Shakespeare:

> By giving us unfamiliar text and text outside of our area—it was like, "Whoa! My gosh, I forgot what this is like." In some ways I think I'm more compassionate with the kids, it put me back in the position of not always knowing what that text is about. Just in going through that myself, as a teacher, it helps me shape the way that I present material in my class—places that I need to help them out and sort of catch them through, and then where I need to let them sort of struggle a bit.

When Lisa describes her heightened awareness of how to "shape the way I present material in my class," she is talking about Reading Process Analysis, such as showing students how to capture their reading processes or use a class Reading Strategies List. She is also talking about the detective work teachers undertake in the Text and Task Analysis to figure out what a text will look like through students' eyes. Team Tool 5.4, Ways to Use Various Reading Process Analyses, is a quick look at the range of RPAs described in this chapter.

TEAM TOOL 5.4

Ways to Use Various Reading Process Analysis Routines

Reading Process Analysis can serve different purposes: to make one's own reading processes more apparent and available, to make disciplinary conventions more apparent and available, to plan lessons incorporating student use of RPA routines, and to plan lessons understanding what scaffolds or strategies to incorporate.

	Investigate Own Reading Processes	Investigate Disciplinary Reading Processes	Plan Lessons	Use with Students
ALL-PURPOSE ROUTINES				
Capturing the Reading Process Create a Reading Strategies List to make public and more visible the ordinarily invisible processes of reading.	✓	✓	✓	✓

(Continued)

	Investigate Own Reading Processes	Investigate Disciplinary Reading Processes	Plan Lessons	Use with Students
Thinking Aloud Make verbal and public the ordinarily invisible processes of reading.	✓	✓	✓	✓
Talking to the Text Think Aloud internally with note taking about reading processes.	✓	✓	✓	✓
Metacognitive Logs, Journals, and Note Takers Record concrete observations and interpret their meaning/ask questions or make connections/argue for their significance.	✓	✓	✓	✓
ROUTINES TURNED TO SPECIFIC PURPOSES				
Processing Previews Talk to the Text with the purpose of anticipating how to approach a text's affective, cognitive, and knowledge challenges.	✓	✓	✓	✓
Querying Questions Talk to the Text with the questions only, to puzzle through ambiguous or confusing sections of a text.	✓	✓	✓	✓
Interrogating Inferences Use Evidence/Interpretation to unpack the inference process to discover textual and other evidence for "knowing" something.	✓	✓	✓	✓
Wondering About Words Apply a Word-Learning Strategies List to clarify word meanings.	✓	✓	✓	✓
DISCIPLINARY INVESTIGATIONS				
Interpreting Disciplinary Practices Find patterns in how successful disciplinary readers approach a disciplinary text.	✓	✓	✓	
Exploring Argumentation Recognize the challenges of making a disciplinary claim and supporting it with text-based evidence and reasoning.	✓	✓	✓	
Text and Task Analysis Identify knowledge demands of a disciplinary text and useful reading strategies. Plan appropriate student tasks and supports for processing the text.	✓	✓	✓	

As team members go through these various RPAs, they will likely be struck by many comparisons between the team's inquiry and a classroom inquiry: How often are students granted the freedom to set their own reading purposes or decide how important it will be to understand particular sections or ideas in a text? What social pressures might students feel revealing their reading processes? How do students' knowledge and experience influence their understanding of the text in ways a teacher might not appreciate or know about? How might students benefit from hearing the thinking and reading processes of others?

Thinking Aloud

The Think Aloud reading process inquiry takes place "online," as readers first encounter a text. They verbalize their thinking processes, interrupting their reading to, for example, intersperse mental pictures or questions, to puzzle over words or meanings, to make connections from their own experiences or to other texts, to make predictions about the direction the text will take, or to share feelings about the text or author. They interact with the text—out loud.

For some teams new to metacognition or to one another, two companionable inquiries for first practicing Think Aloud involve cards or pipe cleaners rather than text, providing a low-risk introduction to making thinking visible. (See Close-Up 5.5, Text-Free Think Aloud Practice.) The first of these activities, Falling Cards, has the additional benefit of drawing in science colleagues, who will see that Think Aloud also supports their students in learning investigatory reasoning. The second activity, Pipe Cleaner Creatures, is also described in *Reading for Understanding* for use with students. Adults like it, too!

For teams ready to practice the Think Aloud with text, the selected text should require some work of an adult reader to comprehend and should be new to all readers, to provide the important opportunity for everyone to be working to comprehend the text, not simply recall it. Team Tool 5.5, Think Aloud Inquiry, lays out the general directions for this inquiry. Close-Up 5.6, *The Red Badge of Courage* Think Aloud, shows how two non–English teachers began their inquiry into this literary classic.

When Think Aloud is approached as an authentic reading process inquiry, team members externalize their meaning making as they work with a text. The gist of the text emerges and is reconsidered and revised as readers work—in the moment—to make sense of the reading. Readers will experience a loss of fluency as they slow down to deliberately process the text and externalize their thoughts. Teachers Thinking Aloud will likely experience some difficulty

CLOSE-UP 5.5

Text-Free Think Aloud Practice

Teams wanting a low-risk opportunity to practice Thinking Aloud report that these two text-free activities are very successful. When cognitive tasks are not demanding, as these are not, team members are able to have fun and get comfortable with how available their thinking is to them. They can more easily relax and notice the metacognitive responses they have as they engage with a task and solve problems that come up.

Team leaders find that with two tasks available, they can use one for modeling, before partners take on the remaining task. During the model task, the team leader's partner records the leader's Think Aloud comments for everyone to see. In a debrief, the team can refer to the recorded comments and talk about which ones strike them as interesting examples of metacognition. In this way, everyone can rehearse thinking about thinking about thinking!

Falling Cards*

- Give each partnership a set of four cards and two pieces of paper.
- Explain that one partner will drop the cards one at a time while the other partner observes and records the card dropper's Thinking Aloud. Encourage team members to try different card-dropping techniques and see what happens.
- Some ideas for the card dropper to Think Aloud about:
  - What card-dropping technique will I try and why? What do I predict will happen?
  - What am I thinking as the card falls?
  - What am I thinking about how the card lands? About where the card lands?
  - What am I wondering?
- Have partners trade roles.

- Ask partners to compare the notes about their Thinking Aloud and choose one or two examples to share with the team.
- Facilitate a discussion of the shared Thinking Aloud comments and the specific elements of metacognition. Ask partners to describe what they noticed about each other's Think Aloud and how it influenced their own thinking.

Pipe Cleaner Creatures

Give each partnership five pipe cleaners and a piece of paper for each person.

- Explain that one partner will create a pipe cleaner creature that can stand on two feet; the other partner will observe and record the creature creator's Thinking Aloud. Encourage team members to be inventive with the pipe cleaners. Set a time limit of two or three minutes.
- Some ideas for the creature creator to Think Aloud about:
  - What do I predict will be tricky about creating a creature that won't fall over?
  - What do I want my creature to look like and why?
  - What am I thinking and feeling about each step of joining and shaping the pipe cleaners?
  - What am I going to do next and why?

- Continue the task as before (see Falling Cards), with partners trading roles, choosing one or two comments to share with the team, and a team discussion focusing on metacognitive elements of the comments.

*Inspired by "The Self-Directing Cards," a sophisticated science inquiry around the observation of falling cards by science educator Tik Liem, in *Invitations to Science Inquiry.*

TEAM TOOL 5.5

Think Aloud Inquiry

PURPOSE

Team members experience being deliberately metacognitive while reading by thinking out loud about their reading processes. Partners and then the whole group consider the range of ways team members interacted with the text and how it helped them build understanding (or not).

PROCEDURE

- Distribute copies of the text that partners will read. The text should be unfamiliar and somewhat challenging.

- Have partners decide how to share the reading. Paragraphs often work well when the text is complex.

- Explain how partners will work together:
  - Take turns Thinking Aloud with a section of text, reading either silently or aloud.
  - As the listening partner, take notes on your copy of the text to capture the reading partner's thinking.
  - After each of you has had at least one turn Thinking Aloud, discuss what you noticed about your own or your partner's metacognitive processes.

- Provide a set of questions partners can use to process their Thinking Aloud moves:
  - What did I do?
  - Where did I do it?
  - How did it help (or not)?

- After partners have discussed their Think Aloud experience, bring the whole team together to share their observations and discuss implications for their instruction.

reading, attending to their thoughts, and externalizing them through talk, and all at once. The immediacy of Thinking Aloud can be daunting.

In a Think Aloud, team members who are not taking their turn to think aloud are likely to experience moments of fascination with the mental processing of others and the distinct ways others are making sense of the text. This difference between readers is an inescapable aspect of making the invisible visible and offers opportunities to consider the various meanings that can be constructed from a single text, the various ways skilled readers approach a text, and the intersection of reader knowledge and text at the core of comprehension.

CLOSE-UP 5.6

The Red Badge of Courage *Think Aloud*

The excerpt below is from a paired Think Aloud. One teacher reads aloud from the first chapter of *The Red Badge of Courage*, by Stephen Crane, a novel encountered by many secondary school students. In a Think Aloud format, she reports her reading processes. The other teacher listens and records her partner's thinking. They will then trade roles.

READER 1: I have this image of, oh, the Civil War, I guess, and I don't really have any preconceived notion of it, other than maybe some mixed-up image of *All's Quiet on the Western Front* or something, which is the next war. But I picture youth fighting. But this is chapter one.

"The cold passed reluctantly from the earth, and the retiring fogs revealed an army stretched out on the hills, resting."

READER 1: Hmm, so they're already there, laid out on the ground waiting for the sun to rise, getting ready, I guess, for the next battle. Must be stepping in in the middle of it here.

"As the landscape changed from brown to green, the army awakened, and began to tremble with eagerness at the noise of rumors."

READER 1: So, sounds like they are waiting for instructions. They're about to move on and they're all, uh, anxious about that.

"It cast its eyes upon the roads, which were growing from long troughs of liquid mud to proper thoroughfares."

READER 1: "It" meaning the sun, I guess. It's warming up. I guess there are so many, there must be a lot of people, a lot of soldiers around, because they're tromping the mud into—I can picture them tromping the dirt into mud and that into highways of soldiers.

"A river, amber-tinted in the shadow of its banks, purled at the army's feet; and at night, when the stream had become of a sorrowful blackness, one could see across it the red, eyelike gleam of hostile camp fires set in the low brows of distant hills."

READER 1: So they're on the river-bank, and I can picture them looking at the water and thinking two things. One, it's a river—it's pretty—and it's night, but there are also these dark, there are these red eyes across, um, across the banks, that represent the enemy, which you know would just naturally make them more anxious.

"Once a certain tall soldier developed virtues and went resolutely to wash a shirt. He came flying back from a brook waving his garment bannerlike. He was swelled with a tale he had heard from a reliable friend, who had heard it from a truthful cavalryman, who had heard it from his trustworthy brother, one of the orderlies at division headquarters."

READER 1: Um, I thought he was going to be running from a bullet, but rather he's running from, running with, uh, hearsay, rumors of perhaps where they're going and what they're going to be doing next.

"He adopted the imported air—uh, important air—of a herald in red and gold."

READER 1: So, he became sort of a standard-bearer with the news, and he's running among the soldiers.

As team members Think Aloud, they may experience the kinds of social pressures many RPAs offer, for example to look bright, demonstrate understanding rather than confusion, and move through text at a brisk pace. Such pressures again raise to awareness the ways reading in the social context of the classroom can affect students. Teachers may also experience the need to edit or even censor their thoughts, selectively choosing which responses to externalize to their colleagues. This gives team members an opportunity to talk about the ways different texts tap into the experiences and privacy of readers, and how to manage the social and private dimensions of reading in a classroom.

In Close-Up 5.6 of the partners engaged in *The Red Badge of Courage* Think Aloud, for example, the teacher Thinking Aloud begins to notice her own reading "knowledge" that had up until this point been tacit and hidden from view—for instance, that at times novelists choose to step a reader into the middle of the action rather than lead into it, and that skilled readers will not only tolerate the ensuing bewilderment, but will enjoy the possibilities, waiting to see what will settle into place as they read. This reader is watching herself clarify pronoun referents and draw inferences about character motivation, make predictions about the action, and then relinquish these conceptions as the story unfolds. All of these insights into skilled reading have implications for the partners' instruction with students—what, for instance, might they do in the classroom and in metacognitive conversation to help students not only tolerate but relish the ambiguity and confusion of those opening pages?

Talking to the Text

Talking to the Text can be thought of as a written Think Aloud. (Team Tool 5.6, Talking to the Text Inquiry, outlines this process.) It begins as an individual reading and writing activity that is then debriefed with a partner or small group. Essentially, Talking to the Text means annotating texts with one's thoughts and musings. Differences between Think Aloud and Talking to the Text will become apparent as team members engage in deliberate inquiry, sharing their annotations with one another, and subsequently discussing what they notice or wonder. As with all reading inquiries, the real interest of the group will be on hearing from others the specific ways they worked with the text, encountered road blocks to comprehension, and pursued their own traces of meaningful engagement. In Close-Up 5.7, Talking to Dr. Seuss, the annotations made by individual teachers to a political cartoon suggest just how valuable it can be to share thinking and perhaps improve on it. The last step of the Talking to the Text inquiry—reflect on implications for instruction—is illustrated in Close-Up 5.8, Why Have Students Talk to the Text?

Of course, when team members reflect on implications for instruction, concerns as well as potential benefits arise. Team members who may already have some Reading Apprenticeship classroom experience can be a reminder of the cycle of inquiry everyone undertakes to move from anticipation to reality. In a group where teachers wondered about the amount of time it might take for students to incorporate Talking to the Text, teachers Dawn Putnam and

CLOSE-UP 5.7

Talking to Dr. Seuss

Six high school teachers first encounter Talking to the Text by each inquiring into a political cartoon that appeared in U.S. newspapers three days after Pearl Harbor. The cartoonist, Dr. Seuss, was better known to the teachers for his children's books—for example, *The Cat in the Hat* and *Horton Hatches the Egg*. Teachers then shared their thinking. This graphic compiles all the teachers' Talking to the Text annotations.

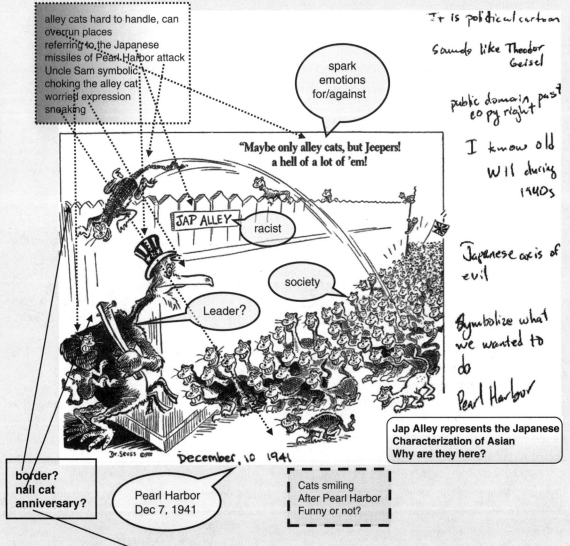

Source: *Dr. Seuss Goes to War: The World War II Editorial Cartoons of Theodor Seuss Geisel*, by Richard Minear, Theodor Geisel. Published by The New Press, 2001. The cartoon Maybe only alley cats, but Jeepers! A hell of a lot of 'em! is in the Dr. Seuss Political Cartoons. Special Collection & Archives, UC San Diego Library. Copyright unknown.

TEAM TOOL 5.6

Talking to the Text Inquiry

PURPOSE

Individual team members put their metacognitive responses to a complex text on the text itself, annotating it with their confusions, questions, connections, and other thinking about how they are reading and thinking about what the author has, in effect, put in front of them. The Talking to the Text inquiry raises awareness across the team of the wide range of ways to read and make sense of complex text.

PROCEDURE

- Explain that in this inquiry, individuals will Think Aloud in writing—or Talk to the Text. Ask everyone to record on their copy of the text their metacognitive conversation with the text, in terms of questions, agreements, confusions, and connections. Set a reading time limit, with the understanding that people should read at whatever pace is comfortable for them because grappling with rather than completing the text is the goal.

- Ask team members to really press themselves to externalize their thoughts and reactions to the text, making notes that capture their thinking.

- At the time limit, ask partners to share their annotations and what they noticed about their own or their partner's reading processes.

- Bring team members together to reflect on what they learned and the implications for their instruction.

CLOSE-UP 5.8

Why Have Students Talk to the Text?

A team of New York City middle school science and social studies teachers analyzed their own reading processes with a Talking to the Text inquiry. When they finished, they took another moment to consider how this kind of inquiry would benefit their students and guide their instruction. A sample of their posted responses is reproduced as follows.

How can analyzing students' Talking to the Text give us insight into our students' reading, and support responsive instruction?

- It can help identify areas of struggle the students may have—for example, vocabulary, fluency, comprehension, connections.
- It helps us cater our instruction. Helps us with recognizing student thought processes.
- Analyzing students' Talking to the Text gives teachers the opportunity to see what students really know based on what is observed. Mini lessons can be created to drive learning.
- It gives us a window into their thinking—what they do on their own. We can support and encourage what they do well and support and reshape areas that can be improved. We can group for instruction.
- Allows us to set student learning goals to address areas of concern. Insight into strategies utilized by students. Assist students in monitoring comprehension.
- Analysis can help reveal the level of thought (whether superficial or critical) and if they are monitoring their understanding, trying to connect to bigger ideas, or even marking/highlighting everything because they can't determine what is/isn't important.

Laurie Lintner, who had already been using Reading Apprenticeship in their high school English classes, shared what they had observed:

> DAWN: From my watching the kids, once they've had some really meaningful experience with Talking to the Text, and they see how much it helps them—because there are a lot of kids that haven't had that meaningful experience yet, they're just sort of randomly writing stuff—but once they see, there's this weird shift that happens by the end of the year. Instead of saying, "Okay, don't forget to Talk to the Text," they'll say to you, "Can we write on this?" It's like, "Whoa, what just happened?" Or the kids will come in and they'll have their own way of doing it because they've seen, "This helps me." And so it becomes not an assignment any more. It becomes how they read.
>
> LAURIE: I had a similar experience. By the end of the year, I didn't have to say, "I want you to Talk to the Text." And the kids did very different things on their papers. Even though I had them in a group of four, one kid would come and he would have questions and writing all over, and another kid would come with drawings and underlines and circles. It was just interesting to find how they took ownership of the Talking to the Text, and of all the strategies, and made it work for them. And some kids still never wrote on the text. Even if I said, "You can write on this," they liked a double-entry journal [see as follows] and would take notes on a separate piece of paper.

Once teams have experience with Think Aloud and Talking to the Text inquiries, they may sometimes choose to narrow the focus of those reading inquiries to particular aspects of the reading process—to shed light, for example, on how skilled readers carry out high-leverage strategies such as previewing, questioning the text, drawing inferences, or working with unfamiliar vocabulary, and how these strategies support comprehension and subject area learning. The following sections of this chapter provide examples of this type of focused inquiry.

Metacognitive Logs, Journals, and Note Takers

One of the most transparent ways for teams to surface reading processes is with a two-column metacognitive note taker clear enough for first graders: I Saw/I Thought. In secondary and college classrooms and in professional settings, the column headings might be labeled Evidence/Interpretation (or not!), but the purpose is the same: to record evidence from a text and give it meaning, whether by making a connection, asking a question, noting a confusion, paraphrasing or restating an idea, or attributing text-based significance.

In Reading Apprenticeship classrooms, various metacognitive note takers are used over and over as a concrete way for readers to track their thinking and build meaning. Teams may also find themselves using metacognitive note takers for looking at student work, interpreting graphics, building an argument, observing colleagues—whenever evidence-based reflection is called for.

Team Tool 5.7 shows a sample of note takers that lead readers from evidence to wondering or interpretation. In the following section of this chapter, Close-Up 5.10 shows how teachers used metacognitive logs to track the meaning elicited by their particular questions about a text, and Close-Up 5.11 shows how specific evidence in a text allowed teachers to infer more than was written on the page.

TEAM TOOL 5.7

A Sampling of Metacognitive Note Takers for Multiple Purposes

When teams use metacognitive note takers for a variety of purposes, teachers come to see how these seemingly simple structures shape-shift for multiple purposes, all with the intention of making thinking visible. (Numerous metacognitive note taker applications are described in Chapter Four of *Reading for Understanding*.)

I Saw (notes and quotes from the text)	**I Thought** (my questions, connections, clarifications, comments, wondering, understanding)

Evidence (notes and quotes from the text)	**Interpretation** (how it supports my thesis or not)

Evidence (what I noticed in a student's work sample)	**Interpretation** (what it makes me think about the student's next steps)

Turning All-Purpose RPAs to Specific Purposes

When teams meet to inquire into various Reading Process Analyses, they will be *using* those processes themselves, with a specific disciplinary text, and often with a specific purpose. In the following examples, one team used Talking to the Text as a previewing tool, another team previewed a text by asking questions and reflecting on how the questions spurred their thinking and how the questions served a disciplinary purpose. A third team reversed their use of the Evidence/Interpretation note taker, stating first what they thought they knew from a text and then citing the textual evidence for their inferences. Yet another team focused their Reading Strategies List to attend to unfamiliar vocabulary. All of these team experiences build teachers' confidence using RPAs with students, for particular instructional purposes.

Processing Previewing

What do skilled readers do before they even begin a challenging piece of text? Previewing is a high-leverage strategy for anticipating the affective, cognitive, and knowledge challenges of a text and recognizing, perhaps, supports for smoothing the way. A valuable inquiry teams can do with any complex text is to capture their *previewing* processes. Before they dig into a text, what do they do as first steps, to get ready for the reading? Close-Up 5.9, Previewing a Research Paper Abstract, is an example of the motivational, cognitive, and schema-building processes a team of high school science teachers employ simply to *preview* a very short piece of geophysics text.

Querying Questions

All active readers ask questions of a text. When teachers query a text, disciplinary interests and practices can shape the questions they raise. In Close-Up 5.10, Querying Questions with a Disciplinary Focus, a team of science teachers Talk to the Text with a single metacognitive purpose, to identify questions that help them think about and comprehend the text. When asked to think about the *purpose* of each question, they quickly recognize the disciplinary strategies they automatically employed when engaging a disciplinary text.

Teachers of any discipline might identify the types of questions they ask with particular genres of text. What are the questions an English teacher raises while reading a poem in *The New Yorker*? What questions come to the fore when a history teacher reads a political speech? By exploring question asking with disciplinary texts, teachers often discover that people's knowledge in a subject not only leads them to ask more informed questions, but that the type of questions they ask can differ a great deal. These insights have implications

CLOSE-UP 5.9

Previewing a Research Paper Abstract

A group of science teachers confront the 241-word abstract of "Methanotropic bacteria occupy benthic microbial mats in shallow marine hydrocarbon seeps, Coal Oil Point, California," an article from the *Journal of Geophysical Research* (Ding & Valentine, 2008). Just reading the fifteen-word title of the article, the teachers realize they are about to be plunged into the deep waters so familiar to many of their science students.

Group members scan the text with two kinds of questions in mind:

1. What connections can you make — What do you know about this kind of text, the topic, the language being used?
2. What predictions can you make about your reading—How hard will it be? How will you adjust your reading processes to get ready? What do you already know that might help?

After a 30-second preview, teachers exchange ideas about the strategies and learning dispositions they are going to need as they grapple with this dense text:

— I saw this is an article from a science journal, and that sort of scared me.

— I read the title three times. I thought, I'll need to buckle down, take some notes.

— I saw big words, tough words. Some of the symbols, I wasn't sure what was going on. But on the other hand, I know a lot of it too, so that pulled me in.

— I ignored the words I didn't know in the title and used a lot of prior knowledge. Being an earth science teacher, I knew that *benthic* is a layer of the ocean. I knew the word *bacteria*, of course. And I knew *hydrocarbon seeps* because I'm in the fracking center of Pennsylvania.

— I'm going to have to take the complex language and put it into plain English so I can tuck it away and remember what this article is about.

These teachers' experiences, of sharing clues to what they may already know and of taking comfort in the recognition that everyone will be engaged in effortful reading, suggest to them that students might benefit from similar experiences to make the hard work ahead more manageable.

for teaching—what questions are essentially literary questions? Scientific ones? Historical or mathematical in nature? How can I develop a more robust questioning repertoire in my students, for my discipline?

Interrogating Inferences

As with questioning, all active readers draw inferences from text as they read. But the inferences happen so automatically that readers are often unaware of them. They come to conclusions, but may have difficulty explaining precisely what in a text led them to a particular inference, or how it triggered prior knowledge. Getting a deliberate handle on *how* they draw inferences can help teachers figure out how to help their students do this vital, invisible meaning making with text.

The Interrogating Inferences inquiry engages team members in using an interactive log, similar to a reading log or dialectical journal, which many

CLOSE-UP 5.10
Querying Questions with a Disciplinary Focus

A team of science teachers Talk to the Text of a professional article that is reporting a "mini-revolution" in scientific thinking about the tectonic history of North America's Pacific Rim. Team members have two tasks: "Write questions that help you think about and comprehend the text," and "Explain the purpose of each question, or how it helps your thinking."

The disciplinary focus of teachers' questions reveals itself organically. After all, these readers are members of a science discourse community—reading and talking about science!

Questions We Asked and How They Helped

Before the Reading

Questions We Asked (after a two-minute scan of text)	How They Helped (Purpose)	Disciplinary Focus
Does anyone know when the Farallon plate entered into the discussion of continental drift?	I was never familiar with the Farallon plate.	Participating in a community of scientists
Is this going to be different from what I taught a few years ago?	Piqued my interest that it might be different.	Recognizing that scientific understanding evolves
How many scientists are on board with this new theory or hypothesis?	I teach students to look at who is doing the study and that there are many different views.	Understanding scientific sourcing and corroboration
How much of this research was done using computer modeling?	Maybe this could lead into a unit on computer modeling, and how useful it is in science.	Understanding the uses of various scientific tools

During the Reading

Questions We Asked	How They Helped (Purpose)	Disciplinary Focus
How would they distinguish between the slabs after they had subducted? If the two slabs disappeared into the mantle, how do they know anything about them?	I was asking a lot of clarification questions. It forced me to go back and reread sections or go back to the diagram.	Understanding the challenges of science text structure and text density
Can I get a better visual to picture this?	I went to the diagram trying to sort out how can you tell anything about multiple slabs or anything!	Understanding the role of visualization and the uses of scientific documents
How can scientists use seismic waves to identify different layers of seafloor crust, etc., especially when you're talking 1,800 kilometers down? How did they figure that out? How can they prove that?	I'm not sure I believe or understand everything they were doing.	Understanding the rules of scientific evidence
How does this change our understanding of plate tectonics?	It was many years ago when Wegener first proposed the theory of plate tectonics and got us to where our understanding is prior to this article.	Monitoring schema on the lookout for conceptual change

(Continued)

After the Reading		
Questions We Asked	**How They Helped (Purpose)**	**Disciplinary Focus**
Now that we have so much more technology, how is that going to change science and some of the things that we thought we knew for a fact?	Kids today are so bound by technology that if you start to say something even technology related, you've got them hooked because it's like you're speaking their language.	Helping students evolve a scientific identity
What prompted this research in the first place?	What was under review that they felt they needed to look into this more? Just the whole process of how geological science happens.	Setting a purpose for future inquiry
How does the conversation go between scientists to determine whether new theories are accepted? How do scientists work with each other?	That's one of the big things we always talk to the students about.	Understanding the process of scientific inquiry

This inquiry is based on "How the West Was Done," by Erin Wayman, in *Science News*, May 4, 2013; Volume 183 #9 (p. 19).

teachers may use to actively engage their students with texts. Whereas those classroom inquiries usually focus on responses to content, this one focuses on connecting the reading process to the content of the text.

Team members investigate *how* they draw inferences from text, slowing down the inferencing process by charting what they think they know about the content and, specifically, what in the text makes them think they know it. As they construct meaning from the text in front of them, teachers consider what information and other clues are offered directly in the text and what knowledge about people, events, situations, or ideas the reader brings to the text. Team members identify what it is in the text—or about the text—that has prompted their inferences, assumptions, and associations.

Charting their text *inferences and interactions* helps teachers better understand how text interpretations emerge from the complex relationship between such things as the reader's strategies, the text's idiosyncratic features, the text's direct information, and the reader's schema, including knowledge about how particular kinds of texts usually work. Close-Up 5.11, Inferences and Text Interactions, is an example of the way one teacher unpacked her inferences about a James Thurber short story.

CLOSE-UP 5.11
Inferences and Text Interactions

In this English teacher's two-column metacognitive log, she is making her way through the first paragraph of "The Catbird Seat," by James Thurber, tracking what the text is causing her to think she knows, and why.

> Mr. Martin bought the pack of Camels on Monday night in the most crowded cigar store on Broadway. It was theatre time and seven or eight men were buying cigarettes. The clerk didn't even glance at Mr. Martin, who put the pack in his overcoat pocket and went out. If any of the staff at F&S had seen him buy the cigarettes, they would have been astonished, for it was generally known that Mr. Martin did not smoke, and never had. No one saw him.[1]

Inferences What do you think you know?	Text Interactions What in the text makes you think you know it?
OK, I think this is in New York.	Because it's crowded and it's Broadway.
But I realize it could be, really be anywhere.	But the theater time also makes me think that it's in New York.
I think the store is F&S. But I'm not even sure about that.	I think that's true because "if any of the staff at F&S had seen him" and "the clerk didn't even glance," so that's one person who didn't see him.
	But I realize that F&S could be something else also. It could be the place where he worked and so . . . I don't know too much for sure there. Could be going to the theater, but no, not necessarily. So, I mostly have questions at this point.
I don't know that he smokes. So I don't know if he's starting to smoke or buying it for somebody else then. At this point in the paragraph, what I have are a lot of questions.	I mean, it says he doesn't.
I don't know if it's his writing here, but I think he's doing something perverse. He has a scheme. He's doing something that he normally does not do, and the author makes a point that he puts it in his overcoat pocket. Even though it didn't say he was concerned about not being seen, they pointed out that he was not seen. That implies that he's doing something. . .	Because of the overcoat.
It's interacting with the genre. Because no one saw him could be a very objective, trite statement. But there's a lot of implications that there is something covert.	
So there's that subtext. Something out of the ordinary that doesn't usually happen. He's building a little bit of mystery.	So that "no one saw him" fits in with that genre of "there's a mystery here." Whereas in another kind of genre, it wouldn't have that implication.
You could even say he wants to be invisible.	He's in the most crowded place on Broadway. Something surreptitious.

(Continued)

When this teacher and her colleagues complete their reading and note making, they come together and discuss what they noticed and what it might mean for their instruction. They note James Thurber's ironic nod to film noir and discuss how they might foreground literary genre signals for students by using and exploring film. They recognize the mystery genre and, thus, their willingness to suspend an immediate need to know what is going on.

They also see how following a trail of inferences throws light on the hidden work readers do, in concert with authors, to appreciate the layers of intended meaning in a literary text.

Teachers conclude that students can learn these disciplinary moves and dispositions through metacognitive conversation with texts of this kind.

Wondering About Words

Subject area teachers frequently find words an instructional worry. They wonder, for example, whether they should teach all the new vocabulary students will encounter in a text before they begin reading, to clear away stumbling blocks to meaning. But if they define all these words explicitly up front, will students even have time for the reading? If they must choose a few words to focus on, how do they choose? It helps teachers set aside these worries once they focus on building students' repertoire of word-learning strategies, so that students have tools to build their own vocabularies as they read.

Because words so often seem to be in the way of students' comprehension, an inquiry to identify the word-learning processes teachers themselves engage in when meeting new vocabulary can be highly motivating, and relieving. Team Tool 5.8, Wondering About Words Inquiry, outlines one way teams raise their awareness of how they approach unfamiliar vocabulary—and how their students might as well.

Close-Up 5.12, Word Learning Strategies List, is a glimpse into an inquiry a group of science teachers did to reveal some of the ways they take on unfamiliar words. In this inquiry, teachers read a text that is challenging for them as adult readers and focus specifically on how they are meeting and working to clarify novel words. What do they do to clarify word meaning, exactly? What skills and knowledge about language and text structure and even grammar do they draw on? How could they apprentice their students into becoming better word learners, and thus boost them along to reading independence?

After teams take up their own word-learning inquiry, they might profitably follow it with a careful look at an instructional text they use with students. What are the ways definitions are given, explicitly and implicitly, in the text? How might students be engaged in discovering their word-learning strategies and building a shared Word-Learning Strategies List?

Another way the team of science teachers in Close-Up 5.12 worked with words was to mentally track any new definitions of a key term that kept

TEAM TOOL 5.8

Wondering About Words Inquiry

PURPOSE

As experienced readers, teachers automatically incorporate a number of strategies for approaching unfamiliar vocabulary. This inquiry reminds them of what they do, and what their students might learn to do.

PROCEDURE

1. With an unfamiliar text that includes a range of unfamiliar vocabulary, team members Talk to the Vocabulary, using the following questions to guide their responses.

    – What words are new or partially known to you? What did you do to make meaning of them?

    – Which words do you recognize as having multiple meanings? How did you figure out the "right" meaning?

    – Which words have familiar parts but the meaning is unknown to you or appears to be inconsistent with your knowledge of the parts?

    – Which words do you think you understand the gist of even if you don't know their actual definitions?

    – Are there unfamiliar phrases or expressions that contain individual words that are familiar to you? What did you do to make meaning of them?

    – Are there words that might have Greek or Latin roots or Spanish language cognates?

2. As a group, team members share the words they attacked and how they made sense of them, learning from one another's strategies.

surfacing during their reading, using evidence from the text to update their understanding, and comparing this emerging understanding with what they previously thought. A simple example from their Word-Learning Strategies List is the way they built their understanding of *chondrite* from clue to clue.

A more complex example would involve conceptual change and the reading habit of using parts of a text to continually explore and update understanding of a key concept. *Prebiotic,* from the teachers' list, might be a concept worthy of this kind of examination across a text. Sample metacognitive note takers for keeping track of this kind of change appear in Team Tool 5.9, Tracking Concept Development. (Tracking conceptual change is also discussed in Chapter Eight of *Reading for Understanding*.)

When teams take the time to practice building the habit of tracking their own conceptual change, their students can become the ultimate beneficiaries of this powerful strategy for deepening disciplinary knowledge and understanding.

CLOSE-UP 5.12

Word-Learning Strategies List

In this word-learning inquiry, a mixed group of middle school, high school, and community college science teachers bend their heads over an article from *American Scientist* about the origins of Earth. As they read, they stop at ten-minute intervals to capture their word-learning processes: What precisely are they doing to understand unfamiliar words?

After a spell of reading and reflecting, they debrief together and build a Word-Learning Strategies List. As they work, they press to fully describe their process of zeroing in on a satisfactory definition, rather than settle for a generic label such as context clues. This enables them to build a set of explicit supports they could well imagine students discovering and documenting in a similar classroom inquiry around an instructional text.

As these science teachers work, they discover their facility at something they begin to call *finding hidden definitions* in the text. With growing pleasure, they call out, "Here's another one!" as they read on and notice the many different ways definitions of new words and concepts are proffered by the author in the process of setting forth a particular scientific argument.

Word-Learning Strategies List

Location	Unfamiliar Word	Description of Strategy
page 1, paragraph 3	*extrasolar* planets	Divide into meaningful word parts (extra + solar), think of other words or phrases containing these parts (solar radiation, extracurricular): outside our own solar system.
		Use context, identify ideas that might be repeated or synonyms, in this case, "other stellar systems" in a previous sentence.
page 2, paragraph 1	*planetologists*	Divide into meaningful word parts (planet + ologists), think of other words or phrases containing these parts (biologist, cosmologist): a person who studies planets or perhaps the formation of planets.
page 2, paragraph 1	*prebiotic* molecules—organic building blocks that could be used to get life started	Divide into meaningful word parts (pre + biotic or pre + bio + ic), think of other words or phrases containing these parts (preschool, biotic zones, cosmic): before life, before something characterized by life.
		Use punctuation, in this case, the dash that precedes the definition.
page 2, paragraph 2	Certain meteorites, the variety known as *chondrites*, are	Use grammar, in this case, the commas framing the phrase containing the unknown word tell the reader that chrondrites are a variety of meteorite.
		Look for definitional statements, in this case, "Certain meteorites, the variety known as chondrites, are."

Location	Unfamiliar Word	Description of Strategy
page 2, paragraph 2	Examine a *chondrite* under a microscope and you'll see that it consists of very fine dust grains of various compositions	Look for descriptions, in this case, "it consists of very fine dust grains."
page 2, paragraph 2	*nascent sun*, or *protosun*	Use punctuation and grammar, in this case the comma followed by the word <u>or</u> marks the word protosun as an alternate way of saying nascent sun (and vice versa).

TEAM TOOL 5.9

Tracking Concept Development

These two samples of metacognitive note takers can help readers recognize (or backtrack to recognize) how their conceptual understanding evolves in relation to their processing of textual information.

Key concept	My understanding before reading	New ideas and examples from the reading	My revised understanding	How I arrived at this understanding

My prior knowledge (schema)	What I read in the text	My revised schema

Interpreting Disciplinary Practices

As teams get comfortable with RPAs in general, they find ways to use them to apprentice students into the discourse practices of a discipline. Generally speaking, skilled readers set goals, use their background knowledge, question, visualize, clarify, summarize, paraphrase, predict, monitor comprehension, and apply other reading strategies. But how do such strategies play out differently for readers in different disciplines? What idiosyncratic tools, knowledge, or expectations does a proficient reader of science texts bring to his or her reading that may differ from what a reader of history or literature brings? The Interpreting Disciplinary Practices Inquiry aims at helping teachers develop a deeper understanding of what is involved in their own disciplinary reading, preparing them to better support the development of these processes in their students.

In 1987, Peter Rabinowitz[2] described how readers construct understandings of literature by recognizing and using the signposts authors design into their writings. He called these *rules of notice, rules of signification,* and *rules of configuration* and suggested that readers apply these interpretive practices to the understanding of a literary text. This idea of interpretive practices is now, these many years later, still working its way into academic discourse about how readers of different disciplines understand disciplinary text.

Just as authors of literature leave signposts for readers, authors of historical texts, scientific explanations, and the like leave conventional signposts throughout their writings to guide the disciplinary-specific interpretative practices of their readers. However, readers who do not share the interpretive practices and conventions relied upon by writers in a discipline may have difficulty understanding authorial intent.

As teams get comfortable with Reading Process Analyses, they find ways to use them to apprentice students into the discourse practices of a discipline. The next two RPAs help teachers remember what those practices might be! Even experts in a field lose track of how they got that way, and these inquiries can serve to remind them.

In Team Tool 5.10, Interpreting Disciplinary Practices Inquiry, teachers in the same subject area all tackle the same challenging discipline-specific text. A group of science teachers might read a difficult piece from *Science* or *Scientific American*. History teachers might read a complex primary source from a former era, replete with archaic language forms. Teachers of literature might choose an unfamiliar drama or poem from a distant time. Math teachers might explore an article from a science or economics journal focused on the use of math models to explore complex natural or social phenomena.

Before doing any reading, teachers record their expectations about the text and their predictions about what they will be reading. This alone can be an interesting focus of inquiry. In one inquiry session, when experienced science readers began an article from *Scientific American,* they anticipated that it would review the current knowledge on its topic and end with a set of questions about the things that were still unknown. Some of them even skipped the introductory narrative, remarking that they knew it functioned as a hook for the reader but would be irrelevant. When a literature teacher started to read this same article, however, he focused closely on the introductory narrative and did not anticipate (or appreciate) the exposition that rapidly followed this soft opening.

As part of the Interpreting Disciplinary Practices Inquiry, after answering the preliminary questions about their text expectations and predictions, readers experience at least two cycles of reading for ten minutes and then writing responses to particular questions about how they just read. These questions help teachers zero in on how they are using the signposts in the text to guide their construction of meaning. The note taker in Team Tool 5.10 includes all questions the reader will answer before and after a given ten-minute reading session.

TEAM TOOL 5.10

Interpreting Disciplinary Practices Inquiry

PURPOSE

This inquiry is a way for teachers in a discipline to identify common disciplinary reading practices—practices that are then more available to them as they consider how to stage them for their students.

PROCEDURE

- Distribute the disciplinary text team members will be reading and the following note taker. Ask that everyone answer the two "Before You Read" questions on the note taker (or in a journal):
  - As a successful reader in this discipline, what *expectations* do you have about this text?
  - As a successful reader in this discipline, what *predictions* do you have about what you will be reading?
- Allow ten minutes for team members to read the text—as they would read any text of the same kind, feeling free to write in the margins, underline, or circle words.
- After ten minutes, alert everyone to write answers to the "After You Read" questions.
- Have the team cycle at least once more through reading for ten minutes and answering the "After You Read" questions.
- Allow a few minutes for everyone to review their notes individually and generalize about their disciplinary reading in these areas:
  - The kinds of things they were *focusing* on or paying particular attention to and the roles these things played in comprehending the text
  - The kinds of *questions* they were asking themselves and the roles these questions played in comprehending the text
  - The kinds of *images* they were forming and the roles these images played in comprehending the text
  - The kinds of *predictions* they were making and the knowledge or information on which they based the predictions

(Continued)

- Facilitate a discussion of any patterns or generalizations team members noticed about their own reading processes. Record their responses for all to see.
- Invite discussion about the disciplinary practices that emerged from team members' reading of this kind of disciplinary text and how it applies to their classrooms.

Interpreting Disciplinary Practices Note Taker

Before You Read

Disciplinary Expectations: As a successful reader in this discipline, what expectations do you have about this text?

Disciplinary Predictions: As a successful reader in this discipline, what predictions do you have about what you will be reading?

After You Read

Focus: Which parts of the text did you focus on? Why did you pay particular attention to those parts?

Questions: What questions were you asking as you read? What were the purposes of your questions?

Images: What images were you forming as you read? What were the purposes of those images?

Predictions: Based on your reading of the text so far, what predictions do you have for the remainder of the text?

What emerges from this inquiry is the identification of some common ways that people in a discipline tend to approach certain texts of that discipline. When different subject area groups share their reading inquiries across disciplines, they are often surprised to see how ways of reading vary from discipline to discipline. All this sharing helps subject area teachers become more attuned to the tacit rules, ways of thinking, idiosyncratic vocabulary, and background knowledge needed to read effectively in their disciplines. This knowledge in turn prepares teachers to help their students learn to work more effectively with discipline-specific texts.

With experience, any of the reading inquiries offered in this chapter can be used to surface disciplinary expertise and contrasts between what skilled readers of particular disciplines know and do. As an example of the kinds of cross-disciplinary insights that can arise, in one reading discussion of an excerpt from the novel *The Perfect Storm*, by Sebastian Junger, English teachers skipped a technical passage describing the scale of the wind and waves battering a small commercial fishing boat—in favor of getting to the plot. A disbelieving science colleague explained what her English colleagues were missing. "Unless you read this part carefully," she admonished, "and understand the scale comparisons he is making here, you have *no idea* how terrified you should be right now!"

An important advantage of reading across disciplines in professional inquiries is this—it uncovers the expertise of the relatively skilled subject area reader in contrast with the out-of-subject-area colleague's more novice attempt to make sense of the text. Such exchanges foster a deeper understanding of the nature of expertise each subject area teacher uniquely brings to students and recognition of the role literacy plays in each discipline.

Close-Up 5.13, Expert and Novice Readers All, describes a cross-disciplinary challenge used in preservice classes where Reading Apprenticeship is introduced to secondary school teacher candidates. These preservice students are paired by dissimilar disciplines to apprentice one another to a text that each reads more expertly than the other.

Exploring Argumentation

Although many teachers think of argument in terms of its structural elements—thesis, supporting evidence, refutation of competing arguments, and the like—they may be less aware of disciplinary differences in how argumentation occurs, and to what ends.

Scientists employ argument in order to build knowledge about scientific phenomena, investigatory methods, and interpretation of findings. Science arguments very often take this form: This is how things work, this is how we know, and this is why it cannot be otherwise. This type of argument is designed to create the best scientific explanation or model, given the available evidence. Scientists know that what is now understood may tomorrow be overturned as new tools and methods of investigation make new evidence available.

Historians use argument when they share their interpretation of the historical record. Historical arguments often take this form: This is what must be the case, given the available historical record, here is why, and this is how we can know. Historical arguments must be gleaned from competing accounts and from records that are often incomplete. The documents that leave misty trails for historians to follow unavoidably embody particular perspectives and interests. Acknowledging perspective is a part of the interpretive work, and comparing varied accounts of events offers clues to corroborate or to clarify differences in points of view and positions.

Team Tool 5.11, Exploring Argumentation Inquiry, is a protocol teams can use to investigate their own argumentation processes and build understanding

CLOSE-UP 5.13

Expert and Novice Readers All

At Mills College, David Donahue's preservice students learn about Reading Apprenticeship in part by experiencing themselves as reading "experts" as well as reading apprentices.* In cross-discipline pairs, students conduct an investigation of their own disciplinary reading expertise, what it means to apprentice a disciplinary outsider to reading text outside of his or her expertise, and how it feels to be apprenticed, in turn.

Students' assignment includes the following rationale:

> All of you are expert readers in your subject area. Some of you have read countless poems. Others have probably lost count of how many scientific reports you've read.
>
> All of you are probably novice readers in some area . . . .
>
> This assignment is designed to help you think about reading as a complex activity of making meaning from text. You will be making explicit your own strategies for understanding a text in your subject area to someone from a different subject area.

For three weeks, students read a book in their discipline, of their choosing (*The Beak of the Finch*, for example, or a collection of Mary Oliver poems). They meet weekly with their partner to share the metacognitive journals they are keeping—notes about their reading processes, including their reflections about the role of the Reading Apprenticeship social, personal, cognitive, and knowledge-building dimensions in taking on their particular subject area text.

A future English teacher wrote about how she first cased the covers and front matter of *Their Eyes Were Watching God* and then dove into the first two paragraphs:

> I took a deep breath, like you do when you're about to jump into a pool or a lake— a huge breath, then holding it to test and see how that first line goes. The first line is huge. The first line bears all of the weight of anticipation and all of the promise of the

rest of the book. . . . It's the portal to the new world—sometimes I have to read it four or five times. Sometimes, as was the case here, I read the first line twice (it's a doozy), then read it again with the second line, then read the two together with the third and so on through the first paragraph. After I'd read the first two paragraphs, I went back and started over. I find that this helps me to gather together my thoughts and to ease in to the language of the work. It also helps me to catch any missed meanings or descriptions as I accustom myself to the new world of the novel.

After three weeks, partners trade books, and for three more weeks keep metacognitive journals as they read a new text in a different subject area. They are advised to "bear in mind what you learned by reading your partner's journal in the previous weeks." Those journals turn out to be important scaffolds as students approach a text outside their own area of expertise.

The culmination of the assignment is a metacognitive conversation in which partners explore their thinking about reading and write a joint summary of their conversation, addressing the following questions in particular:

> What have you learned about reading in your own subject area?
>
> What have you learned about reading outside your subject area?
>
> How will you use this learning to help your students make meaning from the texts you assign in your class?

What these prospective teachers discover in the process of this assignment is an appreciation of the disciplinary reading expertise they have and will be able to offer their future students and reading apprentices.

*This account is based on an activity described in *Rethinking Preparation for Content Area Teaching: The Reading Apprenticeship Approach*, by Jane Braunger, David M. Donahue, Kate Evans, and Tómas Galguera, published by Jossey-Bass, 2005. Used by permission of Jossey-Bass.

about how to help students carry out these increasingly ubiquitous academic tasks.

When teachers have repeated opportunities to engage in argumentation using multiple texts in their disciplines, they begin to appreciate the role argumentation can play in fostering deep subject matter learning. For example, as teachers work together to consider what may have happened during a historic event by examining and interpreting multiple historical documents about that

---

TEAM TOOL 5.11

Exploring Argumentation Inquiry

PURPOSE

With a topic-focused text set, disciplinary teams explore the reading and thinking processes they engage in to develop claims across the texts and then to build an argument for a claim. Their experience informs ways they may want to scaffold their own classroom instruction.

PROCEDURE

- In advance, invite discipline-alike members of the team to create a topic-specific set of two or three short texts they might want to use with students.

- Provide copies of the texts to all team members and ask them to read and Talk to the Texts. Teachers may expect more of a purpose for reading multiple documents, but invite them to explore—to wade in and see what they find.

- Bring the team together and create a Reading Multiple Texts Strategy List:
  - What did we find interesting?
  - What connections did we make?
  - What problems in reading the texts did we have to solve and how did we do that?
  - What questions do we still have?
  - What issues are raised?

- Have teachers work individually to make two or three claims based on their reading. Ask them to pay close attention to what they have to do to make a claim.

- Have teachers gather in discipline-alike small groups to share with a partner both their claims and the processes they used to make them.

- Bring everyone together and begin an Argumentation Strategy List:
  - What did we do to make a claim?
  - What problems did we have to solve and how did we do that?
  - What questions do we still have?
  - What issues are raised?

- Have each disciplinary small group choose a claim for which they will develop an argument.

(Continued)

- Ask teachers to work individually to begin to develop an argument.
- After a few minutes, ask teachers to reflect on their process of developing an argument and discuss this stage of their process with their partner, and then their small group.
- Bring everyone together and debrief by adding to the Argumentation Strategy List:
  - How did we go about identifying evidence to use?
  - What makes particular excerpts from the text helpful in supporting a claim? Less helpful? How do we know?
  - What else are we doing to develop our argument? What are the internal argumentative voices we hear and respond to as we work? What actions do we take mentally?
- Facilitate a discussion of how team members can use this experience in their classrooms.

event, they often realize that argumentation is a *way* of learning, not merely a product at the end of the road.

In fact, negotiating the meaning of a text can be understood as a form of argumentation, especially when it occurs in a community of engaged readers tussling with the text's complexities: What does this data suggest about the relationship between recreation facilities and obesity rates within a community? How does this document shed light on what life may have been like for children during the 1800s? Discussions of texts and text meaning—the process of argumentation—can be as valuable as the concluding performance—constructing an argument. Without deep understanding of a topic, after all, it is hard to construct a compelling argument about it. Arguing to learn, through reading and discussing the meaning of texts, can support the process of learning to argue more skillfully in a discipline.

By exploring their own argumentation processes, teachers often discover that making a claim about a text or from the information offered in a text (when a claim is not given) can be quite a difficult task. Further, they may notice that finding or citing evidence is not necessarily the hardest part of argumentation, despite what they may have believed. Instead, what is often most challenging is the process of explicating the reasoning that connects text evidence to the claim they want to support.

As anyone who has ever carried out a heated argument knows, what counts as persuasive and compelling evidence for one group of people may be quite different from what counts for another. But what may be surprising is that the process of argumentation may differ substantially from one academic discipline to another. Close-Up 5.14, Differing Disciplinary Claims, is such an example.

CLOSE-UP 5.14

Differing Disciplinary Claims

In one inquiry group, teachers of history, science, and literature explored the process of argumentation from a text set on the topic of disease in medieval times. The text set was one that middle school history teachers planned to use in their classes. Each disciplinary group developed claims for an argument.

Having read the same group of texts, these subject area teachers nevertheless made very different claims about them, through distinctly disciplinary lenses.

History

- During the Middle Ages, illness like leprosy and the bubonic plague had an impact on society, culture, and science.
- The history of disease and health care reveal human power dynamics in action; some people gain power, while others are disempowered.
- Being sick in medieval Europe was scary, debilitating, and often hopeless.

Science

- During medieval times, there were many diseases that were difficult to treat and were more easily spread as a result of living conditions and lack of modern medical knowledge.
- People who were sick should have been isolated from healthy people to reduce the spread of disease.

Literature

- When faced with the unexplained, people rely on prior ways of thinking, resulting in isolation/ostracization to protect themselves.
- Without understanding of a disease and how it spreads, people's response to an outbreak of disease is often worse than the disease itself.

This same group of teachers also took a step back to create a Claim-Making Strategies List, a metacognitive survey of how they created claims, with the purpose of recognizing how to help their students tackle the claim-making process.

Claim-Making Strategies List

- Categorize topics . . . into groups . . . to see what connected together
- Wonder: if I could use background knowledge
- Linked overarching idea . . . and specific evidence in the texts
- Compared interesting vs. important ideas . . . felt my claim was a summary but less debatable
- Looking for a claim that the author is offering
- Re-evaluate the purpose of the task—to be controversial—not to summarize
- Stay focused on the facts rather than be drawn into the philosophy—do we bring in our own knowledge?
- Choosing text will impact the level of claims presented—range of types/structures
- How to use the text features in ways that support the claim
- Looked for <u>claim</u> for which text provides evidence
  - Felt backward b/c I could not do research
  - Worried about reliability of texts
  - <u>What other info/resource I would want?</u>
- Looked for big picture for the text set . . . looked for relevant, conflicting arguments
- Looked for something I cared about
- Purposefully didn't qualify argument . . .
- Ask questions—then turn them into statements
- Respond from gut—but realize I need outside resources
- Evaluate the usefulness of each text—eliminate unnecessary
- Revise claim by changing important word/verbs to best express intentions: caused → contributed to (qualify)
- Remove prior conceptions from the claim—personal beliefs don't matter
- Looked for rebuttal . . . b/c interesting articles usually have rebuttals

Engaging in Text and Task Analysis

> So this is like chess. You think ten moves ahead of your students. Then when you are
> teaching, you are ready with the next move.
>
> —Abdiel Salazar, Fremont Elementary School team member

Previous inquiries in this chapter have focused on reading processes. Text and Task Analysis focuses in addition on the knowledge-based challenges a text is likely to pose. Teachers are often so familiar with their course texts that they become inured to the challenges they present. Deliberate focus on these challenges through a process of Text and Task Analysis provides teachers with new insights into sources of potential reading difficulties and strategies students might use in overcoming them. The Text and Task Analysis is an inquiry teachers can use over and over when selecting text and planning how to use it.

With the increasing focus on the importance of text complexity and of matching texts to students, Text and Task Analysis is a particularly valuable tool for preparing teachers to read with students in mind.

Before teachers take on Text and Task Analysis with student materials, however, teams may want to undertake a Text and Task Analysis with a complex text written for an adult audience, to raise their awareness of what makes a text hard and what kind of supports a reader may need. Team Tool 5.12, Text and Task Analysis Inquiry, is written for use with student materials but may easily be adapted for inquiry with adult materials.

One such inquiry might be designed for teachers in disciplinary groups, with a set of texts that offer discipline-specific text structures and features. In this inquiry, focusing first on their reading processes and strategies, teachers

---

TEAM TOOL 5.12

Text and Task Analysis Inquiry

PURPOSE

When teachers know how to identify the demands a text makes on the reader, and in relation to a particular task, they are able to select appropriate texts for classroom use, plan appropriate tasks, and anticipate necessary supports.

PROCEDURE

Note: Many teams use step 1 of this inquiry with texts at an adult level before using the inquiry with student texts.

1. **Read the text** you plan to have students read, paying close attention to your own reading process. What strategies are you using to make sense of the text that students will need to learn or remember

to apply? What knowledge are you drawing on to make meaning of the text? Use the following Text and Task Analysis note taker to record your thinking.

- What schema challenges may this text present for readers?
  - Specific content knowledge that readers may not yet know?
  - Specific content knowledge that readers have studied previously but will need to review or need help to recall?
  - Vocabulary that is unfamiliar?
  - Familiar words used in subject-specific ways?
  - Unfamiliar forms of texts or new text structures and features?
  - Difficult or unfamiliar sentence structures?
- What learning opportunities may this text present for readers?
  - Opportunities to encounter key curriculum ideas or concepts?
  - Opportunities to explore discourse conventions of the discipline?

2. **Try the task** you plan to have students do with this text, paying close attention to the work you are doing to complete the task.
   - What challenges does the task present?
   - What kinds of discipline-specific thinking are required?
   - What experiences have students had with tasks like this previously?
   - What new skills and strategies are demanded?

TEXT AND TASK ANALYSIS NOTE TAKER

What's involved in reading this text? What reading strategies are helpful? What knowledge is necessary (including personal experience)? What teaching and learning opportunities does this text offer?

Knowledge of Content and the World A learned and lived knowledge base	**Knowledge of Texts** Text genres and text structures; visuals and formatting features	**Knowledge of Language** Words and morphology; syntax and text signals	**Knowledge of Disciplinary Discourse and Practices** The particular ways members of a subject area community communicate and think

Reading Strategies

Teaching and Learning Opportunities (Tasks and Supports)

share how they made sense of the text, as they might in Team Tool 5.2, Capturing the Reading Process. What reading strategies did they invoke?

They then complete a Text and Task Analysis note taker, noting these strategies and the knowledge demands they encounter. What knowledge of the world, of texts, of language, and of a particular academic discipline must a reader call on to make sense of the text? It often helps if teachers work in pairs or trios on this charting, puzzling out what knowledge the text requires of them, before turning to a larger group for sharing. In conversation with colleagues, these experiences analyzing text demands increase teachers' understanding of the disciplinary expertise they have gained over time from their experience of disciplinary texts.

Teachers will naturally reflect on how Text and Task Analysis can inform their lesson planning. Having learned how to discern a text's challenges as well as potential opportunities for learning, they can plan lessons in ways that support students' developing competencies. With enough experience engaging in Text and Task Analysis, teachers find that they begin to unconsciously analyze texts' challenges for potential classroom use.

When a team undertakes Text and Task Analysis with student materials, they might individually read such texts as a Robert Frost poem, the Declaration of Independence, or a textbook description of geometric conjectures and respond to the range of challenges and opportunities the text provides: What particular opportunities does a text present them, as teachers, to mentor their students' literacy and disciplinary learning? What concepts or topics, text structures, language, and disciplinary conventions will be difficult, and why? Which of these might productively invite a classroom investigation? Or require particular scaffolding? What will they want to listen for as students work together to make sense of the text? What reading processes or strategies might a text lend itself to? Is this an opportunity to focus on paraphrasing? visualizing? predicting? What part of this text warrants whole class's Think Aloud attention? Are there valuable relationships to other texts for students to uncover?

Finding Texts (and Matching Them to Inquiries)

One of the things we're very committed to is making our professional learning institute a model of a Reading Apprenticeship classroom. Any text we use, a video or reading, we always embed a metacognitive routine. We'll do a reading in the institute and be Talking to the Text and then build a Reading Strategies List together. Or we might do a paired Think Aloud and take notes on each other. We might watch a video keeping a metacognitive log and then debrief it. So we really do try to do all the things in professional learning that we are expecting instructors to do with the students in the classroom.

—Shelagh Rose, Pasadena City College instructor and First Year
Pathways faculty lead

Texts selected for any reading inquiry should be challenging, adult level reading but not so difficult that they discourage team members from participating. Because readers' expertise, experience, and interests vary widely, this is another instance of the importance of establishing a team environment where "It's cool to be confused."

Even if team members all share the same disciplinary background, when initially developing an inquiry community, it may be best to choose a text that is not within the subject area expertise of any of the team members. That way, everyone is likely to be on equal footing with the reading, and surprising areas of individual knowledge or experience can build interest in the collaborative inquiry. Such a text should offer word challenges for many, complex sentences that may require deliberate attention, and background knowledge assumed by the author that may be specialized or at least out of the realm of most teachers' areas of study.

Texts such as "Notes of a Painter," by Henri Matisse, "Father's Butterflies," by Vladimir Nabokov, abstracts and articles from *Scientific American*, and chapters from books like Oliver Sacks's *Awakenings* meet these criteria. *The New York Times*, *The New Yorker*, *Science*, and *The Atlantic* are also reliable sources for complex but not inaccessible texts. Current nonfiction titles and memoirs also serve up appropriate text for teams to explore in initial inquiries.

It's not the point to completely stump teachers, so in cross-disciplinary inquiries when readers will encounter the complexities of a text outside of their area of expertise, finding a text that will help team members build insight into specific aspects of reading requires intentional text examination and choice.

With a carefully chosen text, in which the discourse style is unfamiliar, for example, proficient readers have an opportunity to focus on the role of fluency in reading. In particular, they are invited to see that fluent reading involves more than word recognition or fluent decoding. Unfamiliarity with academic language structures and complex syntax is often a barrier to fluency for inexperienced readers. Selecting a text to present fluency challenges to adult readers is therefore important.

The texts "Notes of a Painter" and "Father's Butterflies" mentioned earlier offer challenges in word recognition and sentence processing. Modern textbooks can also be a source of suitable texts for surfacing fluency issues for otherwise fluent adult readers, since they are often composed of multiple discourses and text styles. History textbooks, for example, are replete with primary sources. Science textbooks often embed historical narratives and short biographies.

Advanced textbooks may also offer opportunities to surface disciplinary dispositions in reading. History teachers may read with a critical eye toward point of view and the selection of historical examples offered in textbooks, while English teachers often critique expository segments as poorly written, while perhaps appreciating the voice and figurative writing of the primary documents.

Many essays or authentic texts can be read from a variety of disciplinary perspectives, as well. Consider Martin Luther King's "Letter from a Birmingham Jail." This piece of persuasive writing could be read as literature, as history, as rhetoric, as psychology, as theology, and as social science. Similarly, many reports of new science advances can be read for their scientific claims as well as for their potential impact on ethics, politics, the economy, and society in general.

To explore the range of textual materials that constitute modern communications, however, it will be important to move beyond traditional text sources to explore reading processes with visual texts such as science diagrams or models, graphical displays of data, maps, political cartoons, advertisements, and the like. How does a reader make sense of such information? What are its important features? What are the structures in the text that support readers in drawing inferences? What conventions are at work in these visual displays? How do we know?

Beyond traditional printed sources of compelling texts to explore, the Internet offers an almost limitless supply of complex texts of various kinds. As savvy readers, teachers and teacher leaders are likely to be aware of reliable and authoritative online sources of texts to engage and challenge themselves and their colleagues.

■ ■ ■

Teachers' inquiries into reading in this chapter prepare them to see and support their students in new ways. The complex processes that a reader orchestrates to make meaning from text become wonderfully alive in these firsthand experiences. In the next chapter, teachers have the opportunity to bring these insights about reading to their inquiries into students' work and their own instructional practices.

Notes

1. Thurber, J. (November 14, 1942). The catbird seat. *The New Yorker*.

2. Rabinowitz, P. (1944). *Before reading: Narrative conventions and the politics of interpretation*. Ithaca, NY: Cornell University Press.

CHAPTER SIX

Exploring Instruction as Colleagues

By sharing what you're doing, it changes the climate of your school.
—Sara Jones, Titusville High School teacher leader

WITH COLLABORATIVE inquiry as the central dynamic of team meetings, teachers' inquiry into their instruction is the natural partner to the inquiry into their own reading described in Chapter Five. In this chapter, we focus on ways to help teachers look closely at classroom practice and student work and to build pedagogical knowledge through professional reading and discussion. We also describe protocols for learning from observing in one another's classrooms and for reflecting on professional and student growth.

Team meetings that engage teachers in repeated opportunities to reflect on their own teaching, share their teaching successes and dilemmas with others, and capture the insights of their colleagues serve to foster ongoing learning from practice and to reinforce an inquiry stance toward teaching. At the same time, the work teams do to normalize the complex, ongoing struggle of teaching in response to diverse learners can be risky—demanding a learning environment of mutual respect in which the resources and contributions of all are genuinely valued.

Protocols can be an important help in establishing a safe and equitable way for teams to organize their inquiries into instruction. Many are included in this chapter. Teacher leader Heather Arena remembers the importance of protocols when her Exeter High School team began their work together:

> We definitely used protocols a lot the first year. We made sure our
> meetings ran according to the protocols so that everyone got to share and
> we didn't get burdened with complaints about our struggles. Now our
> meetings are a little more relaxed. We do still use protocols, but maybe
> not for the entire span of the meetings, or maybe just if we're looking at
> a professional document or looking at student work.

Team Tool 6.1, Collaboration Protocols for Exploring Instruction, previews the team meeting protocols that are described in this chapter. Their selection and use will depend on a team's goals.

Collaboration Protocols for Exploring Instruction

These protocols are designed to help teams organize their inquiries into instruction and provide choice in setting meeting topics that meet a team's goals.

Looking Closely at Practice

- *Planning and Support Conference Protocol:* Teachers envision the beginning of a school year, plan how to introduce key Reading Apprenticeship routines, and then debrief. This protocol can also be used when teachers plan lessons that they present to team members for feedback.

- *Check-in, Exchange, Reflect:* Teachers report on their Reading Apprenticeship practice, exchange information about what they are learning or wondering, and reflect.

- *Chalk Talk:* Teachers respond in writing only (on a chalk board or other public space) to a colleague's question—and to other team members' written comments as well.

- *Reading Apprenticeship Descriptive Consultancy:* Teachers respond as critical friends to a colleague's Reading Apprenticeship classroom case—a lesson, problem, or success—to help develop deeper understanding of Reading Apprenticeship practices for the team and possible next steps for the presenter.

Looking Closely at Student Work

- *Student Work Protocol with Text and Task Analysis:* Teachers respond to a colleague's set of student work samples after completing the assigned student task and a Text and Task Analysis.

- *Student Work Gallery:* Teachers respond to a contextualized piece of student work from each team member, in a gallery format.

- *Analyzing Student Work with the CERA:* Teachers use a rubric to respond to students' pre- and post-CERA samples.

Building Professional Knowledge

- *Book Club Protocol:* Teachers read a professional article or book chapter and share responses, clear up confusions, and discuss implications for practice.

- *Golden Line and Last Word Protocols:* Teachers read a professional text and individually select passages they agree or disagree with or are otherwise interested in discussing with the team (which they do).

- *Classroom Close-Up Cases:* Teachers select a Classroom Close-Up from *Reading for Understanding* and explore what it offers for thinking about Reading Apprenticeship goals for teachers and students.

(Continued)

Observing in Colleagues' Classrooms

- *Focused and Evidence-Based Observations:* Teachers use an Evidence/Interpretation note taker to observe a colleague's requested areas of focus.

- *What Does a Reading Apprenticeship Classroom Look Like?:* Teachers refer to this overview to organize an invited observation.

Reflecting on Growth

- *Reading Apprenticeship Teacher Practice Rubric:* Teachers use the rubric to set and then reflect on team and individual goals.

- *Reading Apprenticeship Student Learning Goals:* Teachers plan how to share the student learning goals with students.

Looking Closely at Practice

> People felt so good about listening to each other share their successes or share the problems they encountered. The problem solving was just as good as the successes.
>
> —Arlene Buchman, Souderton High School teacher leader

Most teams find that inquiry into Reading Apprenticeship classroom practice is always on their agenda, even when the main focus of the meeting is a different topic or inquiry. At Titusville High School, teacher leader Sara Jones thinks of the team meetings as the way teachers can see into one another's classrooms and appreciate their shared commitment to improving their practice:

> Unfortunately, we don't have time in our schedules to go visit somebody else's class. So the team meetings allow us to see what people are doing, what they bring to share, but also to recognize that everybody has challenges. Sometimes you have a lesson that goes bad and it seems like you're the only one. Or it might be a strategy that everyone's struggling with, and then you get some ideas about how to work around that or to do something else instead. We focus on how to make it better and what the kids *can* do. Nobody leaves feeling they failed at something or their students aren't going to be able to do it. The team meetings validate what we're doing and the fact that we're all working on this.

From Anderson High School, Kay Winter describes an example of how inquiry into practice at a Reading Apprenticeship team meeting contributed a key metaphor that has spread throughout the school:

> One teacher said of her students, "We're talking about what they know, their background knowledge and activating that background knowledge,

but my students get sidetracked when they're bringing in their own knowledge, and they go off on something else."

Then another teacher said, "Well, I talked to them about that voice in their head, and I call it their *minion*. I said, "That little minion sits on your shoulder, and that minion can distract you or that minion can help you focus on your work. But you have to train that minion so it knows what to do."

That's become part of the Reading Apprenticeship language in our building, the minion—it can make me wonder what's for lunch today, but it can also be directed to help me wonder about what this really means and how I can better understand it. So the meetings have been very useful. We look forward to them.

When teams have participated in Reading Apprenticeship professional development, they have had a head start getting to the kind of concrete experiences that can be shared with team members. Sometimes, however, teams are starting from scratch. When this is the case, the next two sections offer support for teachers to collaborate to do the necessary planning for a Reading Apprenticeship classroom and for designing Reading Apprenticeship–infused lessons. These sections are followed by two others that include protocols that make the sharing productive.

Planning for a Reading Apprenticeship Classroom

What is it, after all, that characterizes a Reading Apprenticeship classroom? What classroom goals and instructional practices are team members aiming for? Where do they focus and how do they get started?

Goal setting and planning start with the Reading Apprenticeship Framework, a few key Reading Apprenticeship routines, and each teacher's subject-area goals and texts. Even though team members will end up with customized plans for their own courses, everyone on a team benefits from envisioning the beginning of the school year or semester and exchanging feedback about initial plans.

A number of tools can help teams organize their planning and feedback processes. A sequence many teams have used includes these tools:

- Teams discuss Team Tool 6.2, Implementing Reading Apprenticeship: The First Four Weeks, to refresh their understanding of important beginning goals and some routines for supporting them.

- Team Tool 6.3, A Progression for Building Metacognition, shows a suggested sequence for introducing metacognitive routines and suggests their recursive nature.

TEAM TOOL 6.2

Implementing Reading Apprenticeship: The First Four Weeks

What are the most important goals to hold onto during the first weeks of school or a semester? What are some specific routines or activities that support those goals? Teachers can keep these goals and activities in mind as they envision introducing their own students to Reading Apprenticeship.

GOALS

- Begin building the social and personal dimensions of the classroom

  - Personal connections, interests, motivations, experiences

  - Norms for respectful collaboration, risk taking, sharing of resources

- Begin the metacognitive conversation about reading and thinking

  - Classroom inquiry into reading, thinking, and learning

  - "It's cool to be confused"; problem solving to make meaning

- Establish conversational routines for paired, group, and whole-class work

  - Individual, pair share, foursomes, whole-class collaboration

- Introduce, model, and practice key metacognitive conversation routines

  - Think Aloud, Talking to the Text, metacognitive logs/journals

- Extend class time devoted to reading and talking about reading

  - Daily warm-up readings, paired reading, silent reading

- Collect and use a variety of reading materials that offer different levels of difficulty

  - Extend reading opportunities for all students, for the first topic or unit of study and then subsequently for all topics or units

PLANNING NOTES

Ideas for Week 1

Student Reading Survey

(see Reading for Understanding Assessment Appendix)

Have students individually fill out the survey and share their responses with a partner, followed by a whole class discussion about students' responses. What do students read outside of school? What are they interested in and good at? Acknowledge and value students' dislikes and difficulties, and share yours as well. Have students bring materials they read at home into class.

(Continued)

Personal History-/Math-/Science-/English-Reading History

(see Reading for Understanding Box 3.9)

Have individuals reflect on and capture their own subject area reading history with words, pictures, or a combination of both. Have students share their history with a partner, and then combine two sets of partners into a foursome to discuss commonalities and differences. End with a whole-class discussion of what discourages and supports students' reading and learning in a subject area, what resources they are bringing to the class, and what kind of classroom community they want to create. Use that discussion as a means to create norms for class work.

Developing Norms

(see Reading for Understanding Box 3.4)

Let students know that they have the power to create a safe, productive classroom and that you will help them. Invite them to describe what is important to them in a learning environment: What helps and what hurts?

Capturing the Reading Process/Reading Strategies List

(see Reading for Understanding Box 4.3)

Using a high-interest and accessible text, have students read individually and write about what they did to make sense of the reading. Have them share with a partner and then in a whole group discussion. Make a list of the reading strategies they share and post it on the wall in the classroom. Emphasize how much they know about reading and how much they can offer one another as learners. Let them know that they will continue to add to this class Reading Strategies List.

Introduce Metacognition: Think Aloud with Pipe Cleaners

(see Reading for Understanding Box 4.2)

With a nonreading task such as this one, have students learn to externalize their thinking processes. Explain how becoming metacognitive will help them monitor and control their thinking and learning, and how sharing their thoughts will help the whole class. Debrief as a class: acknowledge the difficulties associated with thinking aloud, and value students' willingness to take risks.

Model Think Aloud

(see Reading for Understanding Box 3.10)

Using materials from students' outside-of-class reading, demonstrate your own comprehension processes and problems with these unfamiliar materials. Model the Think Aloud with other high-interest reading materials. Have students use the Metacognitive Bookmark (Box 4.7) to identify your thinking processes.

Use Think Aloud to Model Discipline-Specific Reading Processes

(see Reading for Understanding Box 4.6)

As you introduce course materials, again model the Think Aloud to help students see how you approach these disciplinary materials. Model discipline-specific reading strategies—such as wondering about point of view, identifying rhetorical devices, or comprehending data arrays—and help students see how discipline-specific reading processes can help them read more productively.

Other Ideas

Ideas for Month 1

Practice Think Aloud

Have students contribute to a group Think Aloud using the Metacognitive Bookmark. Ask them to contribute to each prompt: Does anyone have a picture? A question? Is anyone confused? Give students practice Thinking Aloud in pairs with bookmarks. Add new strategies to the Reading Strategies List.

Model Talking to the Text

(see Reading for Understanding Box 4.9)

First model Talking to the Text with the overhead or document camera. Have students contribute to a whole-group Talking to the Text on the next part of the text. Add new strategies students are using to the Reading Strategies List.

Practice Talking to the Text

Have students individually Talk to the Text and share their work with a partner. What did they do to make sense of the text? What comprehension problems did they solve? What comprehension problems do they still have? Have pairs share highlights from their conversations, and debrief the process with the whole class.

Help Students Choose Materials for Extensive Reading

(see Reading for Understanding Box 5.2)

Offer students a variety of reading materials to choose from as they complete class assignments focused on curriculum topics. Model ways of choosing texts according to interest and difficulty. Have a class conversation about ways to choose accessible reading materials. At the beginning of a unit, encourage individual students to choose text selections that are at their comfort level in terms of comprehension and to move on to more difficult selections as they progress in the unit.

Begin SSR or Independent Reading (if applicable)

(see Reading for Understanding Chapter Six)

Introduce Metacognitive Logs/Journals

(see Reading for Understanding Boxes 4.10–4.12)

Introduce metacognitive prompts for reading logs and journal assignments to accompany all class reading. Model the kind of responses you are looking for. Identify good responses in students' logs and journals and share them with the class. Always have students share their metacognitive logs and reading experiences with each other, looking, for example, for especially good responses or interesting new strategies. Add new strategies to the Reading Strategies List.

Other Ideas

TEAM TOOL 6.3

A Progression for Building Metacognition in Shared Class Reading

In this model sequence of metacognitive reading experiences that build students' reading independence, the first three activities occur once, and the others recur in increasingly refined or increasingly expansive iterations.

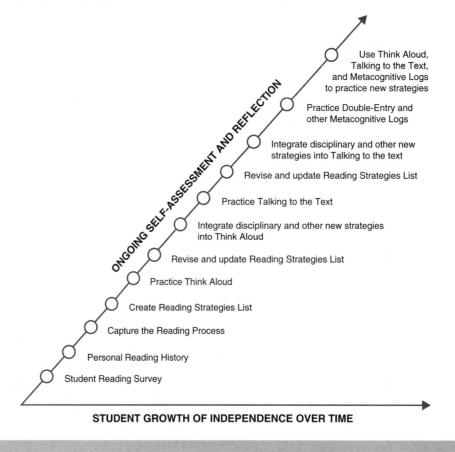

- Team Tool 6.4, Identifying Routines and Scaffolds Note Taker, then invites teachers to review *Reading for Understanding* with a stack of sticky notes at hand, tagging specific routines and scaffolds that could support their beginning instructional goals.

- With those ideas from *Reading for Understanding* in mind, teachers fill in a matrix that relates goals, content, texts, activities, the Framework, and

TEAM TOOL 6.4

Identifying Routines and Scaffolds Note Taker

PURPOSE

Team members take a few minutes to review *Reading for Understanding* , marking with a sticky note any routines or scaffolds they may want to consider as they plan their first weeks of instruction.

PROCEDURE

In advance: Ask team members to bring their copies of *Reading for Understanding* and the texts they plan to use in the first four weeks of their course. Have pads of small sticky notes on hand.

- Ask team members to spend about ten minutes finding and flagging routines and scaffolds in *Reading for Understanding* that may be useful in their planning for the first few weeks in which they introduce students to Reading Apprenticeship.

- Have pairs follow these directions:
  - Take turns sharing routines and scaffolds you identified and their location.
  - Discuss what the routines and scaffolds support students to do.
  - Borrow ideas for your own list.

Routine or Scaffold	What This Scaffold Supports	Page

assessments—Team Tool 6.5, Reading Apprenticeship Framework Activity Planner. They also refer to Appendix C, for the Reading Apprenticeship Teacher Practice Rubric and the student learning goals, as they complete the planner.

- When team members have completed their initial plans, they present them to colleagues for feedback. Team members can record their responses (and ideas to borrow) on Team Tool 6.6, Planning and Support Conference Protocol.

Infusing Reading Apprenticeship into Lessons and Units

Having sorted out their thinking about what Reading Apprenticeship goals, routines, and strategies they want to focus on first—the kind of community they want to establish and the classroom practices they want to cultivate—teachers can begin to design Reading Apprenticeship lessons that reflect those goals. Team Tool 6.7, Contextualizing Your Reading Apprenticeship Lessons, can serve as a touchstone during lesson design.

Teachers all have favorite templates for designing lessons, but Team Tool 6.8, Reading Apprenticeship Lesson Design Template, includes the various

---

TEAM TOOL 6.5

Reading Apprenticeship Framework Activity Planner

PURPOSE

This planner is one way to guide the generation and recording of ideas about how to integrate Reading Apprenticeship goals into subject area instruction. The resulting plan should be thought of as part of a design process that will continue to evolve.

PROCEDURE

In advance: Have copies of the Reading Apprenticeship Teacher Practice Rubric for team members (Appendix C) and the Reading Apprenticeship Framework or student learning goals for any relevant content area(s) (Appendixes A and C).

- Ask team members to look over the planner. Note that the planner can be used at any point during a school term, but the focus now is on the first four weeks of school.

- Move the team through some examples with the planner.

- Fill in a team-nominated content topic or goal for the first week.

- Fill in a team-nominated goal from the teacher practice rubric.

- Invite team members to nominate content area texts that could be used, keeping ideas about extended reading in mind.

- Continue with as many additional examples as needed.

- Note that knowledge-building goals are tied to opportunities in the selected text(s) and are identified through Text and Task Analysis.

- As team members begin planning, point out that they will want to focus on social and personal goals and on metacognitive conversation.

- Provide time for team members to give one another feedback about their plans. (See Team Tool 6.6, Planning and Support Conference Protocol.)

(Continued)

(First Four Weeks) Activity Planner				
Reading Apprenticeship Teacher Practice Goal				
Student Learning Goal				
Time	**Week 1**	**Week 2**	**Week 3**	**Week 4**
Content Topic/Goals				
Extensive Reading/Texts				
Knowledge-Building Goals and Activities Content and World Text Language Disciplinary Discourse and Practices				
Social and Personal Goals and Activities				
Metacognitive Conversation Goals and Activities				
Cognitive Goals and Activities				
Formative Assessment Goals and Activities				

considerations inherent in designing a Reading Apprenticeship-infused lesson. It asks teachers to think about their own practice goals as well as goals for students, to include a Text and Task Analysis (Team Tool 5.12) to inform the design, and to incorporate the key elements of the Reading Apprenticeship Framework. Before trying out a new lesson, team members may choose to present their drafts to colleagues, using Team Tool 6.6, Planning and Support Conference Protocol.

Teachers may need help recognizing how important it is to get into the habit of completing a Text and Task Analysis before assigning text for students to read. In Close-Up 6.1, Text and Task Analysis of an Instructional Unit, history teacher Gayle Cribb's experience is an example of how such an analysis smooths out the teaching and learning of challenging disciplinary skills and concepts.

Planning and Support Conference Protocol

PURPOSE

As team members share their plans for initiating a Reading Apprenticeship classroom, tentative ideas may change, new ideas may be suggested, and a clearer sense of the interaction of goals and activities may emerge.

PROTOCOL FOR TRIOS: TWENTY-SIX MINUTES

ROUND 1: DRAFT: FIVE MINUTES TOTAL PER TRIO MEMBER (FIFTEEN MINUTES)

1. As a presenter, share your plan: Three minutes

- Overview of your plan, including the flow, goals, routines, and texts

- One thing in your plan you are proud of

- A question you have

2. As a listener, take notes on the following:

- Good ideas to borrow

- Questions that will help extend thinking about the plan

	Ideas to Borrow	Questions
Texts		
Knowledge-Building		
Social and Personal		
Metacognitive Conversation		
Cognitive		
Formative Assessment		

3. Each of you make two comments of one minute each when offering feedback:

- An affirmation or good idea to borrow

- A question to help extend thinking and further revision

REVISE PLAN: FIVE MINUTES

4. Revise your plan based on thinking that emerged from your partnership.

ROUND 2: REVISION: TWO MINUTES PER TRIO MEMBER

5. As the presenter, describe what you revised and why.

At Pasadena City College, the faulty leaders who designed the College 1 first year experience seminar infused Reading Apprenticeship into every aspect of this three-credit course. Faculty and staff who sign on to teach the course find themselves learning about metacognitive conversation, reader identity, norms, Reading Strategies Lists, Talking to the Text, metacognitive logs, Think Aloud, and so forth—all as part of a four-day professional development institute.

The College 1 course was a great success as measured by student persistence, credits completed, and equity statistics, but it was a challenge for some of the teachers, especially those who were new to Reading Apprenticeship and lesson planning (in addition to all faculty, non-teaching staff who hold a master's are invited to teach College 1).

Shelagh Rose, who is the faculty lead for College 1, raves about the difference it has made to have an early draft of the model curriculum retooled by one of the course teachers who reflected on her own experience teaching College 1 to scaffold the use of Reading Apprenticeship routines for others:

> Tiffany (Ingle) took the curriculum we had started to create, but that was very messy, and turned it into this very beautiful series of lesson plans where you had the course content and then you had the metacognitive routines and some of the other discussion protocols that we've learned from Reading Apprenticeship very thoughtfully embedded and also scaffolded so you would not just do, say, Think Aloud once. You would be coming back to these metacognitive routines over and over again, and they're completely explained to the instructors along with the theory behind them.

Tiffany's motivation for her work on the College 1 model curriculum is described in Close-Up 6.2, Oh, This Is What Student-Centered Means. The model curriculum is intended to support the College 1 teachers beyond the seminars to help them embed Reading Apprenticeship strategies into their regular courses.

Consulting

When team members inquire into their practice together, they serve one another as collaborators and consultants. They look closely into their Reading Apprenticeship classroom experiences—what is going well and why, and where help may be needed. The expectation is that with everyone on the team trying out new classroom practices, no one will be an expert, but everyone will have a shared context for thinking through challenges and appreciating success.

For many teams, a consulting format is the primary way they build a sense of collegiality and confidence. As Cindy Miceli describes Anaheim High School's first year of Reading Apprenticeship, team members started out hungry for one

TEAM TOOL 6.7

Contextualizing Your Reading Apprenticeship Lessons

Team members can consider the following prompts as they design, participate in, and reflect on the classroom environment they are hoping to promote through Reading Apprenticeship–inflected lessons.

Designing Lesson Routines. . .

- For students to do more extended reading, more often, as they learn in the subject area
- For students to become metacognitive about their own reading and thinking processes
- For students to share their thinking processes with the teacher and with one another
- For students to work together to make sense of reading and subject area content
- For students to gain specific tools and strategies for approaching reading in more powerful ways
- For students to be mentored in the ways of reading and thinking characteristic of the subject area
- For students to become active participants in their own learning process

Being There. . .

- To listen to students' thinking as they work
- To encourage students to tap into everyone's knowledge, experiences, and successful approaches to classroom tasks
- To support students' thinking and collaboration as needed through prompts, questions, or suggestions on the fly
- To see how well students understand and are prepared to carry out assigned tasks
- To make informed decisions about next steps to support student learning

Reflecting. . .

- On where in the lesson you are designing for metacognitive conversation
- On where metacognitive conversation is happening in the social dimension
- On who is doing the reading for understanding—do all students actually have to read to move forward in the lesson
- On whether there are additional places in the lesson where students can read or talk more and you can talk less
- On where in the lesson formative assessment can help you adjust your instruction
- On what options you can have in reserve in case more scaffolding is needed
- On how feedback from colleagues might help in strengthening a lesson

TEAM TOOL 6.8

Reading Apprenticeship Lesson Design Template

This template prompts the inclusion of all aspects of the Reading Apprenticeship Framework in lesson design, and assumes that a Text and Task Analysis informs instructional decisions.

Course/Unit			
Lesson Title **Lesson Duration**		**Extended Reading Texts**	
Teacher Practice Goals			
Insights from Text and Task Analysis			
Lesson Events	**Participation Groupings**	**Teacher Role**	**Student Goals**
Event 1		Some things I might do Some language I might use to do this	Content Literacy Metacognitive Social/Personal Cognitive Knowledge-Building Assessment
Event 2		Some things I might do Some language I might use to do this	Content Literacy Metacognitive Social/Personal Cognitive Knowledge-Building Assessment
Event 3		Some things I might do Some language I might use to do this	Content Literacy Metacognitive Social/Personal Cognitive Knowledge-Building Assessment

another's help thinking through their questions about practice and later found themselves eager to share successes:

> In the beginning our meetings went longer because each teacher wanted time to find out, "Am I doing it right?" "What about this?" Toward the end of the year it was more, "Oh, I have this cool thing and let's look at it."

CLOSE-UP 6.1
Text and Task Analysis of an Instructional Unit

High school history teacher Gayle Cribb developed an instructional unit on the Japanese internment during World War II. Key texts in the unit included the U.S. Constitution, Presidential Executive Order 9066, Civilian Exclusion Order No. 34 of the U.S. Army, and arguments written by two Supreme Court Justices in the case of *Korematsu v. United States*.

Gayle prepared for the unit by rereading all the documents she planned to use and doing all the activities she had planned herself:

> I thought this lesson was very challenging. So in trying to prepare it, first I did everything that the students would be doing. I had a couple of things I thought would make sense that, it turned out, wound up not making sense.
>
> I made my own notes about the Constitution, my own summaries of those notes, which I actually used during class to refer back to, like, "Well, what did I make of that," and to keep myself grounded in my own interpretation.

Leveraging her own efforts to make sense of the material, Gayle identified potential challenges and learning opportunities for students and devised note takers that helped students see connections across texts, events, and ideas.

She also looked up unfamiliar vocabulary and legal terms, and created a timeline of events related to the Korematsu case. Rather than teach the vocabulary up front, Gayle allowed students themselves to identify and grapple with unfamiliar vocabulary:

I chose not to give those definitions to them because I thought most of them they could intuit or figure out by context.

On the other hand, she decided to give students the timeline of events related to the case:

> I set up a list of important events for this particular case because I needed to do that as a reader and, while I think they would have come to that themselves, I am just so aware of the time, the precious time, so I gave that list to them as a reference.

In the interest of time and efficiency, she also identified relevant sections of the Constitution and chose two opinions from *Korematsu v. United States*, those that represented the most compelling argument on each side of the decision:

> One of the things I did as a result was to chunk the text and figure out how I was going to label it and what we were not going to read, because the whole thing was too much. I made the decision to give them the complete set of opinions [even though students would read only two] because one of the ways that I have been training them as historians has been to look at what's left out.

Gayle's Text and Task Analysis was also important in another way:

> The main thing that I understood from the Text and Task Analysis was that this was a lot of intellectual work, and I needed to break it up for them.

Consulting about Reading Apprenticeship practice can be built into any team meeting—at the beginning of the agenda for exchanging questions and discoveries, or as the main topic of the meeting for making an in-depth inquiry. What follows are descriptions of a range of protocol-structured inquiries into classroom practice.

CLOSE-UP 6.2

Oh, This Is What Student-Centered Means

At Pasadena City College, Reading Apprenticeship practices are at the heart of the first year experience seminar, College 1. Faculty leaders Shelagh Rose and Nika Hogan designed it that way and built a four-day institute for campus faculty and staff who would teach the course. In the beginning, they put most of their energy into the course design and the supporting professional development for the seminar teachers. They also managed to put together what they call a "messy" curriculum.

Instructor Tiffany Ingle took care of that. Her motivation to improve her teaching of College 1 led her to create her own scaffolded lesson plans, which have now been polished into model curriculum that benefits everyone who teaches the course:

When I first attended the four-day institute for College 1 teachers, I fell in love with Reading Apprenticeship. After I finished teaching two sections of College 1, I was really thinking about what I would do differently, how I could do it really well. I challenged myself to create lesson plans that activated metacognitive conversation more deeply.

I also realized that I needed more Reading Apprenticeship training. I went to the institute again, I did the Reading Apprenticeship 101 course, and then I got a chance to go to the Reading Apprenticeship Leadership Community of Practice. So I was bringing all that knowledge to help write model lessons.

When I scripted out lesson plans, every time I used a routine from Reading Apprenticeship I had the sidebar on the left where I would explain the reasoning behind that, and I would try to summarize what that was so that it didn't seem like some jargon you would have to look up somewhere. Those explanations created a bridge between people being, "Oh, I get Reading Apprenticeship, I don't need to learn more about it," to realizing, "Oh, wow, I wasn't using it to the best of its potential, I wasn't really leveraging Reading Apprenticeship." Our main hope was that people would see very clearly the routines and how to use them.

When we first did a training using the model curriculum and asked for opinions, one veteran, well-respected teacher was the first to respond: "This is really student-centered, way more than anything else I've ever done." So it was a really good starting place for a lot of conversations like redefining what does student-centered really mean.

These are not magical lessons, but each lesson is based on a text set and at least one of the texts is using a very clear metacognitive routine from *Reading for Understanding*, straight out of the book. When teachers see these routines as a focus of a lesson plan, not just a supplemental piece, or something to do at home, there's a realization for some instructors, "Oh, this is what student-centered means. Students actually do it. I don't tell them what to think."

Some teams begin every meeting with a protocol-structured ten-minute check-in about their recent Reading Apprenticeship classroom experiences. These regular, predictable exchanges are a motivating constant for everyone on the team, allow team members to learn what others are doing, and allow the team to monitor problems or issues that may need attention.

Some of team members' biggest discoveries come from these quick exchanges. Cindy Miceli, for example, recalls her introduction to vertical text sets:

> We were sharing and English brought in vertical text sets, I think that's what they were called, and I thought, "Oh my gosh, I think I can do that in biology." Just pick different articles at different levels, and they would all say the same thing, but make it easy, medium, and hard basically, and let kids have a choice. So, they feel like they're picking something they're comfortable with, and then vary it. Give them an easy one, and then throw in a more difficult one to keep the sense of accomplishment there. So they can read when it is easy, and then when they see the same subject harder, they are already comfortable with it because they've got a little schema built in there: "Oh, I already knew this word. I already know this concept. So, even though it's hard to read, I have an idea what's going on." I got that from English, "Oh, that's smart."

For opening a team meeting with an opportunity to share practice, Team Tool 6.9, Check-in, Exchange, Reflect Protocol, begins a team meeting with a focus on practice but also leaves time for taking up another topic.

TEAM TOOL 6.9

Check-In, Exchange, Reflect Protocol

PURPOSE

Teachers report on their own Reading Apprenticeship practice since their last meeting, exchange information about what they are learning or wondering, and reflect on what they may have learned from the exchange.

PROCEDURE: TWELVE MINUTES

1. **Team members respond to two think-write prompts:** Four minutes
   - Since our last meeting, what did you do to use Reading Apprenticeship approaches or routines in your classroom?
   - What successes and challenges did you experience?
2. **In a whip-around, all team members share answers to the first prompt:** Two minutes
   - Listening team members do not respond or comment.
3. **Volunteers share answers to the second prompt:** Four minutes
   - Facilitate discussion in which team members clarify their experiences and sort out commonalities and differences. Record for the group.
4. **Team members reflect in writing about one thing they can take away from their discussion:** Two minutes

At Buchanan High School, the Reading Apprenticeship team has grown to include over a dozen teachers. The group meets all together but often breaks into smaller content area teams. At a meeting that began with a check-in and exchange of practice, the social science table was looking at one teacher's experience having students "read" political cartoons, the English table considered how students could benefit from their Talking to the Text notes when writing a persuasive response to that text, and the science table was reminded of the power of student talk:

> What I've really been working on is having the kids talk. I'm trying to do more of the social dimension, having them talk to each other and really get that if you don't know what's going on, ask your partner.
>
> When we read they always go through and Talk to the Text. Their focus in this lesson was how do you calculate a half-life, what is a half-life. Then as a group they come up with the definition. And then we make our hypothesis. I tell the kids, "Talk to each other. Take that expert mentality of making a conclusion. Then, I'll give you five minutes to write your conclusion."
>
> So they have that good conversation together and then actually write it. I have seen a very nice improvement on conclusions.

Chalk Talk is another protocol for looking at classroom practice. When a team member wants feedback from the team, he or she writes a question or briefly describes situation in writing on a chalk board or other public space. Silently, team members write responses to the initiating question and iteratively to comments that others write. These silent discussions can become more involved than anticipated. At Wyomissing High School, teacher leader Rob Cushman sometimes saves them for the end of meetings. Team members who must leave do, but others may stick around and around—and eventually even break into discussion. Team Tool 6.10 outlines the Chalk Talk protocol.

Check-ins and Chalk Talks about practice are typically part of a meeting that has a different kind of inquiry—into, for example, student work, Reading Process Analysis, or lesson planning—as its main course. However, when a team wants an in-depth focus on practice, Team Tool 6.11, Reading Apprenticeship Descriptive Consultancy Protocol, is a satisfying format for looking closely at Reading Apprenticeship practice. The protocol can be adapted to look at complete lessons or at particular implementation issues or successes. Timing can be adapted accordingly, ranging from fifteen to fifty minutes. One member of the team brings a classroom situation to the team, and the team responds.

Reading Apprenticeship descriptive consultancy makes three particular demands on team members: to take a descriptive rather than evaluative approach, to maintain focus on the presenter as the team's client, and to anchor

TEAM TOOL 6.10

Chalk Talk Protocol

PURPOSE

Responding in writing to a team member's question about Reading Apprenticeship can have the effect of producing more thoughtful feedback and more equitable participation among team members. Note: Teachers also find that Chalk Talk can be a successful classroom activity.

PROCEDURE: EIGHTEEN MINUTES

In advance: A team member prepares a question that has come up for him or her related to a Reading Apprenticeship classroom experience and posts the question on a chalkboard or other public space with room around it for team members to write comments or add sticky notes.

1. **Explain the directions:** One minute

   – No talking!

   – Write or post at least one response to the question and at least two responses to comments of other team members.

   Responses may include:

   – A question about the question

   – A question about a colleague's comment

   – Agreement or disagreement with the question plus evidence/rationale

   – Agreement or disagreement with a comment plus evidence/rationale

   – An additional idea to an existing idea

   – A new idea

   – A connection between two or more ideas, explained

2. **Team members write responses to the question and to others' comments:** Ten minutes

3. **Team members reflect and write to themselves:** Three minutes

   – What new thoughts or questions did I have during this Chalk Talk?

4. **Team members debrief the activity and their learning and questions:** Four minutes

the discussion with the Reading Apprenticeship Framework graphic or the student learning goals (see Appendix A or C).

Although it may be natural for team members to want to compliment or reassure a colleague who is presenting, consultancy aims for a dispassionate, almost clinical approach to the presenter's situation. A consultancy protocol may at first feel overly prescriptive, but team members typically find that the protocol structure invites careful listening, thoughtful reflection, and time limits designed to protect team members' equitable participation.

TEAM TOOL 6.11

Reading Apprenticeship
Descriptive Consultancy Protocol*

PURPOSE

Teachers respond as critical friends to a colleague's Reading Apprenticeship case—a lesson, an issue, or a particular success—in the classroom implementation of Reading Apprenticeship. (A total of fifteen to twenty minutes may be sufficient for a consultancy; sometimes thirty minutes or more is ideal.)

PROCEDURE: ABOUT THIRTY MINUTES

1. **Presenter lays out the situation:** Five minutes

   Presenter distributes lesson materials and describes the lesson or situation in terms of the following questions, referring to the Reading Apprenticeship Framework graphic (Appendix A) or the Reading Apprenticeship Student Learning Goals (Appendix C) to anchor the discussion:

   – What was the context for what the presenter was trying to accomplish?

   – What happened?

   – What were the presenter's initial understandings?

   Team members are silent.

2. **Team members clarify what they do and do not understand and try to develop a shared understanding of the lesson, problem, or success and its complexity:** Five minutes

   Team members speak in terms of these questions:

   – What did you hear?

   – What do you need to know more about?

   Presenter is silent.

3. **Presenter responds to clarifying questions:** Four minutes

4. **Team members refer to the dimensions graphic or student goals and ask probing questions to elicit presenter's thinking:** Four minutes

   – Questions go deeper into the described successes or challenges.

   – Questions do *not* attempt to come up with solutions or ideas.

   Presenter is silent.

5. **Presenter responds to probing questions:** Four minutes

6. **Team members brainstorm possible next steps for presenter:** Four minutes

   Team members offer their suggestions reflexively:

   – What might happen if. . .

   – One thing I might consider/try/do. . .

   Presenter is silent.

(Continued)

7. Presenter reflects on concrete steps to try—if only first steps: Two minutes
Team members are silent.

8. Presenter and then the team debrief: Four minutes

- What was it like going through these steps?

- What was most useful/interesting about this consultancy?

Keep in Mind...

- Practice being more descriptive and less judgmental (in terms of praise and blame).

- Practice keeping the focus on the presenter's experiences (and not those of your own that may come to mind).

- Anchor your discussion with the Reading Apprenticeship dimensions graphic or Student Learning Goals (so that the purpose of apprenticing students into ever more competent disciplinary literacy remains clear).

*This consultancy is adapted from Nancy Mohr's formulation of descriptive consultancy. See, for example, "Descriptive Consultancy" in *The Power of Protocols: An Educator's Guide to Better Practice*, by Joseph McDonald, Nancy Mohr, Alan Dichter, and Elizabeth McDonald (2003). New York: Teachers College Press, pp. 53–55.

At Berkley High School, the team of five teachers who began the school's Reading Apprenticeship journey reserved every monthly meeting of their first year together for consultancy and followed the protocol deliberately. In their continuing work with one another, their focus as a team has evolved and diversified. At the same time, however, in the role they share as teacher leaders inducting other colleagues into Reading Apprenticeship, they continue to privilege the consultancy protocol that carried them through their own first year.

In Close-Up 6.3, History Unit Descriptive Consultancy, Berkeley High teacher Angie Church presents a unit about the civil rights movement to her first year cross-disciplinary team. A team member appreciates that Angie's unit plans specify which parts of the unit attend to which of the Reading Apprenticeship dimensions:

> You always mark what dimension each part relates to, and that's really helpful, to literally see in your head how these dimensions are working through the unit.

By the end of the consultancy, Angie has incorporated a colleague's reflection into a next step she can take, and biology teacher Tracy Francis is already redesigning her phyla unit.

CLOSE-UP 6.3

History Unit Descriptive Consultancy

In a descriptive consultancy meeting of a Berkley High School team, two English teachers and two science teachers are hearing from a history teacher about a two-week unit she redesigned "with a little more Reading Apprenticeship thinking behind it." Group members have copies of sample unit activities and student work. (The following excerpts cover most but not all unit activities.)

Note: To support a team discussion of this Close-Up, consider having each team member read it with an Evidence/Interpretation note taker. What do they notice (evidence), and what do they think or wonder about it (interpretation)?

1. Presenter lays out the situation

> ANGIE: This is a unit about the civil rights movement for U.S. history. In years past we've given kids these sixteen events, and we've spent time in the library, and we've researched these things. I've said things like find out when this occurred, who was involved, what was the outcome of the event, and what do you think is its significance. The kids would do that for all sixteen events. And all kids were turning in things that were pretty much the same. There wasn't much that made it their own, that they could show themselves in.
>
> So I adjusted it this year with a little more Reading Apprenticeship thinking behind it. What you'll see on the front page is simply an introductory activity that we did to activate schema, get them thinking about what they know and why the civil rights movement even begins. We go back in time here and we look at the Jim Crow laws and we look at *Plessy v. Ferguson* Supreme Court opinions. This kind of framed it, it was something the kids did independently and then we talked about it. A lot was activated in terms of what was the discrimination in this country.

> Then, instead of just giving them the titles of each event and saying, go find them, I gave them a little blurb about each event and I gave them an image. So in class, they took some time to read those and talk to that text on their own. They had an opportunity to dig into it.
>
> The next piece is the events research. So this is how I changed it up. They got to select a partner, so there's some personal choice there and some social dimension, and then they selected the five events they were most interested in.
>
> I was able to give all of the groups one of their top five choices. Some of the higher-end groups, I looked at their events and assigned the most challenging one. Some of my kids that tend to have less interest, I gave them what they really wanted—maybe they wanted the Watts riots or the riots in Detroit. At that point, I had them just think about what do you and your partner know about your event already, what are you still wondering about, and what do you want to find out, to kind of drive them.
>
> Then you'll notice that they get to decide how they're going to present this to us, and they could present in any way. They wanted to try to make it as interesting as possible, but notice they have a rubric that also lets them know the requirements.
>
> What I want to show you [on iPad video] is some of the kids presenting. Every kid presented except for one. He came and talked to me separately about his project, but his partner presented. To me, that was fantastic that every kid got up there.
>
> You have two documents kids used in their presentation, and they're both Reading Apprenticeship–sort of activities. The first one is from the *Brown v. Board of*

(Continued)

Education group. They passed one of these out to every kid in the class and asked them, before they started, to Talk to *this* Text and try to come up with questions of what they were wondering about—which I thought was great.

And then the second one, from two students who typically struggle to participate—one of them, she often tunes out and says the reading's too hard, I'm bored, why do we have to do this—their presentation was solely based around this quote they had found. She walked us through that quote as a class and was completely engaged in that. So, to me, that was huge.

Angie shows excerpts of both presentations. In the second one, the student who had previously been resistant to reading stands at the overhead and goes through the quote she and her partner selected. When she comes to the word begrudgingly, she comments, "I don't know what that means, but I'm guessing it's something bad." At the conclusion of the presentation class members can be seen asking the partners questions. Angie explains:

I didn't have a requirement for questions; they just started asking each other questions. One of the other things I did within this unit was I tried doing some claims —make a claim and then use evidence to support it from the reading. You have two samples there, one really high-achiever kid and then more of a struggling student with the bigger writing, but who was really able to make several claims with evidence that supported it. So I felt like it did address various levels of kids, not just the high end or the low end.

2. Team members clarify what they understand or not

TESS: I'm hearing that you are preparing students in terms activating their prior knowledge and schema, that you're using different modes of reading, and you're doing that through a variety of dif-

ferent texts, both small portions and also full-length texts.

KAY: I also saw a lot of student choice both in the beginning when they got to choose their topic but then you also gave them choice in determining how they were going to present that information. Did they choose their partners . . . yes?

ADINA: I'm wondering how that went.

TESS: Are students in charge of giving that content or are they kind of expanding on it?

TRACY: One of the things I really liked was when you gave them the images and the blurbs, instead of just titles, so they could make an educated decision.

KAY: I wrote this down in big letters. Your student who doesn't like to do the reading modeled confusion but made a guess—*in front of the class:* "I don't know what this word means, but I'm guessing it's something bad."

Everyone in the group acknowledges this student's remarkable shift in engagement and risk taking.

3. Presenter responds to clarifying questions

ANGIE: Okay, self-selected partners actually went pretty well. Sometimes I haven't let them do that, to control it, but I was going with the student choice thing here. I tried up front to say, "You're going to be doing a lot of decision making with this partner, so it needs to be a partner you can move forward with."

(Looking over her notes for the next question from the group) All the content in class is related to those topics. They're all responsible for all of the topics at the end. The note taker with these sixteen blurbs in the beginning gives them a pretty good overview of what happened. Everything else throughout is built on those events.

When we watched clips of *Eyes on the Prize*, an amazing documentary from the time, all of those events are embedded. Kids took their own notes on *Eyes on the*

Prize, on an Evidence/Interpretation page, and then I had them use their notes to write for each of the sixteen events: What do you understand about the event? and What questions do you have? They had to come up with one question for each event.

Then another day I had them partner off and they started clarifying each event: What do I know? What do I not know? And they went through and did a whole bunch of questioning of each other and clarifying. Then we talked through what questions do we still have? As a class, can we answer those questions? And *then* we had our assessment. The scores were phenomenal.

4. Team members ask probing questions

TESS: I have a question about motivation for the class when other students are making a presentation. I was wondering what the draw was for your students?

KAY: The claim and evidence, I was just wondering if there's a next step to this, or if you are considering doing a next step with this next year, or if this is where it ends?

5. Presenter responds to probing questions

ANGIE: During the presentations, kids had their note taker [for the sixteen events]

back out, and they're writing down anything else they might need. I think that's what generated the questions because I had said, "Okay, when they're done and there's pieces of this you still don't understand..." So they're trying to find out.

I haven't even thought about the next steps for claims and evidence.

6-7. Team brainstorms; Presenter describes nest steps

KAY: For me, for English, I'm thinking, well, what are they going to write? A paragraph, an essay? They could totally write something.
ANGIE: Right, right.
KAY: That's exactly what we want them to do.

8. Presenter and team debrief

ANGIE: I think it's good to hear, "Okay, here's the claim and evidence. Now what?" I just wanted them to be able to make a claim about what they've read and support it. It's funny I didn't think about it as a building block for writing.
TRACY: I'm really inspired. This is perfect timing. We have a new assessment on phyla, and I knew that we needed to revamp the whole unit. This could work really well. I literally just emailed myself.

Consultancy is respectful of teachers' professional wisdom and good will, and helps a team capitalize on both. Teacher leader Alicia Ross speaks from her team's experience at Blue Ridge High School:

> I think as teachers we sometimes get a little territorial. Creating a culture where we're constantly sharing, and people want to tell you what they're doing, that's a huge shift. Teachers listen to other teachers. At our school, I think we're seeing the dividends of that.

Another important way that teachers listen to other teachers is with student work in front of them to guide the way.

Looking Closely at Student Work

At most meetings, people brought student work, regardless if that's what we were talking about at that meeting. There was a lot of benefit in starting with student work and then deciding what we should tackle, where are the holes, what do we need to work on.

—Heather Arena, Exeter High School teacher leader

For the most part, teachers at the secondary and college levels have to operate on scant information about their individual students' reading capabilities. With few opportunities to see individual students at work with texts of various kinds, teachers may hear a dysfluent oral reading and wonder whether a student has decoding problems. Similarly, when students have little to offer in class discussions about a text, teachers have difficulty pinpointing the source of their silence. Did they do the reading? Are they able to? Teachers often come to us with this puzzle—*My students can't, don't, or won't read*. Consequently, these teachers have developed instructional coping mechanisms to sidestep the text altogether.

When teams engage in metacognitive conversation about specific samples of student work, a better understanding of students' reading processes, strengths, and problems can emerge. Team inquiries prepare teachers to take advantage of the confusions and sometimes unexpected readings that students offer in response to text. Teachers begin to theorize about student thinking, listen differently in class, and perhaps see students more generously.

In Close-Up 6.4, A Reading Interview as a Student Work Sample, a team of teachers demonstrate this kind of response as they analyze a student's videotaped reading and thinking interview.

With samples of student work to explore, teachers can together trace students' reading and thinking processes and draw implications for instruction. At Wayne Memorial High School, teacher leader Kevin English says student work is at the center of the team's collaboration:

The first part of the meeting we spend just talking about what's happening, to acknowledge that we're all working pretty hard. Then we've had one person bring student work to share each time. We use a protocol and we allow student work to drive our conversation. That's been really enriching in terms of what we talk about.

One teacher may not notice certain things happening in that student work until they get here. And then we really start to think about, "Well, what *is* happening in our classrooms, what are other people seeing?"

We're learning how to look at the things that students *are* doing and what they *can* do. Even if our students are doing something that we

CLOSE-UP 6.4

In this inquiry excerpt, a team of teachers discuss a student's videotaped reading interview, an extended and occasionally prompted Think Aloud. They demonstrate the kind of pedagogical sense making that can build insights into students' reading and instructional needs. Earlier, the teachers had read and inquired into their own reading processes comprehending the same text, a James Thurber short story.

KAREN: I have kind of a question. What strikes me about this interview is that there's a lot of sort of stumbling, "y' know," "stuff," and "like," this imprecise stuff. Stuff, I just used it. So, you could say that as she talks, she's trying to, in that moment, comprehend what she's read. And my question is, with her level of reading, is that really what she's doing? And is it only when she's talking about it that she's comprehending? What's happening when she's just alone with the text and reading it?

LYNN: Obviously she reads the text and understands it, but when she talks to us, she drops grammar, slurs words, whatever. And there I am doing the same thing she did. I think all these "y' knows" and "likes" are just like "whatever." It's a padding that teenagers use when they talk, and she gets the meaning. She knows, and if you disregard all those other paddings, what she says are the nuggets that she's already understood. To me.

CAROL: I was thinking the same thing. When we were reading the James Thurber story, we tended to read a paragraph, but then as we began talking about it, we would go back and find other stuff that we hadn't remembered. And that, certainly, you know, that's not the way that I read fiction. When I'm reading fiction, I'm not, you know, I'm just sort of absorbing the sense of it as it goes along and some of the detail. But I miss probably a lot of the detail. And so I've noticed with these interviews—and I mean in terms of your question—how much do we actually retain and how much does the process sort of force us to go back and find it?

KAREN: I'm rethinking what I said earlier. She's having to make all sorts of inferences, and it's not literal for her. I think it's good to sort of have this firsthand experience of that.

might not expect, they're still making moves that we have to analyze, and diagnose what's going on.

According to Exeter High School teacher leader Heather Arena, the time the team spends looking at student work and the time teachers spend on the social dimension of their classrooms has made them very good *noticers*:

In our meetings, we started with noticing what was happening with student work, and in our classrooms, and what were the commonalities. It went from there to a strategy conversation: "What can we do to help students?" I think I pick up on patterns or things students say much better now than I used to, and I think other teachers are doing the same thing. I always hear them say, "I noticed this was happening when we did this piece, or I noticed in their writing that this was happening."

Building Insight into Student Literacy and Learning Processes

How *do* teachers tune their ears to classroom interactions in order to respond effectively to student thinking, particularly when much of their focus in the past may have been on checking whether students know correct content information? How are they to understand partial conceptions or even misconceptions that may emerge to provide learning opportunities that can shape students' partial practices into proficiencies, their inchoate notions into confident learning? How do they learn to see student thinking on the page with insight into its meaning and possibilities? For many teachers, building insight into student thinking and learning processes requires the deliberate effort of shifting their focus from a student's flawed performance on an assigned task to the promise visible in the thinking and reasoning process itself.[1]

Fortunately, the metacognitive conversation routines common in Reading Apprenticeship classrooms put student thinking and reasoning processes in view. To foster insight into student learning, teachers work together, taking an inquiry stance as they pore over student work, learning to notice what is there and to ask what student conceptions or processes or dispositions the work provides evidence of. With inquiry, rather than grading or summative assessment driving the analysis of student work, new understandings and instructional insights often emerge. Working together to build insight into the learning process, teachers increase their experience and appreciation of the multiple ways students can show learning in the moment. Teachers' responsiveness to students during classroom instruction can increase accordingly.

Moreover, when teachers look closely at students' work for insights into *how students are making sense of texts* as well as what content they are and are not getting, they are engaged in formative assessment. This kind of inquiry can provide insights into how one particular student may be growing and areas where he or she needs further support; likewise, looking closely at one or a few students can guide teachers' planning of next instructional steps for the larger class.

When teams inquire into students' learning processes, most often they will work with the metacognitive conversations that students produce in writing, forms such as metacognitive logs, Evidence/Interpretation notes, and Talking to the Text annotations. Unlike small group or classroom discussion or student Think Aloud, written samples fix student thinking in place for examination and facilitate teachers' observation, conjecture, and theory building. Collecting and inquiring into these written samples of students' work is an ongoing way to access student thinking.

Inquiring into Student Thinking with the CERA

A particular tool that we developed for collecting evidence of students' literacy learning processes is the Curriculum-Embedded Reading Assessment (CERA). (Appendix C includes the CERA and guidance for administering it.)

The CERA asks students to Talk to the Text and to assess their own reading facility with a text, giving teachers information about how aware students are of their own level of reading comprehension and comfort. The CERA also asks students to summarize a text rather than answer specific text-based questions, placing value on reading the entire text rather than hunting for correct answers. And, key to the CERA design, a student's responses to different aspects of the assessment can yield competing and even conflicting views of a single student: Why might a student seem to think a piece was easy to read if he or she cannot summarize it accurately? What does it mean when a student provides few annotations but a lengthy description of his or her reading process? And because the CERA is designed to be given twice, over several months, what might it mean if a student who describes a text as easy the first time finds it less so the second time around?

Close-Up 6.5, Representative History Students' CERA Self-Assessments, is an intriguing glimpse of what students can reveal about their reading and learning processes. (The actual CERAs also included the talking to the text annotations students made on the article as they read it.)

CERA annotations can also be used to identify areas in which students are growing as readers and learners. Very often, by looking at pre/post-CERA responses for individual students, teachers come to insights about students who seem at first not to have much substantive interaction with the text. For example, one middle school student's pre-CERA shows his Talking to the Text comments as very basic—"What does this mean?" and so on—and the comments stop after the first page of the story. As teachers look at this student's post-CERA, they notice that he not only finished the story, still with relatively basic questions and responses along the way, but he also raised a literary question: "I don't see what the story has to do with the title?" Although he has in fact not understood the metaphorical nature of the title and how the story relates to it, he has developed stamina for interacting with a text, and he is displaying the understanding that a story and its title should have a close relationship.

When teachers are new using the CERA for inquiry, sometimes their earliest discoveries about students' literacy processes are the most profound. In Close-Up 6.6, Four Teachers' First Inquiry into Students' CERAs, a small group of high school science teachers compare their thinking about what their students' CERAs reveal.

CLOSE-UP 6.5

Representative History Students' CERA Self-Assessments

In September and again in December, a class of grade 9 U.S. history students took a CERA with an article comparing the racial positions of Booker T. Washington and W. E. B. Dubois. Students Talked to the Text as they read and then answered the six items in the following table. For number 5, they could choose from four levels of difficulty: pretty easy, not too hard, pretty hard, and too hard. A team might well take a close look at what three representative students reveal in their answers to these few CERA questions.

Date of CERA	1. In your own words, write a short (one- or two-sentence) summary of this piece.	2. What kinds of things were happening in your mind as you read this?	3. What did you do that helped you to understand the reading?	4. What questions or problems do you still have with this piece?	5. How easy or difficult was this piece for you? (circle one)	6. How well would you say you understood this piece?
John 9-9	President speeches and government stuff.	I kept thinkin How I kept losing focus from reading.	Reread some of it.	So hard to keep reading? I don't know	Pretty hard	I barley understood it honetly
John 12-13	Uhm president and something to do With African Americans.	What the heck am I reading?	Nothing helps	I almost fainted of pointless boredom	Too hard	I didn't
Dalee 9-9	DuBois didn't like Bucker T. Washingtons address	What was happening	I went over words I didn't understand	I didnt understand all the words	Not too hard	Not very well
Dalee 12-13	This piece is about the disagreement of Booker T. Washington and DuBois	There were a lot of words I didn't understand	I read over it again.	What was the difference in what they believed in	Not too hard	Very well
Matt 9-9	This piece is mostly about people taking a stand against racism, trying to get equality, and stop the judgment.	I always thought that racism is stupid, childish, and wrong, so reading this makes me smile for those who thought the same.	I kinda wrote my thoughts down, thought about them, and re-read as well.	I barely knew the men in this story so I'd like to learn more of their background.	Not too hard	I actually understood it quite well considering racism always was interesting and want to learn for me.
Matt 12-13	This piece is mainly about the racial groups (black and white) and about two very influential men with two very different points of view. One wanted separation while the other wants to be equal.	• Frustrated by the racism towards the blacks • Agree with both about the fact that separation must be eliminated • Confused as to why it was needed	• I wrote down summaries of each racial portion • Asked questions • Wrote as much as possible	• None really	Pretty easy	I would say I got a pretty good understanding of this portion with the help of talking to it.

CLOSE-UP 6.6
Four Teachers' First Inquiry into Students' CERAs

When teachers first use the CERA to look closely at student work, sometimes the most important understanding is to recalibrate how their students define "reading."

Anton: *(Points out student's Talking to the Text)* Some marking there, clumping things together, a little bit of underlining.

Dave: No outside commentary.

Anton: Yeah, no questions or summarizing. With her summary, she says, "It's talking about hypoxia, the cause, and what it affects. Talks about two zones where it is more common."

Dave: Yeah, I see that a lot. They kind of tell you what it's about without actually giving any information.

Anton: She also thought it was "pretty easy."

Sheila: I saw that all the time. Did you see that too with your students? They're like, "Oh, yeah, I understood it." And then in the summary, there's like this disconnect.

Dave: Is that like they're able to "read" it—I knew most of the words and could get through it—versus I could actually understand?

Deb: That's their interpretation of literacy. If you tell them you're teaching them some literacy, reading strategies, they say, "I can read."

Sheila: Yeah, in their minds there's a disconnect between reading and comprehension and they're two completely different things, "Oh, yeah, I can *read* it. It's very easy to *read*."

Anton: "But I don't learn anything." I think that's the struggle with a lot of the kids.

Deb: That's interesting.

The particular text selected for any CERA is of great importance. Team Tool 6.12, Authoring Your Own CERA, suggests how to choose the disciplinary text that will anchor a CERA and what to consider if augmenting the standard CERA questions.

Using the CERA for inquiry can be most instructive when it is coupled with the CERA Rubric (see Appendix C). However, teams may want to take the rubric in small doses until they learn their way around it. As a tool for building increased understanding of what student thinking looks and sounds like, the CERA Rubric can be extremely productive, but it isn't a simple place to begin. Team Tool 6.13, Easing into the CERA Rubric, offers several suggestions for how teams might want to structure their introduction to the rubric.

Collaborating to unpack student CERAs can be a powerful activity for professional development. At Pasadena City College, instructor Shelagh Rose engages faculty who will teach the College 1 first year experience class in comparing a sample set of students' pre-CERAs and post-CERAs—with the pre- and post- not specified. To further tantalize faculty, some of the samples are from

---

TEAM TOOL 6.12

Authoring Your Own CERA

To build new understandings of students' literacy and learning processes, the choice of a disciplinary text for the CERA takes center stage. Teachers should think carefully about choosing the text, with several ideas in mind:

- Most important, the text should be representative of the kinds of texts students will encounter over the length of your course. What is the range of texts necessary for learning in your discipline?

- Beyond choosing a text that is representative, teachers might also be drawn to explore specific questions. For example, they may want to build an understanding of how students currently approach challenging materials, which would lead them to consider which of the types of texts common to their discipline students are likely to find the most unfamiliar or the most complex.

- Teachers may want to see how an instructional focus is influencing student work with text; for example, if a history teacher has been emphasizing point of view, she and her colleagues might look for that in students' comments.

- Similarly, teachers often augment the CERA, adding questions for students to complete after they have responded to the reading process and summary questions, to gain insight into how students are understanding particular concepts or engaging in particular skills of interest.

---

classes where instructors were not practicing Reading Apprenticeship metacognitive routines:

> The CERA is incredibly valuable as a professional learning tool, to have faculty look at how does the student shift, how do they not. And also to have a conversation about what differences they saw for students who were using Reading Process Analysis on a regular basis versus those who were just on their own with their reading.

When teachers use the CERA independently, choosing disciplinary anchor texts for their own purposes with their own students, they will still want their colleagues' eyes on the student samples they choose to share—to help build new insights, and broader insights, into student thinking and learning in their classes, and, recognizing the CERA as the formative assessment that it is, to help think about next steps in instruction.

Two Protocols for Looking at Student Work

When teams sit down to look at student work together, they often use protocols that structure the time for sharing student work and engaging in evidence-based

TEAM TOOL 6.13

Easing into the CERA Rubric

The CERA Rubric can appear daunting at first glance. It describes three levels of a student's control of reading processes across a number of items in terms of metacognitive conversation, use of cognitive strategies, and evidence of building knowledge—with items specific to student annotations on the text and to responses to the CERA questions. Teams have several ways to become familiar with the rubric and to simplify or customize their use of it.

- **Talk to the Text.** The three-page rubric is a table ripe for a previewing exercise that includes annotating the text. How is it structured? What are the headings? What's in a column, and what's in a row? How do individual cells relate? Share your annotations with team members.

- **Work with a small, representative pre- and post-sample from a single class.** Initially, the team will benefit from practicing with a common sample of CERAs that represent distinct levels of control of reading processes.

- **Work with one rubric scale at a time.**

  - Start with the Metacognitive Conversation scale. What can you see in student annotations and responses to the short-answer questions? What are you noticing as a group? What implications might it have for instruction?

  - In another session, add the Using Cognitive Strategies scale. What does this lens on student literacy learning offer? What more do you want to know about student use of cognitive strategies? How might these strategies take on different shapes in the different disciplines? [The student learning goals in Appendix C might provide insights here.]

  - In yet another session, add the Building Knowledge scale. Consider breaking into disciplinary groups, with discipline-specific CERA samples per group. Explore interpretations and theories about student learning. Reconvene in the cross-disciplinary group to share your insights.

- **Warm up with the Metacognitive Funnel.** Teams may find the Metacognitive Funnel (Appendix C) a supportive first step in gauging where their students are as a group. Work from class samples of Talking to the Text or metacognitive logs or CERA samples. Where on the Metacognitive Funnel would they place each of the annotations a student has made? Looking across a set of samples, are there patterns in what students are and are not doing, as readers? What does this imply for instructional next steps?

discussion. Protocols can be helpful for keeping the expectations for students clear, the evidence of their performance documented (rather than intuited), and implications for lesson planning more evident. The two protocols that follow incorporate specific Reading Apprenticeship tools. One includes Text and Task Analysis for deepening teachers' understanding of what the student work may show, and the other pulls on the Reading Apprenticeship Student Learning Goals for considering how the student work may reflect or suggest specific areas of growth.

Looking at Student Work with Text and Task Analysis

Teams have many reasons for looking closely at student work, but regardless of what they may be, a Text and Task Analysis makes the process more meaningful. For teachers to fully appreciate the work students are accomplishing with assigned texts and tasks, they must first do this same work themselves. (Chapter Five includes a description of using the Text and Task Analysis routine in lesson planning.) Understanding the demands of the assignment, teachers can then better understand how the assignment contributed, in ways both helpful and not, to students' thinking and accomplishment of the intended learning.

After analyzing the text and task, teams then examine samples of student work from that assignment. Team members collect evidence of what they see in a piece of student work and describe what they infer as a result. When the evidence is out on the table, other ideas, conjectures, and possibilities can arise from the resulting collegial conversation. Such conversations are likely to expand teachers' thinking about the work at hand and spill into evidence-based exploration of implications for teaching and learning. Team Tool 6.14, Student Work Protocol with Text and Task Analysis, lays out a structure for learning from student work in this way.

At Chabot College, faculty in the Reading Apprenticeship FIGs made it a habit to bring in texts that were a struggle for students and to try and figure out why. Instructor Cindy Hicks reports that participating faculty used students' written metacognitive conversations about the texts, as well. A biology teacher, for example, asked her students to focus their metacognitive logs on challenges in the reading, so in addition to the text, she brought in students' logs, which provided some concrete evidence about what in the text was causing confusion and how students were working to make sense of it.

Looking at Student Work Through the Lens of Student Learning Goals

During some meetings, to teams want to spread their attention across student work samples from every team member. Reading Apprenticeship Student Learning Goals (Appendix C) can provide a common focus. In a gallery format, team members respond to what each sample seems to reveal—about a student's relationship to particular learning goals and the support provided by

Student Work Protocol with Text and Task Analysis

PURPOSE

Time spent looking closely at student work should be preceded by time spent doing the work—and analyzing its challenges!

PROCEDURE: FORTY MINUTES

1. **Presenter Describes the Task or Learning Experience:** Five minutes

   Without distributing any student work samples, the presenting teacher passes out copies of the assignment and the text students read. The teacher provides some background on the instructional context and briefly explains the learning experience. For example:

   – Where does this assignment fit into the course? Is it part of a thematic unit? Is it an ongoing classroom routine? How does it connect with topics that precede and follow it? What was the sequence of learning activities?

   – What should students learn and know how to do as a result of this learning opportunity? What were you hoping to see as quality work? How would students know the criteria for quality work?

   – What materials were students given to work with? What were students asked to do with them?

   – For each part of the assignment, how were students grouped? What was their task? What was your role?

   – In what ways were students called on to be metacognitive?

   – What were the outcomes for students? What evidence do you have?

   Team members listen and take notes.

2. **Team Members Analyze the Task:** Ten minutes

   Team members complete the task (or some part of it) with a Text and Task Analysis note taker and talk about what is involved. They do not yet look at student work. Some points to address in the discussion:

   – What reading or content area knowledge and strategies does the student need to accomplish this task?

   – What other knowledge or strategies does the student need (e.g., the ability to participate effectively in small group discussion, to collaborate on a project, to provide feedback on another's work)?

   Presenter listens and takes notes.

3. **Team Members Look Closely at Samples of Student Work and Discuss:** Fifteen minutes

   The presenting teacher distributes copies of the student work from no more than three students. All team members, including the presenting teacher, spend some time individually reading the student samples and making Evidence/Interpretation notes (see following note taker) about what they are seeing and what they think it means or makes them wonder.

(Continued)

The team discusses their observations. This step is *not* a planning or problem-solving session. The purpose is to support all group members' learning from looking at student work samples. Some points to address:

– What, if anything, is surprising or unexpected in this student work?

– What can we learn about the student's reading or subject area learning from this work sample—what schema and strategies is the student bringing to this task?

– Where are there opportunities for metacognitive conversation?

– In what ways does the student's work satisfy the assignment, given the teacher's goals?

– What additional instructional support might the student need to do better on this task?

Presenter will respond to team members' observations after *this discussion but participates here as may be necessary. Presenter takes notes.*

4. **Presenter Responds and with Team Members Brainstorms Next Steps:** Five minutes
If desired, the presenter addresses some of the team's observations.
Together, presenter and other team members brainstorm next steps for this assignment in light of their discussions and feedback.

5. **Reflection:** Five minutes
All team members write individually in response to one or more of the following questions:

– What are some instructional implications you can see for Reading Apprenticeship from this inquiry into student work?

– What did you learn about engaging in a collaborative conversation about student work with colleagues?

– In what ways did this inquiry process offer a window into the student's world? A mirror that reflects on teaching? A lens that focuses on equity and achievement?

Team members share their responses.

Text and Task Analysis Note Taker			
Knowledge of Content and the World A learned and lived knowledge base	**Knowledge of Texts** Text genres and text structures; visuals and formatting features	**Knowledge of Language** Words and morphology; syntax and text signals	**Knowledge of Disciplinary Discourse and Practices** The particular ways members of a subject area community communicate and think

Reading Strategies

Teaching and Learning Opportunities (Tasks and Supports)

(Continued)

Evidence/Interpretation Note Taker	
Evidence (I saw…)	Interpretation (I thought, wondered…)

the assignment. Team Tool 6.15, Student Work and Student Learning Goals Protocol, is designed to allow everyone to get and give feedback and to gain insights from colleagues' implementation of Reading Apprenticeship.

Looking for Growth

It is common for teachers to think of student work in terms of culminating tasks they have assigned—the essays, speeches, reports, and tests that offer a gauge of students' grasp of course content. When Reading Apprenticeship teams focus on student work, it is in terms of helping students embrace the challenge of complex texts, solve problems of comprehension, reason more productively in distinct disciplinary traditions, and use texts intentionally to learn something new. What kinds of student work can help teams recognize how students are taking on these new dispositions and practices, and how they are growing as learners? Team Tool 6.16, What Counts as Student Work, gives examples of the kinds of student work that can provide information on learning targets of interest.

TEAM TOOL 6.15

Student Work and Student Learning Goals Protocol

PURPOSE

With the Reading Apprenticeship Student Learning Goals as a common frame of reference, team members move from work sample to work sample in a gallery rotation so that everyone has the opportunity to get and give feedback and then to reflect on student thinking and learning in relation to Reading Apprenticeship instructional practices.

PROCEDURE: FIFTY MINUTES

In advance: Teachers each select a piece of student work for colleagues to explore. Each work sample is accompanied by a form that addresses these questions:

- *Description of student work:* Why is this work important? What characterizes the activity structure (e.g., partners or small group, student choice, teacher prompt, work we do every day)? Why did you select work from *this* student?

- *Context:* Where does the work fit into your curriculum? What were your learning goals for the work?

- *Framing Questions:* What do you want to know as it relates to particular student learning goals? What are you wondering about?

- *Revised Framing Questions:* After reflection on feedback from colleagues and other student work you saw, what did you learn and what are your new framing questions?

Arrange the room so that each sample of student work has its own station—on a desk, table, or wall where teachers can comfortably read the context form, read the work sample, and write on sticky notes their comments about the work. Be sure teachers each have a copy of the student learning goals.

1. **Teachers read and comment on student work:** Twenty-five minutes
   Teachers pick a station and read the context form and student work in front of them. They write comments related to the student learning goals framing questions on a large sticky note that they affix to the student work or a separate paper, and then move to another piece of student work. The rotation continues for twenty-five minutes.

2. **Teachers return to their own student work and reflect on the comments left for them by their team members:** Five minutes

3. **Teachers share their reflections with a partner:** Ten minutes
   Each partner takes five minutes.

4. **Teachers write a synthesis of what they learned and wonder:** Ten minutes
   On the context form describing the work, teachers reflect on what they learned in relation to their framing questions and new questions they have now.

What Counts as Student Work?

When teams want to know how students are growing in areas of comprehending complex text and engaging in other reading challenges and opportunities, they can broaden the ways they think about the work students have been doing. In addition to the traditional products and culminating performances required of students, teachers can consider some of the less-traditional ways they have guided students to productive work.

Teams might be interested in collecting data about these other kinds of student work listed as follows. Some general guidelines can help:

- Choose a representative group of students to focus attention on.

- Collect data samples from similar tasks at different points in the year. Look for changes over time.

- Compare data regularly and note trends. Use this information to design supports that help increase wanted behaviors such as time on task.

- Create regular opportunities for students to look at this data with partners and in small groups and to discuss and write about what changes they see over time in themselves and each other.

Student Think Aloud Comments

- Record students' comments during Think Aloud in notebooks or on audio or video tape. When comparing samples, ask, is the text of the Think Aloud getting longer, more complex? Is there evidence that students are more engaged, reading with better stamina, using more strategies . . .?

- Record students' talk about and reflection on what they notice about their own and others' Think Aloud experiences.

Personal Reading Histories and Student Reading Surveys

- Give pre- and post-Personal Reading History assignment. How does the pre- compare to the post-?

- Give pre- and post-student reading surveys. What evidence is there that students are, for example, reading more, spending more time reading, or reading more broadly, with better engagement, comprehension, less frustration, and using more strategies?

- Have students look at their pre- and post-records, discuss with a partner, and write reflectively. What changes do they notice?

(Continued)

Talking to the Text

- Collect samples over time, and compare.

- Focus the task on a particular literacy strategy that is challenging (e.g., questioning) and have students Talk to the Text using that literacy strategy (e.g., writing all the questions that come to mind). Do this before and after instruction in that particular literacy strategy.

- Give the Content-Embedded Reading Assessment (CERA) before and after and compare.

- Have students respond to their peers' Talking to the Text.

- Save samples of work from early in the year and later in the year, pass them back, and ask students to talk and write about what they notice about their reading and Talking to the Text.

Metacognitive Logs, Double or Triple Entry Journals, Evidence/Interpretation Records

- Compare samples from different times in the year. Note changes in, for example, number of pages read (fluency), time spent reading (stamina), length of responses (engagement in task), depth and complexity of responses (comprehension or engagement), range, and complexity or choice of reading (any increase in sophistication or difficulty).

- Ask students to look at early samples and current samples, discuss in small groups, and then reflect individually in writing about what they notice.

Reading Task Behavior, Engagement, and Motivation

- During silent reading tasks or responses, keep a roll sheet in front of you, glance around the room at regular intervals (e.g., every three minutes), and quickly mark each student (or focal student) for on-task or off-task behavior. Time how long it takes for students to begin a task. Time how long students engage in reading or writing responses to reading.

- Count the number of students using reading supports (e.g., sticky notes, highlighters, logs). Note who is and who is not.

- Note who finishes first, last, rereads. Compare students' individual patterns.

- Note who responds or participates during group discussions.

- Note who is reading what. Are students' individual selections and preferences changing—more complex, broader range, more difficult, longer?

- Ask students to regularly reflect orally or in writing on their level of attention and engagement. Discuss focusing engagement strategies and risk factors for inattention and how to deal with them. Have students write about learning to deal with inattention and lack of engagement, and design action plans for dealing with difficult, boring, or confusing texts and with challenging reading environments.

- Time how long students remain in discussion about readings in pairs or small groups. Notice whether or not the length of discussion and time on task increase over the year.

- Keep a tally of absences, referrals, tardy slips, and other similar data. Note trends.

Building Pedagogical Knowledge

> As a collaborative group, our team has become, not a literature circle, but a professional development circle, I guess you might call it.
>
> —Kay Winter, Anderson High School literacy coach

Not all team meetings focus on team members and their students. Team meetings can also be an opportunity for teachers to look at practice from a slight remove. As important as it is for teachers to inquire into their own instruction, sometimes it is important to step back and see what other educators have to say. When a team operates as a professional development "circle," as at Anderson High School, their attention may at times turn to calibrating practice with current policy concerns, considering expert perspectives from the field, and deepening their understanding of the Reading Apprenticeship Framework with suggestive classroom vignettes.

Cross-Walking Reading Apprenticeship and Other Priorities

Education policy is continuously in motion, and schools and colleges are hardly impervious to the research and policy conversations that go on all around them. When these conversations result in policy-driven mandates that determine how academic success and teacher performance will be defined and measured, no campus or school building is exempt.

Berkley High School principal Randy Gawel believes that regardless of how education priorities shift over time, Reading Apprenticeship meets his understanding of what students need for the future—as well as the latest priorities of the education establishment:

> You can't ignore these external things that come along. We've put into place Common Core curriculum. Reading Apprenticeship is direct preparation for the requirements of the Common Core. The other thing for us, in Michigan and a few other states, is it's required that the kids have a college entrance exam. In our case, it's the ACT, and, as people in education know, the ACT is 85 percent a reading test.
>
> So in terms of the outcomes that students can realize—academic outcomes, of course, but also the reality that the world they face will be complex and challenging—I think Reading Apprenticeship is the single most important program we have in place. Priority number one for me is that our students are capable of adapting, of learning, of understanding, of working together—all of the things that prepare kids for the world they are entering, that we don't fully understand.

To help teachers see more specifically how what they value about Reading Apprenticeship supports or aligns with school priorities such as Common Core, standardized tests, and teacher evaluation systems, teams sometimes take on explicit cross-walks. In these inquiries, teachers are likely to discover that Reading Apprenticeship is a valuable ally.

In Pennsylvania, for example, teachers must figure out how Reading Apprenticeship supports college and career standards, the state's adoption of the Danielson model of teacher evaluation, and the requirement that teachers develop and monitor student learning objectives (SLOs) for each student.

Pennsylvania teacher leader Alicia Ross describes what it has meant for the Blue Ridge High School team to support one another in working through the state's multiple mandates. An important support for the team is principal Matt Nebzydoski's understanding of Reading Apprenticeship:

> On the team we've talked about Common Core connections because people are working on their unit plans or their curriculum. When I put into a unit plan, "This unit will be taught within the Reading Apprenticeship Framework, and here are the texts I'm using," Matt knows what that means. He gets that.

As for the Danielson Framework for Teaching, it may cause a certain amount of anxiety for teachers across the state, but Alicia points out that teachers on the Blue Ridge team approach it with comfort:

> At one team meeting we looked at the connections between the Danielson domains and Reading Apprenticeship. We can check a lot of boxes just because this is how we do things. You don't have to *find* something; this is something we're doing every day.

Finally, Pennsylvania teachers are being asked to develop SLOs and collect growth data. Alicia and her team think they have it under control:

> SLOs are where the rubber hits the road for a lot of teachers. You're saying that this is your student learning objective, this is where they are at the beginning of the year, and this is where they are two months in or whatever time frame you have for that SLO. Did they show growth? You need a tool to demonstrate that, you need evidence. You as teacher provide that evidence.
>
> So our team had a meeting about the CERA [see Appendix C]. The CERA is a tool you can use to guide you to guide the kids and to provide evidence. People were really excited about that.
>
> All that stuff that people are stressed out about, it's not a big deal if you're doing Reading Apprenticeship.

Mapping tools can help teams increase teachers' understanding of how Reading Apprenticeship brings coherence to some of the new demands they may be facing. Team Tool 6.17 describes how to investigate the Danielson Framework for Teaching from a Reading Apprenticeship perspective. Team Tool 6.18 describes a similar approach to investigating standards such as the Next Generation Science Standards and the Common Core standards. Appendix C includes protocols for using the CERA to guide formative assessment and the management of student learning outcomes.

TEAM TOOL 6.17

Mapping Reading Apprenticeship onto the Danielson Framework

PURPOSE

A teacher evaluation system that focuses teachers on developing students' confidence, competence, and independence and on reflecting on their own practice, such as Charlotte Danielson's Framework for Teaching, is highly consonant with the Reading Apprenticeship Framework, goals, and approaches. When teachers discover the ways Reading Apprenticeship aligns with and supports them in meeting such teaching goals, their understanding of both frameworks deepens and their effectiveness increases.

PROCEDURE

In advance: Have a copy of the Danielson Framework for Teaching on hand for reference. Make copies for each team member of the following note taker and have teachers bring their own copies of *Reading for Understanding* to the meeting.

- Have partners work together to answer the following questions:

  1. How is Reading Apprenticeship aligned with the Danielson framework?

  2. In what areas in particular do you see congruence with Reading Apprenticeship protocols and routines in terms of observable classroom practices and evidence of learning as defined in the Danielson framework?

  3. How does Reading Apprenticeship add value to teaching, learning, and assessment as described in the Danielson framework?

- Facilitate a team discussion of the partnerships' findings and questions. Create a document that captures all ideas.

- Invite partners to add to their own lists new ideas generated by the team.

(Continued)

Note Taker for Mapping Reading Apprenticeship onto the Danielson Framework for Teaching
Consider ways Reading Apprenticeship approaches and routines support teacher professionalism as outlined in the Danielson Framework for Teaching.

Domain 1 Planning and Preparation	Ways Reading Apprenticeship supports teachers in this area of professionalism
1a Demonstrating Knowledge of Content and Pedagogy	
1b Demonstrating Knowledge of Students	
1c Setting Instructional Outcomes	
1d Demonstrating Knowledge of Resources	
1e Designing Coherent Instruction	
1f Designing Student Assessments	
Domain 2 The Classroom Environment	**Ways Reading Apprenticeship supports teachers in this area of professionalism**
2a Creating an Environment of Respect and Rapport	
2b Establishing a Culture for Learning	
2c Managing Classroom Procedures	
2d Managing Student Behavior	
2e Organizing Physical Space	
Domain 3 Instruction	**Ways Reading Apprenticeship supports teachers in this area of professionalism**
3a Communicating with Students	
3b Using Questioning and Discussion Techniques	
3c Engaging Students in Learning	
3d Using Assessments in Instruction	
3e Demonstrating Flexibility and Responsiveness	
Domain 4 Professional Responsibilities	**Ways Reading Apprenticeship supports teachers in this area of professionalism**
4a Reflecting on Teaching	
4b Maintaining Accurate Records	
4c Communicating with Parents	
4d Participating in a Professional Community	
4e Growing and Developing Professionally	
4f Showing Professionalism	

TEAM TOOL 6.18

Mapping Standards with Reading Apprenticeship Student Learning Goals

PURPOSE

New standards such as the Common Core and Next Generation Science Standards expect students to become independent readers and thinkers in the disciplines. When teachers discover the ways Reading Apprenticeship supports students in meeting such standards, teachers' understanding of the standards and of Reading Apprenticeship deepens and their effectiveness increases.

PROCEDURE

In advance: Ask team members to bring their copy of *Reading for Understanding* to the meeting. They will need to refer to the student learning goals in Appendix C. Have copies for partners to share of the standards your team will investigate. Make a copy for each team member of a note taker such as in the following example. On the note taker, you may want to include the relevant standards, or you may leave it for the team or subject area partners to complete.

- Have team members read over or write in the standards they will be working with.

- Ask partners to work together to answer the following questions:

  - How are the Reading Apprenticeship Student Learning Goals aligned with the Common Core State Standards/Next Generation Science Standards/Other Standards?

  - In what areas in particular do you see congruence with Reading Apprenticeship protocols and routines in terms of observable classroom practices and evidence of learning as defined in the standards?

  - How does Reading Apprenticeship add value to teaching, learning, and assessment as described in the Danielson framework?

- Facilitate a team discussion of the partnerships' findings and questions. Create a document that captures all ideas.

- Invite partners to add to their own lists new ideas generated by the team.

Note Taker for Mapping Standards with Reading Apprenticeship Student Learning Goals

Consider ways Reading Apprenticeship and the student learning goals support students' achievement of _____ Standards.

Standard	Ways Reading Apprenticeship supports learning toward this standard

Book Clubbing Professional Texts

How often do teachers get a chance to read professionally together and talk about it? Not so much. But team meetings can offer just such an opportunity. Especially when teams have cleared the way through their first year together, taking some time for professional reading can infuse new ideas and energy into meetings.

Sometimes teams go back to the well, revisiting sections of *Reading for Understanding* to deepen a particular understanding or area of practice. As Alicia Ross relates, the team at Blue Ridge High School made their review of questioning a model Reading Apprenticeship routine:

> We decided to do a reading from *Reading for Understanding*, the section in Chapter Seven on questioning. We all did Evidence/Interpretation sheets, which was fun as many of us shared with our students that we were doing E/I sheets for our homework! In the meeting we did all the stuff that we are practicing in our classroom—like citing the text—and we would all turn to the page the speaker was referencing. We had a great text-based discussion. It allowed us to go more deeply into the text and the Reading Apprenticeship approach to questioning. What was even better was that we naturally shared out what is happening in our classrooms with questioning and sought help from each other on how to help students generate their own questions. It was just very energizing.

At Renton Technical College, the FIGs facilitated by instructor Michele Lesmeister have been experimenting with a new kind of book club. These particular book clubs feature a very applied focus, with faculty choosing a series of challenging classroom texts and taking turns introducing them to colleagues as they would to students—using Reading Apprenticeship routines and developing a shareable curriculum in the process.

Michele finds these monthly book clubs exhilarating, both personally and for her colleagues:

> We started the book clubs to help faculty move into using Reading Apprenticeship routines as the new normal. I start us off by modeling a wide variety of routines for several chapters of a selected book. Book club members then present chapters, using any of the modeled routines. Their ideas about why they chose which routines lead to much discussion about how to choose a routine to best scaffold the text for our use, and then for our students' use. Thus, a sharable curriculum is made.
>
> The quality of these talking and learning sessions is superior to anything we have previously seen, as new models are put into place along with new protocols for professional development. Faculty take new ideas about how to engage texts back to their classrooms and build the routines into their classes.

The level of inquiry continues as groups meet monthly over selected texts, to share confusions and new understandings as we work through a wide variety of texts together.

This book club model of professional development appeals to teachers as engaging and efficient at the same time. They have a chance to experiment with the Reading Apprenticeship Framework and routines and in doing so develop deep understanding of the instructional scaffolds that can become their new normal.

When teams choose to investigate articles from professional journals or magazines, they may be looking for more support for what they already understand or are doing or they may want to learn how what they are doing meets other ideas in the field. Teacher leader Rob Cushman describes how the Wyomissing team reads together as another model of Reading Apprenticeship classroom practices—providing time to read:

> Sometimes we're finding articles that support our work, and we will take a look at those and have a professional discussion. We send the article out early so that if team members want to, they can take a look at it early. But there's always reading time involved for something like that at our meeting itself.

High school and community college team leaders have a few all-time favorite articles to pass along: see Team Tool 6.19, Team Favorites for Professional Reading and Talking, for notes about these classics.

To engage in professional reading and discussion, some teams choose to read with Evidence/Interpretation note takers, others Talk to the Text, and still others use the Golden Line or Last Word protocols for debriefing their reading. These last two are described in Team Tool 6.20.

In Tess Ferrara Berkley high school English class, students tried out a variation of the golden line protocol with a chapter from *The Great Gatsby*. As she explained to her team, she and they were thrilled by the results:

> Kids had to pick what they thought was a golden line from Chapter 4 and explain why briefly in their journals. Then they had to talk to their partner and between them pick one of their quotes. Then the partnerships got together with another set of partners and whittled it down again. They took that one line and wrote it on the board. We went around and each group had to justify to the class why they picked it. The class voted on *the* most important line. And it's funny because by that time they were all pretty much on the same topic, getting out the same idea, getting the crux of what the chapter was about. On the bottom of their journal page, they had to write down the class golden line and explain why. The kids came up to me later and said, "That was really helpful. It actually helped me analyze the chapter and figure out what's going on."

TEAM TOOL 6.19

Team Favorites for Professional Reading and Talking

Reading Apprenticeship teams have gotten great mileage out of the following articles for professional inquiry.

"Teaching Students to Ask Their Own Questions," Dan Rothstein and Luz Santana, *Harvard Education Letter*, Harvard Graduate School of Education, September/October 2011.

How better to engage students in their own learning?

"Insiders and Outsiders," Sheila Tobias, *Academic Connections*, The College Board Publications, Winter 1988.

As learners, what outsiders have to teach insiders and themselves.

"What Is Metacognition," Michael E. Martinez, *Phi Delta Kappan*, May 2006, pp. 696–699.

The best description we know.

"Brainology," Carol S. Dweck. *Handbook School* Magazine, Winter 2008. http://www.nais.org/Magazines-Newsletters/ISMagazine/Pages/Brainology.aspx

When students see themselves in new, more generous ways, they perform accordingly.

"Teaching Adults to Read," Michele Lesmeister, *Techniques*, ACTEonline.org, February 2010.

One community college teacher's experience with Reading Apprenticeship.

"Formative Assessment: An Enabler of Learning," Margaret Heritage, *Better: Evidence-based Education*, Spring 2011.

Assessment as actionable feedback, for teachers as well as students.

"Leading Deep Conversations in Collaborative Inquiry Groups," Tamara Holmlund Nelson, Angie Deuel, David Slavit, and Anne Kennedy, *The Clearing House*, 83: 175–179, Taylor & Francis Group, 2010.

How to trade congenial conversation for honest inquiry, without tears.

Inquiring into Vignettes of Practice

Video and print vignettes of Reading Apprenticeship practice provide a common text that teachers can use to hone their observational skills and deepen their understanding of classroom practices that put student voices at the center of instruction. Instructors at Renton Technical College found the classroom videos both reassuring and provocative:

> Watching the videos allowed me to see what was possible when students have lots of practice. They really analyzed the material and helped each other understand. As with all new activities, I learned to keep at it even when one event seemed to fail. The repetition of routines became more comfortable as we had more practice.
>
> —Beginning ESL instructor

In several of the videos I watched students who were very comfortable and open in group discussions. I can see that I have not structured my classroom in a way conducive to small-group activities. Even worse, I fear that I have structured my classroom as a stage for my daily performances. This is going to require a major rethinking of my classroom environment.

—Automotive service technician instructor

Reading for Understanding includes a number of print vignettes—Classroom Close-Ups—that teams can choose to explore. In addition, the Reading

---

TEAM TOOL 6.20

The Golden Line and Last Word Protocols for Discussing a Text

PURPOSE

These protocols prime engaged reading. Each reader is expected to *react* to a text, not simply swallow it.

GOLDEN LINE PROCEDURE

1. Explain the directions:

– Read silently and Talk to the Text.

– Pay particular attention to these places in the text:

   – Where the text raises questions for you

   – Where it confirms what you already believe

   – Where it makes you say aha

   – Where it conflicts with your beliefs

   – Where it causes you to reconsider prior assumptions

– Choose two different golden lines that you want to share with the team. (You will only share one, but two gives you a choice, depending on what other team members may have already offered.)

2. After the reading, explain how team members will share their lines:

– Read aloud your golden line.

– Direct team members to its exact location in the text, and explain why you chose that line, its significance to you.

– Do not accept comments or questions at this time.

– Take no more than one minute.

3. Facilitate discussion of team members' selections and thinking.

4. Consider how this protocol might be used with students.

LAST WORD VARIATION

Team members explain the significance of their golden line only after other team members have discussed their own responses to the line. Each nominator of a golden line has the last word.

Apprenticeship website has a collection of short videos that teams can make the center of inquiry. Team Tool 6.21 lists the various print and video vignettes teams might want to consider; Team Tool 6.22 is protocol for using the vignettes.

Sources of Classroom Vignettes for Exploration

Reading for Understanding is a rich resource for classroom vignettes. The Reading Apprenticeship website also has a number of classroom video clips that are fascinating to explore.

SELECTED *READING FOR UNDERSTANDING* CLASSROOM CLOSE-UPS

Classroom Close-Up 3.3 Amidst Familial Gatherings

Classroom Close-Up 3.4 That's Cool. You're Isolating What You Don't Know

Classroom Close-Up 3.7 Choosing Not to Fail

Classroom Close-Up 3.9 Becoming a Student

Classroom Close-Up 4.4 Reciprocal Modeling of a Think Aloud

Classroom Close-Up 4.6 Okay, What Else Did You Notice?

Classroom Close-Up 5.4 Disciplinary Inquiry of the Day

Classroom Close-Up 5.6 Framing an Inquiry into Two Poems

Classroom Close-Up 6.1 Book Partying

Classroom Close-Up 7.1 We're Going to Practice This and Get Better at It

Classroom Close-Up 7.3 Chunking the First Amendment

Classroom Close-Up 7.4 "My Name Is Ricardo, Too"

Classroom Close-Up 8.6 "She Was a First Person"

READING APPRENTICESHIP CLASSROOM VIDEO CLIPS ONLINE

http://readingapprenticeship.org/research-impact/videos/classroom/

Middle School ESL
Grade 9 Academic Literacy
Grade 9 Literature
Intro to Chemistry
Biotechnology
Honors U.S. History
Adult Basic Skills
College First Year Experience
Nursing Assistants
College Pre-Calculus
College Physics
College Chemistry

Exploring Classroom Vignettes Protocol

PURPOSE

When teams explore print and video classroom vignettes, the vignettes serve as a common text that allows team members to observe student and teacher behaviors that contribute to students' academic identity and growth. (The vignettes are listed in Team Tool 6.21.)

PROCEDURE

In advance: When using the vignettes from *Reading for Understanding,* choose two or three for team members to read and chose from for further inquiry. Make copies of the vignettes or let team members know to bring their copies of the book.

   With the video vignettes, you or the team may want to use the grade and topic indicators as the way to select a clip to explore. Arrange for a way that team members can easily view the video clips online.

- When using the print vignettes, direct team members to a set of two or three texts. Ask them to read the texts and together decide on one to explore further.

- When using video vignettes, ask team members to select a video for the team to explore.

- Provide the following prompts for team members to consider as they explore a vignette:

   1. What is this vignette about?

   2. What is the teacher doing to support diverse students in this work?

   3. What are the students doing?

   4. In what ways does the instruction provide a rigorous disciplinary-literacy environment?

   5. How does the instruction map onto the interacting Reading Apprenticeship dimensions?

      – Where are the personal and social dimensions in evidence?

      – What are students learning in the cognitive and knowledge-building dimensions?

      – How is metacognitive conversation represented?

      – What can you learn from this inquiry? What seems important to remember?

- Encourage team members to Talk to the Text of a print vignette or to make Evidence/Interpretation notes about a video vignette.

- Facilitate discussion of team members' ideas about the vignette.

- Conclude with a discussion of these questions:

   1. Which students seem to benefit from ongoing opportunities to learn by using Reading Apprenticeship routines and strategies in their subject areas?

   2. Which of the students in our school could benefit from this kind of support?

   3. How can we work as a school community to provide that ongoing support to our students?

Observing in Colleagues' Classrooms

This year we are deepening our practice by inviting each other into our classrooms and videotaping each other to bring to our monthly meetings.

—Adina Rubenstein, Berkley High School teacher leader

Not all schools offer teachers the opportunity to observe in one another's classrooms. But many teachers wish they would. "We don't get to see each other in our classrooms," is a fairly common refrain. At schools where time is made available, however, peer observations and teacher labs can have an important impact in deepening teachers' understanding of Reading Apprenticeship.

Making Framework-Focused Observations

Kay Winter, the literacy coach and team leader at Anderson High School, is a strong proponent of getting teachers into other people's classrooms, if only to let them start thinking about what students *can do*:

> When you have staff who are using Reading Apprenticeship effectively, it's a great professional development tool to be able to allow other staff to go in and observe that, especially if it's in the same subject area. Maybe a social studies teacher who is struggling with primary sources can go into a room where kids are tackling some really hard primary documents and see them digging in and discussing them intelligently, instead of sitting there, "I didn't get it."

In community colleges, opportunities for faculty to observe in one another's classrooms are rare. However, faculty leaders at Pasadena City College and Santa Rosa Junior College have discovered just how valuable those opportunities can be.

At Pasadena City College, instructors of the College 1 course meet in mentor pods to continue the Reading Apprenticeship learning introduced during the four-day institute that prepares faculty and staff members to teach College 1. Shelagh Rose was one of several mentors who opened her classroom for observation:

> We assigned six to eight instructors to a pod and each pod met on average every other week. A lot of the newer teachers requested to sit in on the classes of a more experienced teacher of the course. Of the six people in my pod, three came and sat in on my class in the first couple of weeks and observed what I was doing and took notes. We met afterward for a quick conversation and then we debriefed it more at our next regular mentor group. The feedback was that it was incredibly helpful.

Faculty at Santa Rosa Junior College have also been requesting to see Reading Apprenticeship in action. Accordingly, the Reading Apprenticeship team there is building from the appreciative observation model that has already been introduced on campus and is inviting faculty to observe in their classrooms. Lauren Servais hopes the observations will help to reassure her colleagues that Reading Apprenticeship is a boon, not a burden:

> A lot of my colleagues are worried that Reading Apprenticeship takes so much time. My students don't even know we do Reading Apprenticeship. It's fully integrated. Everything we do in terms of the reading, that's how we do it. I think if faculty came and saw how it can be integrated into a class, if they saw what it looks like, it would ease some of their fears.

Many teams use the observation and reflection tool What Does a Reading Apprenticeship Classroom Look Like? to structure visits to team members' classrooms (see Team Tool 6.23). Appendix C includes another observation tool, *NOT* Reading Apprenticeship, that highlights some common ways implementation can fall short of what Reading Apprenticeship *is*.

At Titusville High School, the Reading Apprenticeship team initiated the school's first foray into peer observation. Team members were good candidates for this experiment because they had established trust among themselves and were working with shared instructional goals and strategies. Principal Scott Davie describes a structured, nonevaluative process:

> As part of their growth plans, Reading Apprenticeship teachers had another Reading Apprenticeship teacher come in and film them. Then the two of them sat down together and talked through the film with a set of questions—how did you plan this activity and how did it work, what questioning techniques, reading strategies were used? It's something I would like to see expanded. I think there's a lot of value in teachers seeing other teachers teach.

Responding to Colleague's Questions

Berkley High School team leaders saw the promise of peer observations early in their thinking about how to spread Reading Apprenticeship across the campus. Over the course of three years, they first planted a seed with administrators about the value of what they term teacher labs, then they decided to use their own meeting time to try labs out—videotaping one another and using the tapes in their consultancy meetings. They now invite colleagues into teacher labs hosted in their classrooms. Kay Cole recalls how support for the teacher labs grew:

> We talked a couple of years ago after seeing a presentation that it would be great if we could make teacher labs happen. So I had a chance to mention it in a conversation with someone in the district. Then we've had a couple of opportunities to see teacher labs in action, and do our own. Our principal is very on board with the idea, and by all of us allowing people into our classrooms, we've really fostered it.

TEAM TOOL 6.23

What Does a Reading Apprenticeship Classroom Look Like?

Teachers can use this snapshot of a Reading Apprenticeship classroom as a reflection tool, for lesson planning, and with colleagues for peer observations. It can also serve as a guide for administrators' classroom walk-throughs. Three characteristics of a Reading Apprenticeship classroom are paramount: a focus on comprehension, a climate of collaboration, and an emphasis on student independence.

A FOCUS ON COMPREHENSION

- Reading Apprenticeship is embedded in subject area learning: students develop strategies, identify and use text features, build topic knowledge, and carry out discipline-based activities while reading course-related materials.

- The work of comprehending reading materials takes place in the classroom; the teacher scaffolds the learning and serves as model and guide.

- The work of comprehending is metacognitive; how readers make sense of text is as important as what sense they make of it.

A CLIMATE OF COLLABORATION

- Class members draw on each other's knowledge, serving as resources to make sense of text together.

- Class members respect and value problem-solving processes: classroom norms support risk taking, sharing knowledge and confusion, and working together to solve comprehension problems.

- Grouping arrangements support collaboration and inquiry: students work independently, in pairs, in small groups, and as a class, depending on the task and the text.

- A shared vocabulary to describe reading processes and text features is evident in classroom talk, materials in use, and materials on display.

AN EMPHASIS ON STUDENT INDEPENDENCE

- Students are agents in the process of reading and learning: they actively inquire into text meaning, their own and others' reading processes, the utility of particular reading strategies, and their preferences, strengths, and weaknesses as readers.

- Students are expected and supported to read extensively: course-related materials are available on various levels, and accountability systems are in place to ensure that students read large quantities of connected text.

- Over time, students are expected and able to do more reading, make more sophisticated interpretations, and accomplish more work with texts with less support from the teacher during class time.

OTHER THINGS TO NOTICE

Reading Apprenticeship classrooms can also be recognized by a number of other classroom characteristics, including how materials and student groupings are used, the types of learning activities students undertake, and the roles of the teacher, students, and classroom talk in the learning environment.

MATERIALS

- What materials are present? How are they being used?
- What kind of work is displayed in the classroom? On the walls? On the board?
- What do these displays indicate about how reading is approached and the role it plays in the class?

GROUPINGS

- How is the classroom arranged?
- What kinds of groupings are students in as they carry out classroom tasks?
- What do these arrangements offer students as learning environments?

TASKS AND ACTIVITIES

- What activities are the teacher and students engaged in?
- What activities seem to be routine in this classroom?
- Who is doing the work of reading and comprehending?

TEACHING AND LEARNING ROLES

- What roles do the teacher and students play in classroom activities?
- Does the teacher model, guide, and collaborate in comprehension as well as give instructions, assign, and question students?
- Do students pose questions and problems as well as respond to questions about course readings?
- Do all members of the classroom community collaborate in comprehension, share their knowledge and experience, inquire?

CLASSROOM TALK

- What does the teacher say—to the class, to small groups, to individual students?
- What do the students say—to the teacher, to each other?
- What do the teacher and the class talk about?
- What kind of language is being used?

TEAM TOOL 6.24

Classroom Observation Protocol

PURPOSE

When teachers allow colleagues to watch them teach, an observation protocol makes the transaction safer for everyone. The teacher being observed sets the parameters of what observers should be watching for, and observers have a clear structure within which to respond.

PROCEDURE: SEVENTY-FIVE MINUTES

Pre-Observation Conference: Twenty minutes

In advance: The teacher being observed prepares copies of the information in step 1 for each observing teacher.

1. The teacher being observed goes over the following information with observers:

- Grade level and course, and in general what observers can expect to see during the lesson

- Content goals for the lesson

- Reading Apprenticeship goals

- Anything unusual or special circumstances observers should be prepared to see

- Framing question the teacher being observed would like observers to focus on, notice

2. Observers ask any clarifying questions.

3. Team members review "What Does a Reading Apprenticeship Classroom Look Like?"

During the Observation: Thirty minutes

1. Observers take notes on an Evidence/Interpretation note taker.

2. Observers focus on the framing question and ways the classroom represents a Reading Apprenticeship classroom.

Post-Observation Debriefing: Twenty-five minutes

1. A team member restates the framing question.

2. Observers ask and the teacher being observed answers clarifying questions—genuine factual questions to better understand what was observed. Observers must be careful *not* to ask questions that are or may be interpreted as thinly veiled criticisms (five minutes).

3. Observers provide specific, detailed information related to the framing question. The teacher who was observed takes notes silently (five minutes).

4. The teacher who was observed presents his or her impression of the lesson in relation to the framing question and has the option of opening comments beyond the framing question. These comments must focus on positive feedback and clarifying or probing questions (five minutes).

5. All team members refer to "What Does a Reading Apprenticeship Classroom Look Like?" while discussing evidence of Reading Apprenticeship practices and routines in the observed classroom (five minutes).

6. The team reflects on the observation process:

- What could you take back from this observation and use?

- What worked well about the protocol process?

- What might you do differently next time to improve the process?

The team members took turns being videotaped implementing Reading Apprenticeship lessons. They followed an observation protocol that can serve for either live or taped lessons. The preobservation portion of the protocol has the presenting teacher outline the content and Reading Apprenticeship goals for the lesson, clarify details about the class and lesson, and ask a framing question that the presenting teacher wants colleagues to pay attention to. When the Berkley team members were using their own lessons to learn from, whoever did the taping selected portions of the tape for the team to observe and discuss.

Team Tool 6.24, Classroom Observation Protocol, helps teams prepare for, carry out, and debrief a classroom observation. Team Tool 6.25, Evaluating a

---

TEAM TOOL 6.25

Evaluating a Range of Framing Questions

These framing questions were developed by teachers of different subject areas and with varying Reading Apprenticeship experience and varying experience using the observation protocol. Teams can consider which of these might yield the richest learning—for the teacher being observed and for the team as a whole—as preparation for writing their own framing questions.

- What supports are evident in this English-ESL classroom to help students comprehend text?

- How can Reading Apprenticeship help students and teacher differentiate instruction/learning while maintaining high-quality engagement with the text?

- What opportunities do students have for reading, thinking, and talking?

- In what ways and to what extent are students engaged with the text?

- What do you notice about students' interactions and discussions? In what ways do these affect student learning and engagement?

- How well are students able to identify the author's purpose in writing "The Ballad of Birmingham"? How well are students able to cite examples of irony, symbolism, and discrimination that support the author's purpose? Capture specific examples, if possible.

- How do the Reading Apprenticeship routines deepen students' understanding and interactions with the chapter from *Kindred*, by Octavia Butler, called "The Fight"?

- How are students building toward independence in their sense-making?

- What evidence of previous learning do you see as students attempt to answer this question: Who was primarily responsible for the Cold War—the United States or the Soviet Union?

Range of Framing Questions, can help teams think about what kinds of framing questions may be more or less valuable to explore as they plan for an observation.

For the Berkley team, in addition to the professional learning the teacher labs promote, the labs have also been a boon in reaching teachers who were previously unengaged with Reading Apprenticeship. Adina Rubenstein thinks it's the seeing is believing factor:

> Where we are now with teacher labs, inviting people in, there's a lot of momentum. I think we might see some real strides with some of our colleagues who aren't entirely on board, when they can actually see it, hear it, taste it.

Reflecting on Growth

> Each time I come to the end of a semester and see my students' growth, it just gives me more and more confidence.
> —Ann Foster, Santa Rosa Junior College English instructor

In Chapter Four, we encourage teams to start out by having members set learning goals for their own and their students' Reading Apprenticeship work. Two tools, the Reading Apprenticeship Teacher Practice Rubric and the Reading Apprenticeship Student Learning Goals, help in identifying those goals and provide a starting point for formative assessment, reflection, and setting new goals.

When teams have been together for a while, and teachers have been using Reading Apprenticeship in their classrooms and reflecting on their practice with colleagues, it can be both instructive and motivating to check in on team members' teacher practice and student learning goals.

Revisiting the Reading Apprenticeship Teacher Practice Rubric

A group of community college instructors who participated in a Reading Apprenticeship Leadership Community of Practice learned to appreciate the teacher practice rubric for guiding their own learning and as a resource to share with colleagues. The rubric-guided reflections of Catherine England and Melody Schneider appear in Close-Up 6.7, Teachers Reflect with the Reading Apprenticeship Teacher Practice Rubric.

Revisiting the Reading Apprenticeship Student Learning Goals

The Reading Apprenticeship Student Learning Goals (Appendix C) that help teachers plan their instruction and reflect on students' growth are written in simple language that can be shared with students. In addition, however, the goals language helps teachers articulate their instructional goals. As Curtis Refior, a Reading Apprenticeship coach who works with several Michigan school districts, notes, the goals help teachers relate concretely to students' needs:

> We take students where they are, and we think about here's the current reality and how do I design instruction that will move them to that next place. The student learning goals give some concrete examples and language for what those ideas might look like. What might be appropriate for this particular student or for this classroom of students in general, where might my instruction go from here?
>
> If a teacher's really struggling to get their kids to pair-share, for example, then we might go to the social dimension of the student learning goals and be thinking about what goals might be appropriate for getting students to be more collaborative. Or if a teacher says, "I really want to increase the writing in my classroom," then we might go to the personal goals and be thinking about how we could use reflection as a way to get kids to do a little more writing.
>
> If we are looking at student work or if we are talking about a particular thing that might have happened that day in their classroom, the student learning goals are a great resource for teachers and for me to be thinking about what comes next.

Reflection on learning, whether a teacher's own learning or the learning he or she facilitates in a classroom, accelerates that learning by bringing it forward, suggesting logical next steps, and reinforcing a sustained focus on growth. Teachers do this kind of reflection independently, but as a team they also find it is a rewarding way to learn from one another and acknowledge what they are accomplishing together.

CLOSE-UP 6.7

Teachers Reflect with the Reading Apprenticeship Teacher Practice Rubric

The Reading Apprenticeship Teacher Practice Rubric (Appendix C) has six main goals, each with a number of subgoals. Teachers can focus in one or more of the goal areas, or they can reflect on their growth across the board as Reading Apprenticeship practitioners.

Goal 1: Reading Opportunities

Goal 2: Teacher Support for Student Efforts to Comprehend Content from Text

Goal 3: Metacognitive Inquiry into Reading and Thinking Processes

Goal 4: Specific Reading Comprehension Routines, Tools, Strategies, and Processes

Goal 5: Collaboration

Goal 6: Instruction That Promotes Equity

Catherine England Teacher Rubric Reflections

When I initially looked at this rubric, I chose Goal 3, "metacognitive inquiry into reading and thinking processes," as my main goal. I do believe I have improved in this area, but it is something that will be a continual process, as will be Goal 4, "establishing routines and strategies." This certainly is an example to me that Reading Apprenticeship is a "work in progress." While I feel more confident than I did last September, I know it will be a constant area of growth and will certainly serve as a reminder that we are all students.

In addition, I have greatly improved on Goal 1, in the area of "relationship of reading to other classroom activities." I have been able to choose some very rich and deep readings that model the type of writing that we expect our students to be able to complete at the end of the course. It has been an exciting opportunity to integrate Reading Apprenticeship into my course, naturally weaving it into what we are expected to do.

Melody Schneider Teacher Rubric Reflections

Goal 1: Reading Opportunities—Reviewing this goal, I seem to be doing pretty well. Students read every day, read multiple genres, and we talk about how and why we read often—especially how we read certain genres, what we look for, what we think about, and how we make it through. Assessment happens on each reading—but I think I can make this more explicit.

Goal 2 was my goal—where I wanted to develop—and from the looks of my self-assessment in this area, for good reason! I think I am still working through the challenges of having limited class time, requirements from OSPI regarding what I cover, and needing to engage students in a variety of learning modes. Students need to read outside of class every week. There is no getting around this. But I am working on focused reading in classes—reading parts of the text either before they read the entire chapter, or reading to solve a problem, or reading for a specific purpose—this we do in class. At the start of the quarter we work

more deliberately on reading strategies, but I lapsed in maintaining this conversation every class . . . maybe once a week. I can see this is why I chose to work on this area . . . it's a bugger of a problem for me and I look forward to solving it!

My assessment of Metacognitive Inquiry also surprised me. Maybe because we talk about this more than I have in the past, but I see from the assessment that I'm in the middle of learning this. I can see ways to improve—to build this practice—taking a few minutes to make this more explicit.

Work in the area of building routines is improving. I frequently and intentionally model and give instructions . . . I'm slowly building practice in engaging students in problem solving in reading, and I see students starting to do this in their journals and discussion boards.

Although I've always used lots of collaborative activities in my classes I was pleasantly surprised to see how my practice has developed so strongly in this area . . . We work diligently to make the collaborative process explicit in all areas and to extend that to reading practices—students working together on reading—sharing texts and ideas about texts with each other in controlled and open ways. I think this is my strongest area in this assessment and I can see that truth in my classroom, watching how well students make learning together.

Equity is also a strong area for me. Over the years I've become very sensitive to the range of students' experience. I know that not everyone will read quickly—especially English language learners who are mixed in with English speaking students—so I use a variety of strategies to ensure their questions are asked, their voices are heard, and their confidence is built.

Having used the rubric as an assessment tool, I see how valuable it is. Now I have a better idea of how to use it with my colleagues!

■ ■ ■

This chapter, as well as Chapters Four and Five, put teams in charge of orchestrating their work together, with a focus on setting the stage for collaboration, investigating their own reading processes, and inquiring into their classroom practice. Chapter Seven moves beyond the team environment to consider institutional strategies for growing and sustaining a Reading Apprenticeship culture of literacy across a school site, district, or college campus.

Note

1. Educator Mike Rose has spent much of his career thinking and writing about students' promise, especially the promise of the underprepared student. See, for example, his enduring classic, *Lives on the Boundary*, copyright 1989, reissued 2005, Penguin Books.

CHAPTER
SEVEN

Building Capacity, Momentum, and Sustainability

It has to be foundational to what you're doing. It has to be your way of doing business.
—Harley Ramsey, Otto-Eldred High School principal

OVER THE YEARS, there have been many instances of Reading Apprenticeship capturing the enthusiasm of a team or school or department but then fading away as faculty and leaders move on to something new. In this chapter, we consider what it takes for leaders to hang tough: to build the Reading Apprenticeship capacity of their staff; to expand the reach of Reading Apprenticeship across grades, departments, districts, and states; and to stay the course over many years despite staff turnover, competing initiatives, and budget crises. To do so is an enormous accomplishment that goes to the heart of educational reform. As principal Harley Ramsey observes, if education systems are to support this kind of investment in Reading Apprenticeship, "It needs to be foundational to what you're doing. It has to be your way of doing business."

Building Capacity System-Wide: A Canadian Case Study

We're looking at our implementation plan in chunks of three years.
—Shelley Warkentin, English Language Arts and Literacy K–12,
Manitoba Ministry of Education and Advanced Learning

In the Canadian province of Manitoba, there are 37 school divisions (districts), with a Reading Apprenticeship culture slowly reaching a growing number of them. After supporting a three-year pilot in three of the divisions, the Manitoba ministry of education gave the go-ahead for the continued spread of Reading Apprenticeship across the province. The goal is to keep expanding Reading Apprenticeship to divisions and schools where educators recognize the power of Reading Apprenticeship to support their existing literacy work and where they agree to support ongoing professional development and capacity

189

building. The ministry of education is contributing Reading Apprenticeship professional development expertise, material resources, and funding for teacher release time.

As a laboratory for learning about how to roll out Reading Apprenticeship, Manitoba provides many promising ideas. Shelley Warkentin, who co-leads the initiative at the province level, describes a process that continues to evolve as it goes along:

> We began with a "slow leak" pilot in three divisions so that we could start experimenting, learning, and building capacity of the school divisions and the people involved in the schools. The pilot sampling included rural and urban contexts, schools where French is the language of instruction, middle and high school teachers, a range of disciplines, different school structures, and varying cultural, linguistic, and socioeconomic contexts.
>
> One of the school divisions really grew their capacity within the two first year pilot schools and within the division. So as time went on, we added more schools there—two the second year, and two the third year. This implementation model was what we had envisioned. Because there was shared vision, clear growth plans, and dedicated supports from the school division, school administration, and teacher leaders, they were able to continue to support and grow the teams in these initial schools, while looping in motivated teams from new schools. This school division continues to deepen and extend the inquiry and collaborative leadership within and across schools. Some of these educators are now supporting rollout across the province.

On the other hand, as she describes successes, Shelley is also very clear about the fact that they have had mixed results, as is inevitable in change processes:

> We did experience other less successful implementation. In another division, we supported professional inquiry in Reading Apprenticeship for three years within schools and expanded within these same schools, but not beyond them. Factors such as limited participation and support of administration and more limited focus on ongoing, job-embedded professional conversations made sustaining the work more difficult. Although implementation did not fully take root in these schools or within the division, teachers continue to speak to the impact of Reading Apprenticeship on their individual practice.
>
> In the third division, we worked with a small team of teachers in a single school. Although there was no expansion within the school or the division during the pilot, this team of teachers was very committed, and there was a lot of discussion about impact—their growing feeling of confidence and their students' increased engagement. Because of increased focus on literacy as a divisional priority, a year after the pilot

ended, we started working with nine other division high schools. The ministry is now committed to a three-year intensive plan with the school division and nine high schools. This includes five days per year of professional learning for teams in each of the schools, including administrators, two to four days of leadership-focused professional learning per year, and locally run monthly professional conversations, collaborative examination of student work, and classroom observations.

The commitment to ongoing, at least monthly, team meetings is a key element of the Manitoba initiative:

> One thing we seeded with our teams early was that we wanted them to commit to at least once-a-month times when they would bring all folks participating—leaders and teachers and administrators—together to continue learning. Initially, they would connect to share their explorations, successes, challenges, and questions and dig deeper into *Reading for Understanding*. As their team's social and personal dimensions strengthened, they would meet to collaboratively examine student work, observe each other and their students in action and debrief, and reflect on and revise individual and team learning goals.

In addition, as described in later sections of this chapter, coaching, administrator involvement, and leadership development are built into what is truly a systemic initiative. The Manitoba program, as it goes forward, continues to offer a three-year intensive model, with materials and instruction now in French as well as English, and has added a one-year model designed to reach additional schools in the pilot divisions and a broader audience of new divisions and schools. Teams in the one-year model are able to return for a second year as a way of going deeper into their understanding and practice. Close-Up 7.1, Manitoba Reading Apprenticeship Professional Learning Program, is an overview of the professional development options for teams and the model for leadership development.

In planning for the hoped for expansion of the program, leaders built data collection for measuring student and teacher growth into the pilot. The result, the ministry reports, is a dramatic, positive transformation of students' engagement and achievement and of teachers' practice:

- Statistically significant gains in reading achievement overall
- Growth in student confidence, engagement, and abilities
- Growth in teacher and leader confidence and capacity
- Increased teacher engagement and efficacy
- Increased collaboration among educators

CLOSE-UP 7.1

Manitoba Reading Apprenticeship Professional Learning Models

The Manitoba ministry for education sponsored a pilot three-year Reading Apprenticeship Professional Learning Program with school teams from three divisions (districts). The ministry collected data from students and teachers, and decided at the end of the pilot to institute a new, three-year, multipronged program of Reading Apprenticeship professional learning.

Four team models now run simultaneously in the province:

- In French, intensive three-year model for one continuing pilot division
- In English, intensive three-year model for selected divisions
- In English, one-year access model allowing for wide participation of new divisions/school teams (with selection for continuation a possibility)
- Continuing supports within the one-year access model for pilot divisions: pilot and new schools

Manitoba Reading Apprenticeship Professional Learning Models

TEAM MODELS
Teams include teachers, other educators, division leadership, and site administrators and meet at three different locations/times

Three-Year Intensive, Responsive Model, in French	Three-Year Intensive Model	One-Year Access Model	Continued Supports for Pilot Divisions
One division of the original three pilot divisions requested a three-year intensive model, in French, for nine schools; growth in each school is responsive to individual site interest	Five divisions were selected from an applicant pool to commit to the three-year intensive model • Year 1: two to three schools per division • Year 2: varied/responsive growth (growth within all schools plus zero to two additional schools per division) • Year 3: growth within all schools plus varied/responsive number of additional schools	Multiple new divisions, many schools; option to return for a second year Also, continued support for the three pilot divisions, both for pilot schools and for new schools	See one-year access model

In addition, the ministry has designed a Leader Institute. Participation is by invitation to team members after participation of several months in any of the team models. It is a two-year commitment.

LEADERSHIP TEAM MODEL
Leaders emerge after a period of participation in any of the team models and meet together in a single institute

Two-Year Invitational Model

Leadership teams from the French intensive model include divisional leader, school leader, and teacher leader from each school	Leadership teams from the English intensive model include new emerging school leaders and teacher leader from each school	Leadership teams from the access model include emerging divisional/school leader and teacher leader from teams showing commitment	Leadership teams from the continued pilot support model include new emerging school and teacher leaders from pilot divisions and schools

In addition, Shelley says, students are aware of the differences in their learning:

> Many students who have experienced teaching and learning in Reading
> Apprenticeship classrooms are now advocating for their learning needs,
> for deeper learning, for conversation and problem solving with their
> peers, and for modeling from their teachers.

The ministry is looking to continue the implementation plan in chunks of three years. As Shelley describes it, just the notion of the work ahead is invigorating:

> We'll learn about the model as we go and tweak it. And because schools
> and school divisions have their different character and culture, we'll try to
> be responsive to that, too.
>   This is the real work, I just keep saying. The conversation, the
> thinking that happens, the learning that's going on—it's so exciting.

Increasing Expertise

> Building capacity to implement the Reading Apprenticeship Framework is something
> you hone over time.
> —Debbie Harmon, Brown County director of student learning

Although it is rare to find the kind of comprehensive, coherent, and sustained implementation of Reading Apprenticeship that has been true in Manitoba, many schools, districts, and college campuses have been resourceful in finding ways to build internal expertise. Some are able to use instructional or literacy coaches, others create innovative connections with new faculty and non-faculty staff. Finally, increasing the expertise of school and district leaders has been an important strategic investment for building institutional capacity to implement Reading Apprenticeship with *flexible fidelity*—holding to the core principles of the Reading Apprenticeship Framework but reflecting local contexts and their particular opportunities and constraints.

Coaching Teachers and Teams to Promote Their Own Inquiry

As the voices in previous chapters make clear, teachers need time and support to learn to integrate Reading Apprenticeship into their classrooms. Chapters Four, Five, and Six offer ideas that school teams can use in their own contexts to bring Reading Apprenticeship alive. Those practices can serve as a solid foundation for accessible, cost-effective, inquiry-based professional learning. In addition, however, sometimes schools are able to afford extra support for implementing new practices, through on-site coaching.

Usually, teachers who have themselves integrated Reading Apprenticeship into their instructional routines are best able to support others to do so. As coaches, they may also hold teaching or other positions within a school or district, or they may be Reading Apprenticeship specialists who work across districts or regions. Key for any coach of Reading Apprenticeship, however, is a deep understanding of and commitment to inquiry-based learning for students and teachers.[1] Perhaps the most valuable role a coach can play is to steer a steady course of inquiry.

Coaches may well be appreciated for the insights they can offer individual teachers and teams, but even more valuable are the ways they help teachers see themselves as investigators of their own practice, their students' learning, and the texts that drive disciplinary learning.

Gayle Cribb, a longtime Reading Apprenticeship teacher and now professional developer and coach, recalls the importance of the small Reading Apprenticeship team at her school in supporting one another in collaborative inquiry. When she works as a coach, her goal is to help teachers establish a similar dynamic for themselves:

> I think that often teachers' experiences of coaching are on the order of someone coming in and checking off, "Did they do this? Did they do that?" Or even just their own thinking of the coach as the person who is going to make the difference for them. I remember one group complaining at first that I wasn't giving them feedback, because they weren't used to being engaged in an inquiry together.
>
> That's what is so different, the whole approach of "What do we see? What are we noticing? What are we learning?" versus "I'm expecting you to do these three things, and did you do them?" For example, just fifteen or twenty minutes of a team discussing challenges or successes from their teaching can be amazing—their sense of each other as professionals and that they are able to tap into each other's teacher minds.
>
> I may be the coach for a while, but when I'm gone, I want to have supported them to have a professional culture that can go forward, with them thinking and learning together under their own steam.

In a coaching situation, the kind of self-propelling team Gayle aims for is one in which the relationships between the coach and the team members and, even more importantly, among the team members have been carefully nurtured.

The Social and Personal Dimensions Are Key to Good Coaching

Many of the ideas for building and maintaining a strong social and personal dimension within teams, such as the norms for collaborative collegial work described in Chapter Four, are equally important in the work coaches do with teams. Coaches supporting others to practice these norms model the value of the Reading Apprenticeship Framework in professional interactions as well as in classrooms.

Anyone who takes on the role of coaching teachers faces the primary task of building trusting relationships with the teachers themselves. Lori Wojtowicz, a Michigan-based Reading Apprenticeship coach, explains how the Reading Apprenticeship Framework helps her think about her coaching relationships:

> We know that in the classroom the personal and social dimensions must be established and continually nurtured to support the rigor of the cognitive and knowledge-building dimensions. Coaching mirrors this understanding.
>
> Meeting teachers where they are, listening to them and allowing them to set their own goals is the essential beginning. It is their inquiry into their own practice that gives validity to this experience. This is not the one-sided PD experience most teachers have come to know and loathe. Initial meetings are spent getting to know the individual teachers, to listen and then imagine how Reading Apprenticeship can best serve teachers' own goals for growth.

Coaches also find that building positive relationships with administrators greatly enhances their ability to work productively with teachers. Mary Ann Liberati, who has spent over a decade coaching Reading Apprenticeship teachers and teacher leaders, reflects on this point in the context of her work in New York City middle schools:

> When administrators feel respected, their support is very helpful with teacher buy-in and intentional implementation of Reading Apprenticeship. It really accelerates the benefits of coaching, because some of the biggest challenges are communication—communicating that there is a meeting, that there is an agenda, that teachers will need coverage and sufficient time. It really helps the communication if you have a good, strong, trusting relationship.
>
> For example, if I notice an administrator hasn't registered for the coaching meeting, I send them a separate email. I ask them to come, that I really hope to see them. Something personal. I have had several assistant principals say to me, "I wouldn't have come to the meeting if you didn't invite me." So just trying to reach out and find ways to be helpful, that goes a long way.

Coaching Whole Teams Versus Individual Teachers

Many schools bring Reading Apprenticeship coaches in to work with school teams rather than with individual teachers. Another common model is to balance a coach's time between team meetings and one-on-one coaching with individual teachers. A third model keeps the team together both for meeting time and for participating in facilitated observations in team members' classrooms.

Reading Apprenticeship coaches work with all these models, recognizing the particular benefits of keeping a team together and the needs of some teachers for individual support. But regardless of the model, coaches recognize the value of spending at least some time just visiting each teacher's classroom. As coach Gayle Cribb puts it, to do her best work, she needs to experience each teacher's reality:

> I want to see what a teacher's classroom is like in action. What their planet is. I want to see their classroom management and what they have in place. It grounds me in their kids, their school, their classroom.

Leveraging Learning in Teams Curtis Refior, who supports Reading Apprenticeship implementation in a number of Michigan schools, has come to believe that the best use of his limited coaching time is to work with teams of teachers and, when possible, administrators who join them. Curtis especially values the social construction of knowledge that happens best in teams:

> The way I like to do Reading Apprenticeship coaching is to engage groups rather than individuals. When we have the inquiry into different parts of the Framework or instruction or formative assessment of literacy, with a group of teachers we have more opportunities for a rich conversation and the fertilization of new ideas. It's more difficult when it's one on one because there are only two people who have ideas to bring to the table. When you work with groups, there might be things that you never even thought about that are great ideas.
>
> When I first started doing Reading Apprenticeship coaching, it was exclusively one on one. We would have really nice conversation or we would plan and something great might happen in the teacher's classroom, but it was a secret between the teacher and me. With a group, all of those bright spots get recognized and can get taken up by others.

Another benefit Curtis finds in working with whole teams is the increased commitment that comes when teachers are accountable to the group, not the coach. Time spent fostering relationships within a team, he believes, contributes directly to that sense of shared responsibility. One of the most potent ways he has found to promote collegiality is through structured observations teams make in members' classrooms:

High school teachers are very much like independent contractors. They come into their buildings, enter their classroom, do their thing, and at the end of the day they'll open that door and go home. So one of the things I try very much in my coaching is to open the doors and have them stay open.

Every year at the end of my coaching cycle, I ask people to write their feedback. It never fails that they reflect on their heightened sense of collegiality and the more comfort they have in working with their peers. And I do believe that is directly related to their opening the classroom doors and seeing each other in their element, with their students.

Meeting Individual Teachers' Needs   Although supporting multiple teachers at a time by working with them in teams has many advantages, there can also be important value in one-on-one coaching scenarios and debriefing with individual teachers. Mary Ann Liberati likes to give teachers options about how they can work with her when she comes into their classrooms:

> When I come in to coach, teachers have options. I can come in and observe them and give them individual feedback, I can co-teach with them, or I can come in and model for them with a text their students are using.
>
> Sometimes teachers can't make the leap from the Reading Apprenticeship practices they experience in professional development to their classroom. I often find that when I do a model in class—it could be very short, ten minutes—all of a sudden they see it with kids and they get it. It's so amazing. I've found that to be a real catalyst for change.
>
> If I'm going to visit a classroom for an individual one-on-one debriefing with a teacher, I really try to honor the effort the teacher is making, but also I try to capture word for word on my computer what they say during a lesson so that we can have evidence-based conversations, and I can shine a light on the opportunities within lessons that would help teachers to support students.

Likewise, when veteran Reading Apprenticeship teacher and coach Janet Ghio is asked to observe and debrief with individual teachers, she makes detailed classroom observation notes that she can then refer to when debriefing the lesson. The notes anchor the ensuing discussion and include questions to deepen the teacher's learning. (See Close-Up 7.2, Sample Classroom Visit Notes.) Janet also emails the teacher a copy of these notes, often prompting an appreciative response to this kind of supportive and rigorous feedback. "It makes a huge difference to them," Janet says.

CLOSE-UP 7.2

Sample Classroom Visit Notes

When Janet Ghio visits a classroom as a Reading Apprenticeship coach, she records what she sees the teacher and students do and inserts a few questions for the teacher's reflection. She then discusses these notes with the teacher and emails the teacher a copy. Teachers are inclined to take these visits seriously since they have the hard evidence that Janet does!

PERIOD 2, March 11

On the whiteboard: Norms, sentence frames for Talking to the Text, Reading Strategies List.

Warm-up: What was Malthus's conclusion about population growth? Industrial melanism?

> Students figure out their prediction of what industrial melanism means using their schema or schema of some of the students.

Text: Industrial Melanism

> You do a whole-class Think Aloud and write down student thinking. Students ask questions and then try to problem solve. At the end of a chunk, you ask them to paraphrase.

> Some students write down notes you are writing.

Question: What if you had debriefed what was cleared up from doing this: What strategies were used and how did they help us understand what we are reading?

> You ask class: Why are we doing this . . . more reading and thinking about our reading instead of me delivering a PowerPoint?

> Student responses: To remember it better, so we can figure it out what it says, so we think.

> Your directions: 7 minutes to finish the rest of the paragraph. Write your thinking. Then we will talk about it. Give this a slow, careful read. I'll check in with you in five minutes.

I [Janet] give you the idea of using sentence frames:

I wrote . . . . when I read. . . (the part of text), because I was thinking. . . .

I am confused about this part . . . I think maybe it means . . . because . . . What do you think it means?

> You write on the whiteboard: I wrote this because . . . I got confused when. . .

I [Janet] listen to two students who just read out to each other what they wrote but don't explain what they read that supports their thinking, so maybe change.

Question: Do you think an expanded sentence frame would support students' thinking and support a deeper discussion?

> You ask partners to use each other's names.

> Many listening partners look at the other person who is talking, but if they look at the text they are talking about instead, it helps make their conversation text-based.

> You have the text on document camera. As students bring up parts of text, you reread it. You ask a comprehension question.

Question: When student has a confusing part, could students do a Think Aloud with pair-share partner, and then you call on someone randomly to share what they figured out?

> You ask them to get the gist. No response, so you ask them to talk in groups of four.

Question: Why did you switch from pairs to groups of four?

Culminating Reflection: What do you notice about whole-group discussion? Who does the talking?

Reading Apprenticeship Coaching Tools

Coaches find that three Reading Apprenticeship tools are particularly helpful for keeping coaching conversations focused on building a classroom culture of literacy: the Reading Apprenticeship Framework itself, Reading Apprenticeship Student Learning Goals, and the Text and Task Analysis for planning classroom instruction.

The Reading Apprenticeship Framework

The Framework gives teachers and coaches a common language for looking at instruction and setting goals. Curtis Refior describes it as a touchstone for coaching conversations:

> One thing that sets Reading Apprenticeship coaching apart is the Reading Apprenticeship Framework, because it gives us very specific common language to have conversations about planning, to talk about classroom observations, and then to reflect. The Framework very much grounds our work and the kinds of conversations we can have.
>
> When we are having conversations within the Framework, I can use it along with the teacher to be thinking about where are the strengths and where are the opportunities. It's almost like a rubric.
>
> One of the biggest goals of Reading Apprenticeship coaching is to instill understanding of the Reading Apprenticeship Framework. But you can't do that if you're not repeatedly using it and talking about it.

Reading Apprenticeship Student Learning Goals

Another way for coaches and teachers to talk together about the Framework is to refer to the Reading Apprenticeship Student Learning Goals (see Appendix C). These goals translate the Framework into student language, and in some instances are easier for teachers to use in thinking about their goals for instruction. Curtis Refior provides an example of how he might help a teacher form an instructional goal by way of the student learning goals:

> Sometimes teachers might begin building a Reading Strategies List, but then it might fade away. They might do it as a singular event but not circle back to it—just have a Reading Strategies List posted on the wall. As a way to encourage teachers to make that a more consistent routine, we might take a look at the personal engagement part of the student learning goals and talk about, "Well, how are you helping your students grow their reader identity, or how are you helping them recognize that relationship between reading and power?" The student learning goals give teachers some language for how to proceed.

Curtis also has found the student learning goals are an entrée for teachers who have trouble articulating their disciplinary expertise:

> Many of the things that teachers do, especially in their disciplinary knowledge, happens intuitively. It just happens, and they don't know why they do the things that they do. So I try to help them break that down, especially metacognitively as we are reading text, but also we can take a look at the specific student learning goals in the knowledge-building dimension—it's right there!

Text and Task Analysis

Text and Task Analysis (see Team Tool 5.12) can be very helpful for clarifying the important connections between the metacognitive conversation teachers have when reading with students in mind and the opportunities they have to help their students meet disciplinary literacy and content goals.

Mary Ann Liberati makes the Text and Task Analysis yet another way to model Reading Apprenticeship practices for the teachers she coaches:

> The Text and Task Analysis is the essential first step in planning. Teachers of content are so close to the content they teach they don't really understand why the kids are struggling with the text. Reading with students in mind is understanding the complexity of the reading task that we're asking students to do. It's a habit of mind that I think teachers really need. I'm like a broken record on the topic.
>
> I do a Text and Task Analysis for every single text I use in teaching or professional development or coaching, and I have a copy to show teachers.
>
> I show them what schema I think students need to make sense of this and what I have identified in terms of a text's challenges and opportunities. I identify the priorities I think students need the most. It might be identifying roadblocks, or previewing, or doing paired reading, or something else.

School teams that Curtis Refior coaches rotate visits to team members' classrooms. Curtis makes it a practice that the presenting teacher plans the lesson using the Text and Task Analysis and that the visiting teachers also read the lesson text and do a Text and Task Analysis preliminary to their observation:

> After the teacher hosting the visit describes the context of the lesson, the content goal and the literacy goal, and a focus question the teacher wants us to pay attention to, then we always read the text that students are going to be reading together. That means every teacher who's coming into that classroom has read the text and analyzed it and has trained his or her ears to listen for some of those same things that we did as we read it.

When classroom observations incorporate Text and Task Analysis, observation debriefs are richer because the hosting teacher and visiting teachers are all primed to identify and discuss patterns in student understanding and participation as they relate to next steps in instruction.

Supporting New Teachers

What do teachers need to know when they join a middle school, high school, or college faculty? Does Reading Apprenticeship make it onto the priority list?

Getting Secondary School New Hires Up to Speed

Many secondary schools have routines for bringing new teachers on board, perhaps including a day or two of orientation and the assignment of a mentor teacher. As for the professional development background that other faculty members already share, new teachers have a lot to learn, and they typically do not have formal opportunities to catch up. In a few places, however, new teachers learn about Reading Apprenticeship as part of ongoing professional development for the whole school.

At Souderton Area High School, principal Sam Varano plans to include Reading Apprenticeship professional development in the school's two-year induction program. He also sees that new teachers and veteran teachers will all continue their Reading Apprenticeship learning as part of the school's focus on Common Core State Standards:

> For us, Common Core standards for implementation are standards 1 and
> 10,[2] and we rely on Reading Apprenticeship leaders to help us accomplish those two standards, because that is exactly what Reading Apprenticeship is all about.

Reading Apprenticeship teacher leaders at Berkley High School include new teachers in the site-based professional development that reaches other faculty members who have not yet been part of a Reading Apprenticeship training cohort. Principal Randy Gawel reports that teacher labs (peer observations) will be a new element in the school's professional learning:

> New teachers will be in another cohort of Reading Apprenticeship
> teachers trained internally. And we are going to expand our professional
> development and do a lot more of the teacher labs, so that teachers are
> working together on a more consistent basis, both in department and
> across departments. Our Reading Apprenticeship coordinators are
> working on planning that.

New teachers at the Excel Centers for adult learners (see note 2 in Chapter One) receive professional development in Reading Apprenticeship as a matter of course—both initially and as follow-up support. Reading

Apprenticeship is a formal part of the professional development plan for all fourteen of their schools. And because Reading Apprenticeship implementation is reinforced with feedback from weekly walk-throughs and four formal evaluations a year, new teachers are continuously upgrading their practice of Reading Apprenticeship.

Building Reading Apprenticeship into Community College New Faculty Academies

In community colleges, it is increasingly common for new faculty to participate in new-faculty orientation or academies that last from one semester up to two years. At a number of community colleges, campus Reading Apprenticeship leaders have put Reading Apprenticeship on the agenda.

At Santa Rosa Junior College, instructors Ann Foster and Lauren Servais serve as co-coordinators of the campus Center for Excellence—the center for faculty professional development—which includes Faculty Inquiry Groups, flex activities (paid professional development), and the New Faculty Professional Learning Program. Ann and Lauren were able to offer their experience with the Reading Apprenticeship Leadership Community of Practice as a model for the campus program for new faculty. Ann describes how the SRJC program is changing:

> New faculty orientation is mandatory at our school. When faculty are hired, they know that for the first two years, rather than have to write curriculum or serve on committees, the outside-of-classroom commitment for college service and professional development is our New Faculty Professional Learning Program. The first few years I coordinated that, and it was a series of workshops that were not connected by topic—a buffet. For faculty, only every once in a while would a topic resonate. Lauren and I knew the faculty had to go deeper, the experience had to be meaningful. So we met with our vice president and presented the community of practice idea and spoke to other deans involved.
>
> We were able to redo the entire structure so that there are five communities of practice. One is Reading Apprenticeship, which I facilitate.

At American River College, instructor Amanda Corcoran describes a very supportive culture for professional development, and a New Faculty Academy just getting off the ground. The college puts together welcome boxes for new hires, in which they include *Reading for Understanding, Habits of Mind, Mindset,* and *College Fear Factor.* Those books are now discussed in book groups offered through the New Faculty Academy. Amanda welcomes the huge potential of the academy for seeding faculty understanding of Reading Apprenticeship and the ideas it promotes:

> Those book groups are a great opportunity for us to have a shared vocabulary across the college in terms of Reading Apprenticeship routines and thinking about students as academic outsiders who want to be insiders. I'm amazed. We're just very fortunate here that administration is so supportive of professional development and innovative pedagogy.

Including Professional Development for Non-Faculty Staff

On community college campuses, many staff members who work with students in tutoring, learning communities, counseling, and other support services resonate with Reading Apprenticeship approaches. The Reading Apprenticeship Framework matches what these student service providers know about helping students engage with learning through the social and personal dimensions as well as the cognitive and knowledge-building dimensions.

Enlisting Community College Tutors as Reading Apprenticeship Allies

At Coastline College, reading and education instructor Danny Pittaway is the student success coordinator with responsibility for about sixty-five tutors on the college's four campuses. Coastline tutors are typically upper-division undergraduate students in transition, not set on a career, but who are at Coastline to fulfill one or two classes they couldn't get into at their own schools. Danny has developed a tutor-training course that includes the Reading Apprenticeship Framework and approaches. Tutors get it, Danny says:

> The responses to Reading Apprenticeship are always touching to me. It's amazing to see how the tutors grasp the significance of Reading Apprenticeship: "Oh, yeah, that makes sense. We *should* have these conversations with students, shine a light on the space of reading, and support the affective domain." Our tutoring course connects the Framework and growth mindset, with Reading Apprenticeship being a way of empowering students.
>
> After they have this experience of tutoring, a lot of tutors come to me, "I want to be a teacher now." I feel like our culture at Coastline is creating the next generation of teachers. We're raising them up as empathetic tutors and giving them the same solid professional learning foundation that we try to give ourselves.

Jennifer Taylor-Mendoza, as the dean of Academic Support and Learning Technologies at the College of San Mateo, sets the tone for a range of support services on campus. But she was sold on Reading Apprenticeship before she was dean, when she was director of the learning center:

> We embedded Reading Apprenticeship in our tutor training, which made a huge difference in regard to students getting the skill set they need, but also in the classroom as well. It was a great partnership between instructional support, classroom practice, and faculty.
>
> Now we have a summer bridge program, a first year success program, student learning communities, a tutoring inquiry group— Reading Apprenticeship is now sort of the foundation, for how we begin to build our programs.

Spreading Reading Apprenticeship Approaches Through Student Counseling

Counselors, too, are learning to put Reading Apprenticeship to use. At Pasadena City College, the open invitation to educators across campus roles to participate as instructors of the College 1 seminar means that counselors like Myriam Altounji are learning about Reading Apprenticeship—and finding that it can help them be better counselors as well knowledgeable College 1 instructors:

> My counseling appointments are available to any student on campus, so I get a wide variety of students who come in and meet with me.
>
> With probation students we have to get down to where they understand the situation they're in, what their strengths are, and how they can move forward and build on those strengths to continue toward their goals. That's hugely metacognition, to get them to reflect on their path.
>
> When students come in to do an educational plan, it's really easy for me to create a plan for them, but once I started learning about Reading Apprenticeship, I found that's a huge disservice to students. If I'm doing the work, they're not learning how to do it for themselves. So I'll start out, for example, modeling Talking to the Text in a catalog, reading and annotating, and then give them five or ten minutes to continue to work through the document. Then we look at the annotations and see what questions they might have. My goal is that once they walk out of my office they're able to access these materials with a stronger foundation, so when they go to register or start working on their next semester plan, they understand why they have selected every single course and whether it fits their ultimate goal.
>
> In the case of a student looking for a potential university to transfer to, if they know their major, I'll show them how to navigate a couple of different university sites, but my homework to them is to find your top three universities that have your major and look through the main site and the major site, and to keep track of things that stand out—good and bad—and why, and what questions they have. It's a lifelong skill for them to develop their own process of making meaning.

Developing Reading Apprenticeship Leaders

Whether at the school, district, college, or regional level, developing leaders to sustain Reading Apprenticeship with fidelity requires teachers and administrators to have deep knowledge of the unique aspects of the Framework and to have a clear sense of the essential elements of a Reading Apprenticeship classroom and Reading Apprenticeship professional conversation. Sometimes it takes time for the right leaders to emerge.

Setting the Stage for Reading Apprenticeship Leaders to Emerge

When the Manitoba ministry for education originally designed its three-year pilot for implementing Reading Apprenticeship in local divisions, leadership development at the school and division level was the first-year priority. Leaders were identified in advance (one or two teachers per school and one or two staff members per division or school administration) and participated in a much more intensive immersion in Reading Apprenticeship than did the rest of the teachers. As Shelley Warkentin, co-leader of the Manitoba effort, points out, that model has changed:

> In our first year we started with five consecutive days with just the leaders. So they were immersed in the Framework, in their own learning, and in learning around what the leadership would look like and sound like for them. That was followed directly by a three-day institute for teams of teachers, where the leaders' role was a little bit different. They were still learners, but they were also observers and there to support their teacher teams, listen to their conversations, and support team building.
>
> We thought we needed the leadership in place upfront. But we found that sometimes the wrong leaders were identified. Not all selected leaders had the mindset or the skill set required for this approach to collaborative professional learning. It was critical that leaders recognize that Reading Apprenticeship is grounded in inquiry and focused on raising teachers' metacognitive awareness of their own disciplinary practices in order for them to apprentice their students in these practices. We quickly learned that leadership practices that promoted surface-level activities, like "get and go" or "tips and tricks," or that placed focus on isolated instructional strategies were counterproductive.
>
> So now we're looking first at team building, working on the concept of team with all divisional and school educators, and focusing on collaborative learning. We strongly, strongly encourage that school administrators be part of the team, so that they get the deeper understandings generated in the team and are able to support teachers in a way that makes sense. In school divisions and schools where administrators

were *active participants,* Reading Apprenticeship became part of the division and school culture [emphasis added].

As we really observe our teams and see the leaders emerge in different ways, then we can bring them into the leadership training later.

We have also needed to clarify the roles of leaders in the context of inquiry in Reading Apprenticeship—emphasizing a distributed leadership model, one where educators work together as a team to support collaborative learning. For some, the word *leader* evoked a pressure to go out and "teach" colleagues about Reading Apprenticeship. Through leadership supports, we co-constructed characteristics of leadership that spoke instead to supporting professional conversation with colleagues; building risk-free, collaborative professional learning environments for teams; participating in rich, exciting conversation in staff rooms to build curiosity; setting a tone for inquiry and action research; and inviting colleagues into professional reading, classroom observations, and shared examination of student work.

Coaching Leadership Teams to Mentor and Coach Others

The Reading Apprenticeship approach to coaching leadership teams is similar to the approach to coaching classroom teachers (described earlier in this chapter). Literacy leadership team members collaboratively inquire into their literacy practice, thinking, and learning to support one another and build their capacity to support others—in this case other educators.

In the New Haven, California, Unified School District, where a focus of the district's successful application for federal Race to the Top funds was a plan to sustain and increase the district's implementation of Reading Apprenticeship at its five secondary schools, building internal leadership capacity was key. The district's plan called for the development of a cross-district Reading Apprenticeship leadership team. Team members included site administrators, literacy coaches, and content area teachers (typically one each in science, history, and English language arts) from each of the five schools.

Recognizing the importance of leading by example (as described in Chapter Two), New Haven leaders brought in Reading Apprenticeship coaches Rita Jensen and Irisa Charney-Sirott to work with the district's leadership team to develop the strong foundation and deep insight into their own Reading Apprenticeship practice the team members would need to effectively lead and mentor others.

The coaching model Rita and Irisa used was a blend of observation cycles in classrooms of teachers on the leadership team and inquiry into professional reading about coaching and team leadership. Integral to the classroom observation cycles were pre-observation close reading of the text that team members would see students work with and post-observation discussion of student work. Rita and Irisa were intent on moving the leadership team members beyond a checklist of discrete Reading Apprenticeship behaviors to an understanding of when and why those behaviors are effective.

Over the course of a year, the coaches met with the New Haven Reading Apprenticeship leadership team five times, once at each school site. In advance of each all-day meeting, Rita and Irisa met individually with the classroom teachers who would be observed, and with the school literacy coach, to discuss the text, tasks, and participation structures each teacher had selected to use. With the literacy coach, they also planned how that site-based coach might support each teacher's preparation for the observation.

During the portion of the meeting days focused on the classroom observations, the team divided into subject-area groups and conducted concurrent observations. In each group, observers completed a Text and Task Analysis of the text students would be working with. During the observations, which lasted for one class period, team members used the Evidence/Interpretation note taker (see Team Tool 5.7) to make notes about what they were seeing and thinking. At the end of the period, all student work generated during the lesson was collected. Group members debriefed their observations using their Evidence/Interpretation notes and the protocol for looking at student work as evidence of student learning (Team Tool 6.15). For the remainder of the day, the team convened as a whole for close reading of professional texts and small group inquiry.

At the end of the year, after debriefing and reviewing feedback from the New Haven leadership team, Rita and Irisa were able to identify a number of strengths of this model as well as things to change. Close-Up 7.3, Takeaways from a Leadership Team Coaching Model, summarizes these findings.

In the three-year Manitoba pilot implementation of Reading Apprenticeship, the idea of helping leaders assume a coaching role took hold after the first year of the pilot. A leader of the pilot project, Shelley Warkentin, describes the tentative first steps:

> We weren't sure where we were going to go with coaching, but our hope
> was to get our leaders to reflect on teachers' practices and to think about
> how they could nudge that. We had to really work on formative assess-
> ment for our leaders. How would they be observing their teachers? What
> would they be looking for? And what do they do next? How do they
> negotiate conversation? What is their inquiry as leaders like?

The first step involved bringing in two expert Reading Apprenticeship coaches to model inquiry-based coaching with two volunteer teachers. Leaders observed the coaches' and teachers' interactions and then debriefed with them,

CLOSE-UP 7.3

How did one school district with five secondary schools leverage five days of coaching for its Reading Apprenticeship leadership team? What does the New Haven, California, Unified School District experience contribute to our learning about coaching as a tool for leadership team development?

At each of the district's secondary schools, the goal was for a site administrator; a literacy coach; and a science, a history, and an English language arts teacher to comprise the site-based Reading Apprenticeship leadership team. In addition, the five site-based teams together constituted the district Reading Apprenticeship leadership team. They met as a group with two Reading Apprenticeship coaches to build their capacity to mentor colleagues at their local sites.

Over the course of a year, each of the five schools hosted one of the meeting days. The days focused on classroom observations in the classes of the host school teachers and on close reading and discussion of leadership and coaching texts. The teachers being observed prepared in advance of each of the five days with the help of the Reading Apprenticeship and site-based coaches.

Strengths of the Model

Varied Meeting Sites. Holding the meetings at the different school sites in the district worked well, as the leadership team members were able to see Reading Apprenticeship in practice outside of their own school—in fact, at all the middle and high school sites across the district. This contributed to the feeling of a district-wide community of Reading Apprenticeship, with no school or teacher operating in a silo.

Classroom Observation Cycles. Some teachers and district coaches on the leadership team were initially resistant to the idea that classroom observations would contribute to leadership development. Yet by the end of the year, these teachers and coaches reported that the observations were the most helpful part of the coaching. In fact, three of the four district coaches participating in the group took the observation model back to their own schools to use with their teachers.

The classroom observation cycles also had the effect of shifting teacher practice toward deeper knowledge of Reading Apprenticeship. Knowing that so many people were going to be in their classroom for a full period caused teachers to revisit the foundations of Reading Apprenticeship–based instruction—such as the social dimension and comprehension routines—to make sure their class was prepared for tackling the planned lesson.

The one requirement for teachers planning an observation lesson—that the class would be examining a text—meant that teachers used the Text and Task Analysis as the main tool for planning and debriefing the observation. As a result, both the teachers and students were deeply immersed in the text and the practice of close reading.

Shifting Conversations. Collecting student work for discussion and debriefing after the classroom observation had the benefit of shifting the discussion about the observation toward student outcomes rather than teacher actions.

Revisions to the Model

More Shared Investment in Lesson Planning. Looking back at their work with the New Haven Reading Apprenticeship leadership team, Rita and Irisa recommend structuring the coaching meetings as two-day events. They found that even though their one-day meetings were powerful—and fit into schools' schedules more easily than a two-day structure would—the classroom observation portion of the meetings would benefit from two back-to-back days. Teams found that while their pre-observation close reading and annotating of student texts often alerted them to text challenges and opportunities, there was no time for the classroom teacher to make changes to lesson plans to incorporate these discoveries.

In a two-day structure, these coaches believe, Day 1 would allow the team more time for collaborative consideration of the selected text and the chance to develop and refine the lesson more collaboratively with the classroom teacher. In this model, Day 2 would then be focused on observation of the lesson and debriefing. Not only would responsibility for and investment in the lesson be more distributed across the team, the learning would be more potently shared as well. (This two-day structure could also be scheduled as back-to-back half-days rather than full days.)

Challenges

Scheduling. In most schools, scheduling is a classic challenge of any kind of collaborative work. Teams may find that scheduling concurrent classroom observations is not always possible; some flexibility in agenda planning should be anticipated.

Mistrust of the Process. As noted, some administrators and coaches initially believed that participating in the classroom observation cycles was of little value to them, thinking that they should simply be told how to be a coach.

Observation Anxiety. Some of the teachers were anxious about having team members—who included their building administrators—observe them. An inherent tension on teams that mix administrators and teachers is whether administrators can maintain an inquiry stance in the team meetings and classroom observations. For teachers, it may be difficult to let go of a sense that administrators are always evaluating them, however committed administrators may say they are to learning with the team and from the observations.

Labor-Intensive. Finally, as with all kinds of coaching, the leadership team coaching approach piloted by Rita and Irisa was labor-intensive. The one-on-one preparation time with teachers in advance of the observation days requires a good deal of support and scaffolding.

reflecting on what they had noticed and wondered. Shelley was pleased with the experiment:

> I think it was really important to model coaching in a way that we hope to explore further, so that it is ongoing and embedded and tied to teachers' goals and ongoing inquiry.

Creating Leadership Communities Across Schools and Districts

The inquiry-based, collaborative model of Reading Apprenticeship professional development is a boon when applied to teams of Reading Apprenticeship leaders as well as to site-based teams. The opportunity for leaders to learn along with peers, to compare notes and problem solve, and to participate in a supportive community is a benefit for the leaders themselves and also for those with whom they work.

Literacy Coordinator Teams   Literacy coordinators in schools and districts have a role that bridges from the administration to the teaching staff, with administrative responsibilities that include professional development, coaching, and teacher evaluation.

In the Dearborn, Michigan, school district, three literacy coordinators serve the three comprehensive high schools, and another coordinator manages the district's middle schools. These four coordinators also meet together as a team and support one another in their hybrid roles.

When comparing their coordinator position with that of a coach, which most of them have been, they acknowledge the tension of being a teacher's evaluator as well as coach-collaborator, but they feel that their administrative role makes them more effective. Gretchen Bajorek, literacy coordinator at Edsel Ford High School, has a perspective on both roles:

> I've been an instructional coach, and you're really supportive. You have the folks who just run with things and it's exciting to collaborate with them, but there are a few who, once the door is closed, go right back to what they were doing. With this administrative piece, you don't have to go in with a heavy hand. You don't have to be explicit about why aren't you doing this or that. They know you're evaluating them, everyone's aware of the potential. But you've got to be really authentic and transparent. You have to put everything out there for the trust factor, so they know where you're coming from.

Laurie Lintner, the new literacy coordinator for Dearborn High School, agrees that the administrative role cuts both ways:

> The evaluative role has been a concern, not that there's a whole lot of pushback, but it's something to be very mindful of. It's been important to me to be in classrooms right away, to build relationships and build that trust in me.

For Catherine Morrison, the Dearborn middle school literacy coordinator, the team is an important support in helping to sort out the issues that come with the territory:

> Just like a Reading Apprenticeship team would do in a building, we can use each other's expertise. As a Reading Apprenticeship teacher you need those teacher meetings, and it's the same with us. We need our coordinator meetings, what's working or not working, what we're struggling with.

Amy Keith Wardlow, literacy coordinator at Dearborn's Fordson High School, provides an example of how the four of them work together:

> We were faced with a situation last semester with a cohort in our Reading Apprenticeship training where a teacher had some problems with the training, didn't think the training was a valuable use of her time away from her students, and she went above us.
>
> It was brought to our attention and we sat in a room and figured out what does that look like, how do we change that? How do we make it worth her while, even though it was only one person? We could turn off an entire building by just that one person who feels this is not worthwhile. We have to be constantly taking a look at ourselves and what we're doing and how we're approaching it. We have to be open to that.

Cross-School or Cross-District Teacher Leader Meetings Reading Apprenticeship teacher leaders value time to meet across schools or districts with others whose leadership responsibilities parallel their own. In some instances, teacher leader meetings are convened by intermediate district staff who are supporting Reading Apprenticeship professional development. Sometimes the opportunity to bring teacher leaders together exists between neighboring school districts or within a district where teacher leaders represent different schools. In Michigan, Pennsylvania, Indiana, and California, regional teacher leader meetings evolved at a time when many Reading Apprenticeship teams in those states were in the early stages of Reading Apprenticeship implementation. Three times a year, for a day at a time, teacher leaders in those states met for their own professional development and support. The design of these meetings focused on deepening the participants' own classroom practice and understanding of the Reading Apprenticeship Framework, on more typical leadership discussions and professional reading, and on trying out Reading Apprenticeship protocols that the teacher leaders could bring back to their teams. For an example of the full range of activities that can structure all-day teacher leader meetings, see Close-Up 7.4, Sample Reading Apprenticeship Teacher Leader Meeting Agenda.

Comments from teacher leaders in California provide a sense of why these meetings are important:

> —I loved how our discussions were always inquiry based. Being involved with this group has changed my teaching and leadership ability.
> —Guidance from the Reading Apprenticeship teacher leader group has helped problem solve some of the issues around developing and planning effective team meetings at my school.
> —Great experience and support! These meetings are a model of how to facilitate our students' learning.
> —I really like how we got to experience the actual Framework as part of this training. This group has been a safe place for me.
> —The protocol for discussing today's professional article was an excellent process for digging into the contents.

In Close-Up 7.5, Please Let Them (Us) Talk!, teacher leader Kevin English writes a heartfelt reflection about what he finds most important in the meetings with other Reading Apprenticeship teacher leaders.

As it turns out, it is not only the teacher leaders who anticipate the teacher leader meetings. Site teams also have a stake in the teacher leader meetings.

CLOSE-UP 7.4

Sample Reading Apprenticeship Teacher Leader Meeting Agenda

This sample agenda is designed to address the goals that drive every Reading Apprenticeship teacher leader meeting:

1. Provide a forum for teacher leaders to network and learn from one another
2. Deepen our own practices in Reading Apprenticeship
3. Learn tools to improve the effectiveness of monthly team meetings
4. Have a space to share challenges and ideas about building a stronger bridge between administrators and teachers implementing the Reading Apprenticeship Framework

9:00–9:10: Opening/Goals/Norms
9:10–9:50: Reflecting on Team Meetings

- Each person reflects and writes about the team meetings: What is going well and what makes the meetings productive? What needs more work? What are you hoping to see as a result of your team meetings? What are some ideas you have for improving your team meetings so they move closer to what you would like them to be?
- Shoulder partner share. (Each person has three minutes to share. One partner listens without interrupting for two minutes, and then there is one minute for questions. Switch roles.)
- Partners report out to whole group any successes, challenges, questions, needs. Facilitator charts, categorizing responses.

9:40–10:30: Topic Inquiry (the six most mentioned topics of interest per registration forms)

1. Constructing formative assessments
2. Facilitating productive team meetings
3. Connecting Reading Apprenticeship, Common Core, and our content
4. Bringing colleagues on board
5. Sustaining Reading Apprenticeship after the cohort training ends
6. Developing successful Reading Apprenticeship routines

Gallery Walk:

- Participants count off in groups of six, go to topic numbered chart, discuss ideas and questions related to topic, use sticky notes to respond on chart.
- Small groups rotate right at timer until all topics have been visited.

Focused Group Discussion:

- Participants go to the topic chart they most want to discuss more deeply (make groups no larger than five), designate recorder and timekeeper, spend fifteen minutes to further discuss the topic.
- A recorder charts group ideas and questions to bring to larger group and hangs chart, group selects a reporter.

10:30–10:40: Break
10:40–11:35: Topic Inquiry (continued)

Report Out, Feedback, and New Thinking:

- Each group reports for four minutes, audience members write ideas and questions for each group on half-slip of paper. Group has one minute to respond to oral questions or comments from audience.
- Audience half-slips are collected for each group, groups consider feedback and make adjustments to their own ideas and questions.
- Groups report out new ideas or insights they will take away with them.

11:35–12:30: Professional Reading and Collaborative Learning

Thompson and Zeuli Chapter Review with Golden Line Protocol:

- Participants have five minutes to look over text (sent as homework) and select a golden line.
- In groups of three and four, participants share golden lines and reasons for choice, groups choose one golden line/idea to share with the whole group and one new learning or question

for further inquiry resulting from the reading and discussion.

- Groups report out and facilitator charts.

12:30–1:00: Lunch
1:00–1:50: Consultancy Protocol

Write and Share:

- In groups of three, each person writes for two minutes about one success and one concern in his or her Reading Apprenticeship classroom the past month.
- Each person has a five-minute period for sharing and feedback: two minutes sharing, one minute clarifying questions by partners, one minute summarizing what was heard by partners, one minute having presenter reflect.

Triad Discussion and Whole-Group Share:

- Each group talks about commonalities heard and makes a list of successes and concerns to share with whole group.
- As each group shares out, facilitator records a list.

Brainstorming for Solutions:

- Triads look at list of concerns and brainstorm for solutions.
- Triads share out to whole group.

1:50–2:00: Closing/Gots and Needs

- Each person reflects and writes what new learning they will take away and questions they still have about Reading Apprenticeship, its implementation in classrooms, or working with teacher teams.

According to members of the Abington Senior High School team, they also gain from the experiences their teacher leader brings back:

> —Allyson Morcom: It was great to have someone who would come back from all the team leader meetings with new ideas for us—presents!
> —Barb Moss: It was not only getting the tools, but helping us implement them. It was never, "Here is something you could try." It was always support to make that happen.
> —Jake Gilboy: A ton of credit needs to be given to our team leader [Krista Carey]. Not only the support that was there through the monthly meetings and trainings, but organizing and keeping us on track and being that resource when we needed it.

The literacy coordinators in the Dearborn district, who meet with the Reading Apprenticeship teams and teacher leaders and meet in their own four-person team, also value teacher leader meetings as an extra source of support. Literacy coordinator Amy Keith-Wardlow characterizes the group consensus:

> Meetings with other Reading Apprenticeship teacher leaders have gotten progressively better as our work together and our conversations have gotten deeper. That's really been supportive for us. Having that time to come together with people who are not on our team and to branch out and go, "Okay, I'm on the right track," or "I need to try that"—just having the time to have those conversations. We're supported by our administrators, we're supported by each other, but that outside support, too, has been invaluable for us.

CLOSE-UP 7.5

Please Let Them (Us) Talk!

Kevin English writes an education blog, *English's Education: Lessons from a Novice Teaching Life* (http://englishseducation.blogspot.com). Reading it is a rewarding reminder of why teachers become teachers, and why it matters. In the following post, Kevin reflects on his experience at a meeting with other Reading Apprenticeship teacher leaders.

Please Let Them (Us) Talk!

I spent Friday at the local intermediate school district, meeting with other teacher-leaders trained in Reading Apprenticeship. I long for these days of quality professional development that isn't scripted, is flexible, and meets my needs. The highlight of the day: *getting to talk to other teachers.*

The power of talk isn't a revolutionary idea. Talk, just like writing, is used for a variety of purposes: to communicate, express, reflect, defend, think, etc. But more often than not, I feel as if academic and collegial conversations are looked down upon in the field. "Talk" and "conversation" have taken on negative connotations to others in a similar way that "test" and "assessment" have with teachers.

More often than not, I've found professional development to limit talking. As a result, I imagine that limits the speaking and listening that needs to take place in our classrooms. If we can't trust our teachers to have meaningful conversations, how will that translate into the trust necessary for student success? Sure, conversations go off on tangents, but so does our thinking! It's at that moment that

we have to help each other bring the conversation back to the task at hand. I would also argue that this is a valuable skill to teach students. And if people talk about other things, they are probably things that matter to them. It's then that we have to learn how to connect the things that they see as important to what we see as important. As a colleague once told me, we all have different questions that need answering. The difficult work is getting everyone to see how each other's answers are valuable—and they *all* are!

In the end, I left training with a list of new ideas—a list that wouldn't have come about if I hadn't had the opportunity to talk with so many colleagues. And this is what I was promised during my training in college: a chance to enter difficult, but necessary, conversations. When teachers have the opportunity to put their heads together, we all benefit from their collective knowledge—especially when teachers don't agree. There is something magical about cognitive dissonance! Teachers, like students, have knowledge that they can share, and varied experiences that enable them to contribute to a larger conversation that becomes enriched because of said experiences. All we need is the opportunity to talk about what is important to us . . . .

As I try to make this a year of strategic talking in my classroom and with the group of Reading Apprenticeship teachers I am so excited to work with, I end with this thought: When we limit talk, we limit our growth as teachers. And when we limit our growth as teachers, we limit students' growth, too.

Expanding Strategically

When we started the district rollout of Reading Apprenticeship, we knew it would be best if people could jump in when they were ready. For the people who were kind of dragging their feet, they're now hearing about the really strong disciplinary literacy work that people are doing. We're generating buzz.

—Becky Graf, Charlotte-Mecklenburg Schools director of humanities

Regardless of whether a Reading Apprenticeship literacy community gets its start as an administrative initiative or as the result of grassroots teacher enthusiasm, in order to move beyond first steps and expand the reach and depth of Reading Apprenticeship practices, it is the *combination* of strategic support and the buzz of teacher discovery that builds momentum to keep the effort growing.

Whether by expanding across a whole district, adding grade levels within a school, or spreading success within particular disciplines or programs, important structural support of Reading Apprenticeship at the institutional level ensures that teachers have time to collaborate, experience success, and build the authentic interest of other colleagues.

Building Momentum for a District-Wide Rollout

Charlotte-Mecklenburg Schools (CMS) is the sixteenth largest school district in the United States. Teachers and administrators in all seventy-five of its secondary schools are learning about Reading Apprenticeship in response to a district initiative that has made literacy its "North Star." The mandate to focus on literacy comes with a somewhat loose timetable, but district support is comprehensive: Reading Apprenticeship professional development for mixed-role school teams, site-based team meetings, integration with other major district initiatives, coaching for schools that are ready to go further with Reading Apprenticeship, and cross-district inquiry communities for teacher leaders and administrators who are pioneering the work.

As might be imagined, there are several threads to this story.

In 2009 when CMS was looking to strengthen its approach to secondary literacy, the district hired Becky Graf to work with the Academic Division and help guide district policy. Common Core was on the horizon, bringing increased attention to disciplinary literacy. District principals were being expected to take more instructional leadership—specifically in literacy. Ideas about distributed leadership were also in the air, suggesting that a range of educators could share responsibility for making schools more effective.

Laying the Groundwork for Administrative Understanding and Connection

As part of her new role with the district, Becky investigated the research in disciplinary literacy, talked with various leaders in the field, and became increasingly curious about Reading Apprenticeship. She visited schools in Michigan where Reading Apprenticeship approaches were well integrated into subject area classes. Impressed, she and a colleague from the district's science, technology, engineering, and math (STEM) division participated in a national Reading

Apprenticeship leadership institute. At that point, she started recommending Reading Apprenticeship to leaders in the district.

As district professional development for Common Core rolled out, Becky says, no decisions had been made about Reading Apprenticeship, but it was clearly in the background:

> In our Common Core work, we really emphasized the research on
> disciplinary literacy, citing a lot of different sources. We knew that
> disciplinary literacy was the path we wanted to follow.

Then CMS changed superintendents, and district initiatives were put into a holding pattern. What could have been a frustrating time turned into an opportunity to introduce Reading Apprenticeship to interested principals:

> That's when we offered a book study for the principals. I said, "Hey, I
> have this really great book about disciplinary literacy. Anybody interested
> in doing a book study?" We bought some copies of *Reading for
> Understanding*,[3] and we shared sections of that with about 40 principals,
> assistant principals, and academic facilitators [coaches].

With this small core of book group leaders showing interest, Becky and her team moved to gain buy-in from a larger group of principals and district leaders. They designed a three-day introduction to Reading Apprenticeship for a group of about forty principals and another group of about forty leaders in the central office and the district's ten learning communities. Becky had a number of goals for this introduction—informational, collaborative, and political:

> We wanted them to see what this was and kind of immerse themselves in
> it. We also wanted them to imagine, if we were to do this, what would
> they recommend for a rollout? We invited people to those three-day
> trainings that we knew were gung-ho, on board, and excited, but we also
> included others we knew would need to be persuaded or it wasn't going
> to go anywhere.

Enough of the invited leaders saw the potential of Reading Apprenticeship so that the CMS central office decided to institute Reading Apprenticeship professional development for all secondary schools in the district, beginning with five days of professional development for cross-role teams of ten from each building.

Inviting Choice Within a District Mandate

There is an interesting tension in the CMS literacy mandate. All middle and high schools must field a literacy team to participate in Reading Apprenticeship professional development, but aside from that, the district's ten learning communities and individual schools within a learning community can choose to implement Reading Apprenticeship or a completely different approach for meeting the district's annual literacy goals—broad goals such as a focus on close reading, vocabulary, and chunking text.

Learning communities and schools are also offered some choice in how soon they must have a team ready to participate in Reading Apprenticeship professional development and who will serve on the team. District guidance is that a school's principal and academic facilitator must be on the team, along with teachers from across content areas. It took about a year after the professional development was announced for schools in every learning community to field a team, which Becky recognizes as a not unreasonable response:

> With ten learning communities and seventy-five schools, some had things on their plates that they were working on, or they didn't necessarily like our time frame, or they just didn't buy in. So it's taken a little bit longer than we anticipated, but at this point, everyone is involved.

Because teachers on the Reading Apprenticeship teams are volunteers, other teachers who are more tentative or even skeptical can adopt a wait-and-see approach to Reading Apprenticeship. Moninda Eslick, a literacy coach at Francis Bradley Middle School, believes this works in everyone's favor:

> Many of our teachers have been trained and several were all in as they began the work. As with anything, some were also hesitant and not quite sure how to make a transition, while some said it wouldn't work in their content.
>
> Based on my experience, the volunteer-to-attend approach seems to have made the buy-in more successful. Not putting pressure on teachers has allowed them to make it work for them in their own classroom and content. The success they have had has generated more interest among our staff.

Moving into Distributed Leadership and Open Classrooms

Along with Charlotte-Mecklenburg's turn to literacy as the district's North Star came the expectation that the principal would be the instructional leader in a building and responsible for working with the teachers to support their literacy learning. Becky says principals immediately recognized the magnitude of this challenge—and the need for more-distributed leadership at the school site:

> When we started with some very intentional work about literacy for principals, and they saw the scope of what would be required, they said, "We can't do this alone. Can we *please* work with a team of people from our school?"

> So instead of having principal meetings on one day and literacy
> facilitator meetings on another day, and the assistant principals on a
> different day, and everybody getting different messages, the principals
> asked for mixed-role meetings so school teams could work together.
> Many asked also to have teachers working side by side with them.

In voicing this request, the principals were discovering the need for a new kind of professional development structure, one that dovetailed with a direction district leaders had already begun to investigate: instructional leadership teams (ILTs). The purpose of ILTs is to drive instructional learning in a building, so the teams are representative of all the stakeholder groups. They include the principal and other instructional leaders and teachers from a range of subject areas and specialties. In CMS, because literacy is the district's instructional focus, the ILTs are charged with deepening their own members' understanding of literacy practices and also with leading literacy learning at their school site. If this sounds a lot like the goals for the Reading Apprenticeship teams, it should.

A school's Reading Apprenticeship team and the ILT have many, if not most, of the same members—the principal, literacy leaders, and teachers representing a range of subject areas. Becky explains that such overlap is intentional:

> When we asked schools to create their ILTs, we encouraged them to
> include people holding similar roles as those we already had on our
> Reading Apprenticeship teams. In schools where a lot of people overlap
> on the two teams, they're really forging ahead.
>
> Principals appreciate the structure of the ILT for how it supports the
> rollout of our literacy practices. I've heard them say they really like this
> way of working and would be really unhappy if the district took it away.

ILT members attend six learning days in the academic year, in cohorts of three partnering teams, and each day concludes with significant time for teams to plan how they will transfer the learning they have experienced to their unique school contexts. Teams consider this "golden time"—time to think about and plan for what to take back to their colleagues and how to connect it to everything else going on at their school.

Becky describes how a team's planning decisions translate into literacy learning and accountability at a school site:

> Say the ILT decides, "Okay, we're going to be working on close reading
> using Talking to the Text annotations." They're also deciding how much
> they're going to push, how fast, what the expectations are depending on
> what all of the teachers are ready for. Whatever level of implementation

the ILT decides, after a month of "safe practice," you're going to be doing that and we can evaluate that.

Then within the ILT, they might be deciding to push themselves. So, they might have a cohort of people that are trying a lot of things, knowing they're not going to share it with the school at large until they're ready. So that's kind of the beauty of the process because they have the ability to make the decisions that are best for their school.

ILTs also participate in periodic cross-school classroom observations. Known as "opening up practice," ILTs from three partnering schools rotate hosting guided classroom visits. The visitors specifically observe for literacy practices that the host team and their faculty have been working on in advance. As Becky points out, the visits are instrumental in supporting teachers' implementation and assessment of their literacy practices:

We're setting it up so that people can see Reading Apprenticeship in other places, and it's a way we're ensuring that implementation is happening rather than just hoping it is because people attended a training.

Fast-Tracking Implementation

In all of the planning for the CMS rollout of Reading Apprenticeship, a key strategy has been support for fast-tracking pilot implementation models. For CMS, this began by crossing state lines. Small groups of CMS administrators and teachers visited schools in Berkley and Dearborn, Michigan, where mature implementation of Reading Apprenticeship is in place. For the CMS visitors, the Michigan models galvanized their support for creating local models of their own.

In a number of CMS schools where teachers or administrators were part of the Michigan expedition, Reading Apprenticeship implementation has been on a fast track. In other schools, overlapping Reading Apprenticeship and ILT membership has accelerated teachers' learning and practice. The district is also supporting implementation with site-based coaching. It won't be long, Becky believes, until teachers across the district can observe in a range of classrooms where Reading Apprenticeship is in action:

We've got people who are moving on this so fast it's scary, and we've got a good base growing. Using the structure of the instructional leadership teams is turning out to be much more powerful than we anticipated— we're getting so much traction so fast. What we need is classrooms where we can send people, where teachers are opening up their practice, just so people can get a look in the basket. It feeds the learning. We're hoping to do that locally, without having to travel to Michigan!

Moving Up and Down the Grades

It is not unusual for Reading Apprenticeship to first take hold at one level in a school, district, or community and then prompt additional professional development up and down the grades. Sometimes it means expanding systematically from ninth grade up through twelfth or from high school down to middle school, or even to cross boundaries between community college and high school.

Many school districts that begin implementation of Reading Apprenticeship at the high school level find that bringing in the middle school feeder schools is a sound decision. Students benefit earlier, and their transition to high school is easier when literacy routines are familiar.

Youssef Mosallam, principal of Fordson High School, has been able to grow his school's Reading Apprenticeship implementation up the grades, from a base in the ninth grade academies, and now to welcome entering freshmen from feeder schools where Reading Apprenticeship is already in place:

> We have invested so much financial and human capital in the ninth
> grade academies, so that each year, as Reading Apprenticeship has built
> through all the grade levels, our students are able to seamlessly use
> Reading Apprenticeship strategies and self-regulate their own learning.
>
> Now, what has taken us to the next level is the implementation of
> Reading Apprenticeship in our feeder middle schools. When our students
> come in as freshmen, we are not taking the month of September to
> prepare them for Reading Apprenticeship strategies. Our freshman
> academy teachers are just diving into content.

For Julia Raddatz, principal of Manistee High School, extending Reading Apprenticeship from the town's high school to the middle school was a no-brainer:

> Even though I'm the high school principal, I do all the curriculum and
> professional development for grades 7 through 12.

In Traverse City, Michigan, the successful implementation of Reading Apprenticeship by the West Senior High School ninth grade teachers led to a school action plan to expand Reading Apprenticeship to tenth grade the following year, and then on up to eleventh and twelfth grades. Close-Up 7.6, West Senior High Five-Year Plan, lays out the schedule for school-wide professional development at West that includes both administrators and teachers.

At Berkley High School, the teacher leader team is hopeful that the vision of a district-wide literacy plan, built on a Reading Apprenticeship foundation, is a growing reality. They have enjoyed solid support of long standing for Reading Apprenticeship at the high school, and with Berkley middle school teachers beginning to take up Reading Apprenticeship, they believe the time is right to become explicit about how Reading Apprenticeship connects with district goals. Teacher leader Tracy Francis argues for a district vision that will inform policy for years to come:

> We need a vision of where we're going. Reading Apprenticeship is not reinventing the wheel. These are good practices and that's not going to change. They've been consolidated in a way that really makes sense. So how do we set that vision?

At the community college level, being strategic about expanding the reach of Reading Apprenticeship can mean preparing the high school teachers of future students to implement Reading Apprenticeship practices.

North Central Michigan College provides Reading Apprenticeship professional development for area high school teachers, and the motivation is not entirely altruistic. Those teachers' students may well wind up in North Central classrooms, where many faculty members have a Reading Apprenticeship bent.

Chris Padgett and Amanda Corcoran, who lead the Reading Apprenticeship initiative at American River College (ARC), have a similar motivation for providing local high school teachers with a taste of Reading Apprenticeship, which they do in summer institute days hosted at ARC. Why not build bridges that can give students a head start for the literacy expectations they will encounter in many classes on the ARC campus?

Promoting Strongholds

Often, a core of committed Reading Apprenticeship–trained teachers band together in a particular department or discipline, where they support one another and become a model of self-sustaining, discipline-based literacy pedagogy for others in their building or institution. The Reading Apprenticeship Academic Literacy (RAAL) course has also proven to be a stronghold of Reading Apprenticeship practice, where teachers celebrate its effectiveness helping students step up their literacy confidence and competence.

Building Disciplinary Cohorts

At American River College, Amanda Corcoran describes the work she and Chris Padgett are doing to promote the strategic growth of Reading Apprenticeship, discipline by discipline:

> We're trying to build cohorts within the disciplines of people who have been trained in Reading Apprenticeship. Chris and I can't be the only ones on campus organizing and supporting Reading Apprenticeship.

CLOSE-UP 7.6

West Senior High Five-Year Plan

In Traverse City, Michigan, when administrators and staff at West Senior High agreed to begin implementation of Reading Apprenticeship, the plan was to begin professional development with the ninth grade teachers and add one grade per year. Professional development for administrators, too, was built into the five-year plan that was approved by the school district.

Action Plan: Five-Year Plan, West Senior High 2013–2015*

Focus Area: Reading Apprenticeship Initiative

Goals:

1. To train all subject area teachers in the Reading Apprenticeship techniques in order to increase student literacy.
2. All students will become better and independent critical thinkers and readers with all texts to align to the Common Core standards.

Strategies/Activities/Initiatives	Persons Responsible	Resources Needed	Timeline
1. Ninth-grade social studies, science, and ELA team teachers will attend Reading Apprenticeship training in summer 2012 through the school year	TBA/Joe Tibaldi	Time out of the classroom provided with sub coverage Copies of the text	August 2012–June 2013
2. Tenth-grade social studies, science, and ELA team teachers will attend Reading Apprenticeship training in summer 2013 through the school year	Joe Tibaldi	Time out of the classroom provided with sub coverage Copies of the text	August 2013–June 2014
3. West administrators will take the online Reading Apprenticeship training course to support teachers in their work to use Reading Apprenticeship strategies to teach literacy in their subject area	Joe Tibaldi, Patti Tibaldi, Charles Kolbusz, Dan Oberski, Stephanie Long	Copies of the text Madonna U. registration	September 2012–May 2013
4. Teachers will self-select Reading Apprenticeship critical friends groups to support their Reading Apprenticeship training	Ninth- and tenth-grade academic teamed teachers	Reading Apprenticeship trained facilitators 90-minute PLC time	September 2012–2015
5. Non-core academic teachers will be taught by West staff Reading Apprenticeship facilitators in groups of thirty at West over two years	Kelly Rintala, Rachel Noller	Texts, PD hourly wage money, sub pay during the year for ongoing training	August 2013–2015

*[Plan for eleventh and twelfth grades to come]

Implications for Professional Development: Time will need to be dedicated for Reading Apprenticeship critical friends groups to meet for ongoing support to be led by Reading Apprenticeship coaches acting as CFG facilitators. Current CFG groups will need to reorganized. Money will need to be allocated to pay for hourly rate, texts, and subs for non-core teachers to get trained over the next two years. All staff PD time to be dedicated to introducing and supporting Reading Apprenticeship as a whole-school intervention for all students across all disciplines.

Implications for Other Stakeholder Involvement (Parents, Community): Parents will need to be informed about Reading Apprenticeship and how to support their child using Reading Apprenticeship strategies at home on their homework. Reading Apprenticeship facilitators and administrators will make a board presentation at the yearly board curriculum meetings explaining the intervention and sharing growth data.

Evaluation Process/Methods: We will collect data on ninth-, tenth-, and eleventh-grade students, tracked in cohorts, to determine if students in Reading Apprenticeship classrooms showed any significant growth in EPAS compared with the rest of the school. Data will need to be tracked for four years.

Evidence of Success: More students will demonstrate growth on EPAS, NWEA, AP, and other standardized tests. Students will self-report more confidence and success with complex reading tasks and texts, and students' grades will improve.

STEM is a good example of how that could happen. Our STEM department has a number of people trained in Reading Apprenticeship. They received some funding to build up a STEM Reading Apprenticeship support network, and they have a growing cohort.

Our perspective is we don't have to reach everyone, we just have to reach a couple of people in a department and emphasize that they need to talk with their colleagues. Get your colleagues in your discipline involved. You can't do it alone, but if you believe in it, make it part of your discipline culture. That's what happened in STEM. It happened in history. It's happening in English.

When the Reading Apprenticeship Framework and classroom routines become more integrated across a campus, people may not use the language of Reading Apprenticeship per se, because its key ideas and ways of working have been absorbed into how a range of campus initiatives occur. According to biology instructor Theresa Martin, who was instrumental in building a strong interest in Reading Apprenticeship across the College of San Mateo STEM faculty, that is what happened there after a few years:

Someone made a comment to me recently, "What's going on with Reading Apprenticeship? Is it only in STEM?"

The reason you don't hear about it is because the Reading Apprenticeship initiative has morphed, expanded, and broadened slightly in its focus to include other student-centered instructional ideas. New initiatives, like Habits of Mind, a first year experience, and a new faculty institute, are being developed on our campus, and we are incorporating the Reading Apprenticeship Framework into those activities.

Shining a Light on Reading Apprenticeship Academic Literacy

Secondary schools have found that the RAAL course,[4] designed originally as an intensive two-semester reading course for ninth graders, can become a showcase for the power of the Reading Apprenticeship Framework.

At Pinckney Community High School, where Dianna Behl works as assistant principal and director of Pinckney's school-within-a-school New Tech High School (and also as district instructional coach), all professional development is based on the Reading Apprenticeship Framework. In addition, RAAL has a special place in Pinckney's approach to adolescent literacy. (See Close-Up 7.7, Pinckney High School's Rock 'n RAAL.)

In the school's most recent North Central Association of Colleges and Schools (NCA) accreditation, the Reading Apprenticeship program was cited as a Pocket of Excellence. Dianna credits especially the district's support for RAAL, which now includes sections that reach students in grades 8–12.

In an email to RAAL teacher Debbie Renton, Dianna notes the results of a deliberate scheduling experiment to assign students to the same teacher for RAAL and English:

> You and your students ROCKED IT!!!! As we suspected, having the same
> teacher for RAAL and ELA 9 made a *huge* difference in student achieve-
> ment! Last year your students' average Lexile growth[5] for the year was
> 25.6 units. This year it was 80.11!!!!

Copied on the email were the district superintendent and assistant superintendent of instruction, assessment, and technology, with a brief thank you for their support in expanding the district's RAAL offerings:

> Thank you so much for making sure we can offer the additional RAAL
> grade 10–12 class this fall so we can help even more students who are not
> at grade level reading.
>   We do make a difference in kids' lives!

Collecting Data

School systems and community colleges collect institutional data as a matter of course—attendance, behavior, grades, state test scores, retention and transfer rates, for example. These data are often used to compel change. Sometimes Reading Apprenticeship becomes part of a school's improvement plan. On the other hand, data collected as part of an inquiry into a teacher's own implementation of Reading Apprenticeship or a school's tracking of its own Reading Apprenticeship program carries particular weight for communicating the value of Reading Apprenticeship in a building or on a campus.

At Harrison High School, assistant principal Allyson Robinson heard from one of the science teachers about a tiny experiment he ran to show the difference

Reading Apprenticeship was making for his students. The data he collected, she says, is just the kind that other teachers can appreciate:

> Last year he gave a unit test that his kids averaged in the D range. This year he gave the exact same test but he used the Reading Apprenticeship approach to teaching the content. The scores rose by 15 percent overall. He explained that he didn't modify the test because he wanted the comparison.
>
> Don't think I haven't been using him to recruit people!

CLOSE-UP 7.7
Pinckney High School's Rock 'n RAAL

When Dianna Behl first encountered Reading Apprenticeship, she was an assistant principal at Pinckney Community High School in the Pinckney, Michigan, district. She attended a summer institute for administrators whose teachers were Reading Apprenticeship–trained and was so startled by her reaction that, she says, "I begged to go back to the classroom so I could teach Reading Apprenticeship."

And she did, spending several years implementing the Reading Apprenticeship Framework with the high school's English students. These days she has returned to administration, where her enthusiasm for Reading Apprenticeship is stronger than ever. She is especially proud of the district's growing commitment to the Reading Apprenticeship Academic Literacy course (RAAL).[6]

School Year	RAAL Implementation	RAAL–English Language Arts Assignment	Student Outcomes
2012–13	RAAL–English 9 hybrid; two sections, full year	Single teacher of hybrid course	Gains in behavior, attendance; average Lexile gain 14.7
2013–14	RAAL is a separate grade 9 course; two sections, full year	RAAL teacher does not have same students for English 9	Gains in GPA, behavior, attendance; average Lexile gain 25.6
2014–15	RAAL is a separate grade 9 course; two sections, full year	*RAAL teacher has same students for English 9*	Gains in GPA, behavior, attendance; average *Lexile gain 80.11*
	Added RAAL in grade 8; four sections, one semester	RAAL teacher does not have the same students for English 8	Average Lexile gain 60.0
2015–16	RAAL in grade 8; four sections, one semester	RAAL teacher does not have the same students for English 8	TBA
	RAAL in grade 9; one section, full year	RAAL teacher has same students for English 9	TBA
	Added RAAL in grades 10–12; one section, full year	RAAL teacher has same grade 10 students for English 10	TBA
	Added RAAL in special education grades 9–12; three sections, full year	RAAL teacher does not have the same students for English	TBA

At Northern Essex Community College (NECC), members of the Reading Apprenticeship staff and faculty interest group (which evolved into the campus Transitions to Academic Success team) decided to get concrete about the benefits they experienced in classes where they implemented Reading Apprenticeship practices. Instructors of courses ranging from business to dental assisting to chemistry quantified their use of Reading Apprenticeship in a variety of course-specific ways. These data helped them gain the attention of colleagues and the support of the college administration. Close-Up 7.8, Getting Concrete at Northern Essex Community College, is a summary of classroom-level data about Reading Apprenticeship implementation that the NECC faculty team shared with colleagues and administrators.

Reading Apprenticeship leaders on a number of community college campuses are tapping their institutional research departments for help telling

CLOSE-UP 7.8

Getting Concrete at Northern Essex Community College

Convincing data are often the data collected closest to home. When the Transitions to Academic Success team at NECC wanted to bring Reading Apprenticeship to the attention of others on campus, they collected data (and samples of student work) that made their assertions about its value concrete.

Faculty-Collected Data	Treatment	Student Outcomes
ALL	**Reading Apprenticeship practices**	**Grades jumped an average of ten points**
Business 101	Reading response journal (four classes)	Treatment students' grade average 82% versus 68%
Dental Assisting 101	Reading journals (all classes for three years)	Pass rate on state boards 100% last two years
Dental Radiology	Double-entry journals (all classes for two years)	Direct correlation between correct use of journals and exam performance
Anthropology 101	Talking to the text (four classes)	Treatment students twice as likely to draw inferences from reading assignment
Biology 101	Reading journals (all classes)	Higher-level student questions and increased engagement in discussion
Biology 202	Reading journals (all classes)	Higher-level student questions and increased engagement in discussion
Biology 115	Double-entry journal (two classes)	Treatment students' grade average 86% versus 74%
Chemistry 111	Reading journals (all classes)	Higher-level student questions and increased engagement in discussion

the student success stories they are witnessing. As described in Chapter One, Renton Technical College is one campus where the initial data collected by a single instructor grew to include a campus study of completion rates in 25 classes before and after Reading Apprenticeship was implemented. Growth from 60 to 90 percent completion was documented, and such data would be difficult to ignore as a factor that has drawn the vast majority of the Renton faculty to Reading Apprenticeship training opportunities.

Pasadena City College is another campus where the research department has had a role in bolstering support for Reading Apprenticeship. At PCC, data were collected about the College 1 first-year seminar course, which incorporates Reading Apprenticeship practices and routines. As part of an extensive first-year experience program called Pathways, students enrolled in College 1 were more likely to finish their first year and more likely to return for a second year. These results were particularly significant for African American and Hispanic/Latino students. (See Close-Up 7.9, The Reading Apprenticeship Difference in a First-Year Experience Program.) The course was still in its pilot phase at the time of the study, but the findings for students who took the course compared with those who did not were so strong that the Pathways program has now scaled up to about 2,500 students per year (or half of all first-year students).

For campuses not so far along in their data collection, Ann Foster, a Reading Apprenticeship leader at Santa Rosa Junior College, voices a consistent message—provide colleagues with local data:

> Do not be afraid to start on data collection, whatever that might be in the beginning. It's really energizing, because people do like to see how it's working on their own campus.

Staying the Course

> As the Reading Apprenticeship support person, I have been a constant reminder to people not to lose focus. I think people are looking for magic potions, which Reading Apprenticeship is not. But if you do it well, you get to the heart of what good teaching is, and it impacts everything that you do.
> —Debbie Swanson, Willow Run 6–8 Intermediate Learning Center
> Reading Apprenticeship teacher leader

How does Reading Apprenticeship fit into an education landscape where the expectations for being college and career ready have never been higher? Too often, new expectations result in a scramble for equally new approaches or at least newly packaged programs. But if educators recognize the power of the Reading Apprenticeship tools they are already using, how can they keep that focus when new initiatives come along?

CLOSE-UP 7.9

The Reading Apprenticeship Difference in a First-Year Experience Program

Educators at Pasadena City College were intent on creating a powerful way for first-year students to launch their college careers. To anchor their larger program, First Year Pathways (FYP), a small team of faculty members interested in working with Reading Apprenticeship approaches took up the challenge of designing a new first-year seminar, called College 1. They focused on improved critical reading and metacognition as course outcomes and designed a rigorous three-credit course approved for transfer credit by the California State University and University of California systems.

To prepare instructors of the interdisciplinary course, they infused Reading Apprenticeship approaches into a required College 1 professional learning institute. Any staff member with at least a master's degree was encouraged to teach the course. Thus, staff from across disciplines and job titles helped to create a truly cross-campus effort on behalf of students.

To assess the effectiveness of FYP, the campus research department gathered the following data.

FYP Differences for Students

2012–13	College 1–FYP Students	Non-College 1–FYP Students
Average credits completed	27.9 units	17.2 units
Persistence fall to fall	93.2%	77.2%
African American students' persistence	87.9%	66.3%
Hispanic/Latino students' persistence	92.5%	74.8%

The College 1 team also collected information about College 1 instructors' sense of self-efficacy before and after participating in the College 1 professional learning institute.

College 1 Differences for Instructors

Fall 2012 Survey	Pre		Post	
	Some	Quite a Bit	Some	Quite a Bit
How much can you do to motivate students who show low interest in schoolwork?	35%	35%	25%	69%
How much can you do to help your students value learning?	31%	40%	13%	69%
How much can you do to improve the understanding of a student who is failing?	36%	32%	31%	69%

Teachers who have had institutional support to implement Reading Apprenticeship deeply, over time, are powerful advocates for focusing in and following through on the promise of the Reading Apprenticeship Framework.

The more they learn, the more effective they become. They understand as well the importance of having colleagues who can share their experiences, whether as members of a school or campus team or as members of a broader network.

Fixing Your Focus

For teacher leaders, teams, schools, districts, and faculty on college campuses—fixing a focus is part of sustaining a Reading Apprenticeship community and the inquiry culture it helps to create. In some cases, the focus may result in convincing a principal or dean to support an ongoing team; in others, it may result in a regional effort to institutionalize Reading Apprenticeship. In still others school board members may be persuaded to extend their support when presented with concrete data and the testimony of students, parents, and teachers. But in every case, the ability to maintain focus in the face of shifting priorities is supported by practitioners' and community members' direct experience of the difference Reading Apprenticeship can make in the lives of teachers and students.

Keeping the Embers Warm

When Kevin English and a team of teachers at Wayne Memorial High School took up Reading Apprenticeship, they were able to meet during PLC time. As school priorities shifted around them, that PLC time became less available for Reading Apprenticeship, so the team made time to meet outside of the PLC. Now, Kevin reports, their sustained effort and focus have made an impression. Their principal is making it possible for them to meet once again as a PLC, and they are also continuing to support one another in other ways:

> Because of a variety of school initiatives this past year, we were only able to meet every now and then during scheduled PLCs, but we also made time outside of the PLCs to make our Reading Apprenticeship implementation work.
>
> Heading into the fall, we have secured a monthly PLC meeting as we bring a few new people on board and work with a consultant in a nearby district. This has developed because of our group advocating to our principal that our collegial conversations are worthwhile, are focused on students, and are focused on building-wide goals that are research based and long-term.
>
> We're even meeting as a team in August to refresh our Reading Apprenticeship work before school begins and to plan for instructional rounds. We want to visit each other more and not work in isolation.

Infiltrating a Campus, One Program After Another

At Pasadena City College, English instructor Nika Hogan was strongly committed to implementing Reading Apprenticeship and sharing what she was learning in her own classroom with colleagues. She offered workshops, started a Reading Apprenticeship Faculty Inquiry Group, and talked with faculty she thought would be interested. Not much happened. But one close colleague, Shelagh Rose, was becoming convinced of the promise of Reading Apprenticeship approaches for students. When Nika and Shelagh had the opportunity to design a summer seminar and yearlong learning community for new faculty, they agreed to use the Reading Apprenticeship Framework to structure faculty inquiry and to model Reading Apprenticeship instructional approaches.

Inspired by the new faculty group's reception to this inquiry into students' disciplinary reading as a means to deeper learning, Nika and Shelagh proposed integrating Reading Apprenticeship into another major piece of program development. As part of a larger Title V grant, they worked with math instructor Carrie Starbird and counselor Cecile Davis to create a first-year seminar with recursive Reading Apprenticeship routines woven in.[7]

When College 1 turned out to be a huge success (see Close-Up 7.9), faculty and administrative interest in Reading Apprenticeship practices grew accordingly.

The PCC College 1 design team recognized that any real campus change initiative would need to involve stakeholders from every area on campus, so they designed it as an interdisciplinary course that any campus employee with a master's degree could teach. This intriguing invitation crosses disciplines and job titles and creates meaningful opportunities for sustained cross-campus collaboration. Deans, tutors, counselors, researchers, librarians and bookstore managers, faculty and adjunct faculty from every division—all attend the College 1 professional learning institute as colleagues and learn how to apply Reading Apprenticeship in their own courses as well as in College 1. (See, for example, "Spreading Reading Apprenticeship Approaches Through Student Counseling," earlier in this chapter.)

From a base in College 1, in addition to spreading into the campus counseling program, the coaching program, tutor training, the summer bridge program, the new faculty institute, the faculty mentor program, and the classrooms of individual instructors, Reading Apprenticeship practices are starting to show up in curriculum redesign initiatives. Whether for acceleration[8] or just to improve how they are delivering their courses, curriculum redesign committees are beginning to incorporate Reading Apprenticeship practices in their courses. For example, new curricula for accelerated math and accelerated English are anchored by Reading Apprenticeship practices, as is a nascent redesign for English as a second language (ESL) courses.

Designing for Scale-Up

Concerned with adolescent literacy in Washtenaw County, Michigan, Naomi Norman and her colleagues at the county's Intermediate School District searched for a literacy approach that would increase students' opportunities to take responsibility for their own learning. They found Reading Apprenticeship and fixed their focus on a program of teacher professional development that would not stop at the end of a five-day institute. Their intention was to support ongoing teacher learning in Reading Apprenticeship practices and to bring it to every secondary school teacher in Washtenaw County.

To accomplish this, they proposed that the county school districts provide, in addition to a program of Reading Apprenticeship professional development, regular meeting time for teachers and release time for teacher leaders. Naomi describes their thinking at the time:

> We were fundamentally focused on the idea that this initiative has to start with classroom teachers, and that they have to have the time to work together and build it as a collaborative piece of work.
>
> This was going to be hard stuff if you think about what's being asked of teachers in the Reading Apprenticeship model. Student agency—how do you create a different classroom culture? This was substantially different from teachers' current practice. And the fact that we were going to include history and science teachers, they didn't have a mindset that it was their job to do this kind of work. We knew the best person to help convince someone to do that would be a peer who's going through it with them simultaneously.
>
> So when we began to think like that, it opened up our thinking about how to get every district to contribute teacher time as part of a larger initiative. We went to every district to start convincing them and figure out where that first set of money was going to come from. We had them participate in building a plan, mapping it out, and building a case for this work.

In 2006, the districts each sent one special education teacher and one general education teacher to the training. The ISD and the districts split the cost of the teachers' participation in the professional development. And teachers had to agree that their participation would include monitoring of their students' reading growth on the Degrees of Reading Power (DRP) assessment.

At the end of the first year, plans for scaling up depended on the decision by members of that first group of teachers to continue their participation—as teacher leaders. The focus Naomi and her colleagues had identified, to build a collaborative piece of work, depended on having won the teachers' trust and commitment:

> At the end of the year, we asked them if they would come back the next year and lead a group of colleagues [who would first attend a five-day Reading Apprenticeship professional development institute] in a collaborative inquiry through a Reading Apprenticeship year like they had just experienced.
>
> Eighteen of the twenty-two did, and we scaled up to about 250 people that next year. We did the DRP in every classroom, pre and post. We were really serious about this student level activity, and we got great results. We were super excited, and it got the attention of our neighboring county.

The scale-up continued, and after five years had reached nearly every teacher, grades 5–12, in Washtenaw County and in neighboring Livingston County. The counties continue to offer Reading Apprenticeship professional development for new hires, to ease them into their department or grade-level teams, where everyone else has already had Reading Apprenticeship training. Naomi believes this sustained focus continues to pay off:

> In our mind, this was sustainable if it just became a part of regular practice—that was our ideal. At this point, everyone's been touched. Without going into classrooms, I don't know whether everyone is doing it, but what I do know is that Washtenaw County has been rising in ranking against all of our other counties in Michigan. We were in the middle of the pack among our peers before Reading Apprenticeship, and now we're the highest performing on the eleventh-grade assessment in reading out of fifty-six regions in the state. So I do know that something right is happening.

Networking for Sustainability

At the community college as well as secondary level, faculty working with Reading Apprenticeship find that networking with colleagues on other campuses enriches and deepens their own efforts. In both California and Washington, statewide community college networks are demonstrating the inspirational and instrumental power of cross-campus exchange and collaboration. Faculty leaders and organizational leaders in other states are looking to these examples and beginning to build similar kinds of statewide communities of practice in Michigan, Tennessee, and Massachusetts.

Communities of Practice: An Educator-Led, State-Supported Network

The California Community Colleges Success Network, or 3CSN, is a professional learning network that connects thousands of educators from across the disciplines and all of the state's 113 community colleges. 3CSN is funded by the California Community Colleges Chancellor's Office and, according to executive director Deborah Harrington, Reading Apprenticeship is at the heart of its success:

> We started 3CSN in 2009 by developing four regional networks where community college faculty, staff, and administrators could connect, share resources, and together learn to incorporate high impact practices and eliminate the equity gap that plagues our students. We wanted our organization to be grassroots and led by community college educators, which turned out to be a powerful launching point.
>
> Within a year, the number of regions expanded, and colleges throughout the state were exponentially increasing participation in regional and statewide activities and events. We realized that these practitioners wanted to connect not just regionally, but based on specific best practices. We added opportunities for structured, sustained professional learning in communities of practice, in direct response to the stated needs of participants.[9]
>
> The Reading Apprenticeship Project (RAP) was one of our first communities of practice, and it is now our largest, having involved more than two thousand participants from ninety-one colleges at some point. Furthermore, the Reading Apprenticeship Framework is so congruent with our community of practice approach that it has significantly impacted the way 3CSN does business.
>
> When we plan events or even our own retreats, we always think in terms of the personal, social, cognitive, and knowledge-building dimensions. We always try to give participants a chance to read together and to engage in metacognitive conversation. Reading Apprenticeship has helped us build this amazing, learner-centered organization.[10]

Under Deborah's leadership, community college practitioners now lead eight regional networks and six communities of practice, all engaging California educators in sustained, recursive professional learning. To guide their work, the 3CSN leadership team draws on and is explicit about the theoretical basis for social learning and communities of practice. Nika Hogan, the founding coordinator of the Reading Apprenticeship Project, explains:

> Theories of situated learning and communities of practice, such as the work of Jean Lave and Etienne Wenger on "legitimate peripheral

participation," are baked into the Reading Apprenticeship Framework, and it might seem odd that we feel the need to call so much attention to them in the community college work. But the truth is many of us are not familiar with these theories or with much of the literature about cognitive apprenticeships or how learning works. College professors have deep expertise in their disciplines. There is no guarantee that we have a strong background in educational theories or pedagogy.

Being explicit about creating and maintaining a community of practice, referring to and citing our sources, has really helped us create an ecology where professionals feel legitimated to invest in their own learning and to develop tolerance for the long-term, recursive nature of it.

Being explicit about our theory of action also helps us explain to campus leaders—who may expect simply to send a team to a one-time "training"—that nothing real is going to happen that way. We constantly cite Wenger and others on the sustained, recursive way that communities of practice work, and it seems to resonate.

Access, Access, Access   In developing and maintaining the California statewide Reading Apprenticeship Project, Nika, Deborah Harrington, and their colleague Ann Foster have focused on three principles of what community college professionals need in a learning environment. The first of these Nika labels *access*:

> We need to make it easy for people to explore these ideas.
>
> If they have to beg, borrow, and plead for institutional funding in order to attend one seminar, one time, the stakes are too high. No single seminar is going to do it. We need people to be able to drop in and connect with the community and to take the time they need to consider how the Reading Apprenticeship Framework might work for them.
>
> Access is also an equity issue. We'd like to reach all faculty, including part-time faculty and those teaching at institutions without professional learning budgets. Participation should not be limited to a privileged few.

To create frequent, low-stakes opportunities to learn about Reading Apprenticeship, 3CSN collaborates with the Strategic Literacy Initiative to host multiple one-day workshops around the state. Early on, participants in these introductory workshops were then invited to apply for scholarships to attend further professional development, such as the online course, the three-day seminar, or, for those interested in supporting others on their campuses, the Reading Apprenticeship Leadership Community of Practice.[11] More recently, as the profile and credibility of Reading Apprenticeship in California community colleges has increased, faculty have been able to secure support from other funding streams on campus to attend these workshops.

Support for Leadership Development The Reading Apprenticeship Leadership Community of Practice is an example of another principle that 3CSN leaders build into their learning initiatives: support for leadership development.

Because 3CSN's experienced Reading Apprenticeship Project facilitators lead so many regional one-day workshops around the state, newer leadership community of practice participants have opportunities to take on parts of the facilitation and gain experience. In these regional settings, apprentice facilitators can build skills and confidence to tackle the sometimes more charged task of leading professional development activities on their home campus. Nika's own leadership trial by fire leads her to appreciate the difference:

> When I first learned about Reading Apprenticeship, I was expected to come right home and teach my colleagues. It was an unreasonable expectation. I needed time and space to learn myself, before putting myself out there as a leader in high-stakes situations. Now, we can support leadership development in a more authentic way.

Designing for Aliveness Perhaps the most important principle of 3CSN's Reading Apprenticeship Project is its respect for the evolving nature of learning and what Wenger and his colleagues refer to as *designing for aliveness* (2002).[12] Nika describes the synergy she sees between the Reading Apprenticeship Framework and learning communities that embody such aliveness:

> We have this amazing Framework to ground our work. I think that is very important. But given that, we have to make sure that we don't have rigid ideas about how the community of practice *should* make progress on their inquiry. Wenger and others have found that the most effective communities of practice design for evolution, open a dialogue between inside and outside perspectives, and invite different levels of participation.
>
> For example, we really emphasize that it's okay to lurk around RAP and observe for a while. You don't have to be all in to be welcomed and accepted. Most college professors, who begin to incorporate the Reading Apprenticeship Framework into their teaching experience significant, emotionally charged challenges associated with changing their instruction. It behooves us to recognize the resiliency and support that are often

needed to try something new and change. People don't need extra pressure—they are internally motivated to improve their practice and to do better for students. They just need a supportive community.

Community college professionals are always being told, "The bus is leaving. Get on board or you'll be left behind." I hate that. We don't do that. The truth is, there is no bus. There is an amazing, challenging, humbling, and worthy career to be had trying to help community colleges live up to their mission to provide high quality higher education for all. We can all expect to be working on it for our whole careers. To me, the Reading Apprenticeship Framework gives us a clear focus for our work. When professionals are invited to get involved and are not judged based on how they are participating, they tend to stick around.

Creating a Reading Apprenticeship STEM Community of Practice

3CSN has helped to change the culture of and attitudes about professional learning in California community colleges. Support for long-term professional learning is growing, and it is coupled with recognition of the importance of promoting academic literacy across the disciplines. For example, in a collaboration between 3CSN and the Strategic Literacy Initiative, and with funding from the Leona M. and Harry B. Helmsley Foundation, STEM faculty from seventeen California campuses have come together in a network of Reading Apprenticeship communities of practice, the Reading Apprenticeship Community College STEM Network, dedicated to increasing students' equitable access to science, technology, engineering, and mathematics courses and careers.

Much research on increasing access to STEM learning points to the value of metacognitive routines—the practice of making thinking visible that drives Reading Apprenticeship—to deepen students' ability to analyze disciplinary texts.[13] Network participants are exploring ways to bring metacognitive conversation into their courses and to involve their students in more active processing of the range of texts their courses demand. STEM faculty members are also investigating how the social and personal dimensions of the Reading Apprenticeship Framework can contribute to a positive context for student learning and to students' stronger academic identities.

The network is also designed to promote leadership development on individual campuses, across the seventeen campuses, and in the wider post-secondary STEM community. The network's differential opportunities for learning, engaging, building, and disseminating knowledge allow participating faculty members to follow individual paths in their own development and to learn from and support others in their communities of practice.

Building a Statewide Network from a Spark

In most states, community college faculties do not have an equivalent of the state-sponsored 3CSN organization and resources available in California. But that doesn't mean good ideas from 3CSN aren't crossing state borders.

In Washington, for example, Michele Lesmeister, Debbie Crumb, and others at Renton Technical College have made RTC a Reading Apprenticeship showcase (see Close-Up 1.4). And they have worked the state as well, presenting at diverse campuses and conferences and providing state-funded workshops for community college faculty.

Several of the state's community and technical colleges have been inspired by Renton's Achieving the Dream (AtD) Leader College narrative, in which Reading Apprenticeship is the featured innovation, and have infused Reading Apprenticeship into their own AtD scenarios.

And, a handful of leaders from these and other Washington campuses have also participated in the Reading Apprenticeship Leadership Community of Practice, which is convened by the Strategic Literacy Initiative and primarily populated with California educators.

Recently a critical mass of Washington leaders attended a two-day leadership community of practice meeting and were happily inspired by the energy and ideas flying around the room. At the end of the two days, when they reported out from their planning session what it was their Washington group would like to accomplish as a next step, they had decided on an outrageously ambitious goal—to hold a Washington statewide Reading Apprenticeship college conference within a year. Michele explains that they were more than inspired by their California colleagues:

> We were so impressed by what a powerful experience it is to be part of
> that learning community that we wanted to bring it to more of our
> colleagues in Washington. How could we bring people along? How do
> you really create a viable, live, energetic community of practice? What
> activities can pull people together and engage them in meaningful ways?
> How can we do it with no centralized funding or support?
>
> We kept talking—at the airport, on the plane. Then we went crazy
> emailing back and forth: "How can we do this?"

Michele and the Renton RATS (Reading Apprenticeship Teachers and Supporters) drew on the deep relationships they had built developing the Reading Apprenticeship presence on campus. RTC administrators agreed to host the all-day event, lend logistical and marketing support, and give fundraising efforts a home within the Renton Technical College Foundation. The Seattle Foundation provided $8,000 in seed money, and additional smaller donations followed.

Across the state, other Reading Apprenticeship leaders called on their networks, and the buzz began. On the morning that the Washington conference, Metacognition and Mindfulness: Academic Literacies for the 21st Century, got under way, 250 participants from thirty-two of the state's thirty-four community colleges and several state universities, colleges, and local service organizations gathered at RTC to share ideas and energy. Reading Apprenticeship practitioners from campuses around the state as well as leadership community of practice colleagues from California colleges presented a rich smorgasbord of sessions, and time for discussion and networking was built into the day. As the conference came to a close, participants were asked about their interest in another Reading Apprenticeship statewide conference. "Next year!" the crowd insisted. Michele attributes participants' enthusiasm to the Reading Apprenticeship Framework itself:

> There was a lot of energy because this was a new kind of conference. We really tried to use the four dimensions [of the Reading Apprenticeship Framework] in our planning and model that. People got greeted and welcomed when they came in—that doesn't happen in such an intentional and explicit way at most conferences. Presenters were practitioners in the field, dynamos, passionate, every single one of them. When you learn Reading Apprenticeship, how you work with other people is totally different. I think that the people who attended our conference saw that. We're not afraid to say, "I tried this, and it didn't work, but I'm going to try again." Participants were walking away with hands-on suggestions for improving their practice. It was teacherly.

With imitation being the highest form of flattery, the California faculty members who attended and presented at this conference left vowing to create a similar statewide Reading Apprenticeship college conference in California—their dates and venue already on the calendar.

■ ■ ■

As inspirational as these various local, regional, and statewide examples of building and growing momentum are, we also recognize that for many individuals or small teams, the challenges to sustained attention on improving teaching are significant—even through a lens as broad and powerful as Reading Apprenticeship.

However, the stories throughout this book leave us with hope that in the midst of challenging times, a vision inspired by empowered teaching, engaged learning, and a culture of literacy not only can endure but can grow—in whole schools and districts, across college campuses and regions, and in small pockets where fresh situations and new opportunities may yet arise.

Notes

1. Sometimes, support providers such as district coaches or site administrators do not have direct classroom experience with Reading Apprenticeship. In these instances, we strongly recommend that they borrow classrooms to build their experience base and credibility in supporting Reading Apprenticeship implementation.

2. Common Core Reading Anchor Standard 1: Read closely to determine what the text says explicitly and to make logical inferences from it; cite specific textual evidence when writing or speaking to support conclusions drawn from the text. Common Core Reading Anchor Standard 10: Read and comprehend complex literary and informational texts independently and proficiently.

3. *Reading for Understanding: How Reading Apprenticeship Improves Disciplinary Learning in Secondary and College Classrooms* introduces disciplinary literacy in terms of metacognition, increased opportunities for classroom reading, and the Reading Apprenticeship Framework.

4. An overview of the Reading Apprenticeship Academic Literacy (RAAL) course appears on the Reading Apprenticeship website (http://readingapprenticeship.org/publications/curriculum).

5. An average grade-to-grade increase in Lexile scores on the Scholastic Reading Inventory ranges from 200 Lexile units in grades 1 and 2 to as few as twenty-five units in grades 9 and 10. Source: Scholastic Inc. (2007). Scholastic Reading Inventory Technical Guide. New York: Scholastic Inc. Education Group. National Governors Association Center for Best Practices, Council of Chief State School Officers (http://encompass.ousd.k12.ca.us/files/SRI_-_Lexile_Scores_Chart.pdf).

6. See note 4.

7. The College 1 course includes an all-campus reading of a selected book and an accompanying speakers' series.

8. Acceleration is an approach for underprepared community college students that shortens the amount of time they must spend in remedial, non-credit-bearing courses while increasing the amount of challenging and well-supported work these courses provide.

9. 3CSN is the hub for a number of related California community college communities of practice. These 3CSN communities of practice (CoPs) share underlying principles of strengths-based instruction that welcomes and supports the legitimate peripheral participation of outsider or novice learners toward increasing engagement. Practitioners experience a coherent approach to learning across the CoPs—in professional as well as classroom learning. In addition to the Reading Apprenticeship Project, 3CSN supports CoPs organized by the California Acceleration Project, Habits of Mind, Threshold Project, Career and Technical Education, and the Learning Assistance Project (see http://3csn.org).

10. After years of experience building 3CSN, Deborah Harrington chose to write her UCLA doctoral dissertation about the impact of the interaction of Reading Apprenticeship and

communities of practice. See "You Can't Just Jump into the Icy Pool of Metacognition: The Value of Networking and Community Building in California Community Colleges' Reading Apprenticeship Project" (http://escholarship.org/uc/item/8tt0s8g0).

11. Although these courses and learning opportunities are still available, scholarships are no longer available through 3CSN. However, as the scholarships were intended, many recipients have assumed leadership roles on campuses that now support their own Reading Apprenticeship CoPs and other ways to learn about Reading Apprenticeship.

12. Wenger, E., McDermott, R., & Snyder, W. (2002). *Cultivating communities of practice: A guide to managing knowledge.* Cambridge, MA: Harvard Business School Press.

13. Kober, N. (2015). *Reaching students: What research says about effective instruction in undergraduate science and engineering.* Washington, DC: National Research Council.

Reading Apprenticeship Framework

THE READING APPRENTICESHIP® FRAMEWORK

SOCIAL DIMENSION
» Creating safety
» Investigating the relationship between literacy and power
» Sharing text talk
» Sharing reading processes, problems, and solutions
» Noticing and appropriating others' ways of reading

PERSONAL DIMENSION
» Developing reader identity
» Developing metacognition
» Developing reader fluency and stamina
» Developing reader confidence and range

COGNITIVE DIMENSION
» Getting the big picture
» Breaking it down
» Monitoring comprehension
» Using problem-solving strategies to assist and restore comprehension
» Setting reading purposes and adjusting reading processes

KNOWLEDGE-BUILDING DIMENSION
» Surfacing, building, and refining schema
» Building knowledge of content and the world
» Building knowledge of texts
» Building knowledge of language
» Building knowledge of disciplinary discourse and practices

METACOGNITIVE CONVERSATION

EXTENSIVE READING

The Research Rationale for Inquiry-Based Teacher Professional Development

THE DESIGN of Reading Apprenticeship professional development reflects the research knowledge base about effective teacher professional development. Research in the field—including our own studies—indicates a growing consensus about essential elements of effective professional development.[1] Among the important characteristics that have emerged from research studies are these:

- Focusing on how students learn in the subject area (in the case of Reading Apprenticeship, how students learn literacy and become more proficient literate practitioners in the disciplines);

- Involving teachers collectively in professional development;

- Providing active learning engagements for teachers, over sufficient time for new learning and inquiry practices to take root;

- Building coherence while transforming existing beliefs and practices; and

- Inviting collaborative problem solving and generativity to address the contexts in which people are working.[2]

A Focus on Student Learning

Professional development approaches that focus on analyzing student thinking, examining cases of teaching and learning, and reflecting on and critiquing one's own and others' teaching have been shown to develop teachers' pedagogical content knowledge[3] and have a positive impact on student learning of both subject area and literacy.[4] For example, Kennedy's review of professional development models (see note 1) succinctly summarizes these findings:

> Programs whose content focused mainly on teachers' behaviors
> demonstrated smaller influences on student learning than did programs
> whose content focused on teachers' knowledge of the subject, on the
> curriculum, or on how students learn the subject. Moreover, the
> knowledge that these more successful programs provided tended *not* to be

purely about the subject matter—that is, they were not courses in mathematics—but instead were about *how students learn* that subject matter. (p. 17)

Contrary to common practice in the field, then, offering teachers specific teaching techniques and prescriptions for structuring lessons turned out to be less effective than focusing on student learning and problem solving, using modeling techniques reflecting a "cognitive apprenticeship" approach to teaching. In studies of professional development, when professional development led to increased student achievement, professional development invariably centered directly on helping teachers better understand both what they teach and how students acquire specific content knowledge and skill.[5] This makes sense to us: to navigate the complexities of teaching, teachers need generative professional knowledge—knowledge that allows them to generate effective responses to students' thinking in the moment of teaching.[6] The lesson we draw from this research base is that while pedagogical repertoire matters, building teachers' deep understandings of how students learn particular subject matter through ongoing inquiries into literacy tasks, student work, and the like will be more effective than professional development focused on teaching technique alone.

Collective Participation

Research into teacher learning has also shown that encouraging discourse, or collective participation, around problems of practice helps teachers to delve deeply into issues of teaching and learning.[7]

When teachers from the same school interact in an ongoing way around problems of practice—whether by grade, department, or school-wide—their collective participation becomes the basis for effective professional learning communities.[8]

Effective collective participation activities include examining and analyzing artifacts of practice such as video cases and student work for evidence of student thinking and teacher decision making.[9] In inquiry communities with a focus on literacy, collective participation would include making sense of literacy tasks, making sense of student literacy performance, and working together to design instruction to support high literacy attainment for particular students.

Active Modes of Learning

Active modes of sense making and inquiry into teaching and learning have long been related to the effectiveness of professional development.[10] Professional development activities of the kind already described will necessarily entail opportunities for teachers to engage in active learning.[11] With teachers' limited time, it is encouraging to know that specific routines can meet several criteria for high-quality professional development simultaneously.

Building Coherence

The beliefs teachers bring to professional development exert a powerful influence on their development of new concepts and understandings, and professional development needs to engage these preconceptions at the same time as it challenges them.[12] Thus, in addition to the qualities of professional development discussed so far, some studies indicate that professional development is most effective when its content and focus are aligned with teachers' existing beliefs and practices as well as with the policies that mandate them.[13] In the arena of discipline-specific literacy, we disagree. In this arena, pedagogy that focuses on literacy in the subject areas is so new for many teachers that their learning must be disruptive of former practices and beliefs. In fact, we think professional development is best when it respectfully engages teachers in overturning prior conceptions—about literacy, about learning, and about student capacity.[14]

Nonetheless, Huberman observes that teachers engage in a process of *bricolage*, or tinkering, by which they unknowingly assimilate new ideas into their current practices and adjust the new to fit prior knowledge and experiences. Yet to *transform* the nature of instruction, it is essential to change the theories that inform teachers' decision-making processes.[15] We have found that transforming instruction—making subject area classrooms different places to think and learn—requires professional development that challenges teachers' beliefs and practices, provides support for resolving the resulting cognitive dissonance, and responds to teachers' needs for pragmatic solutions to problems of practice by offering a repertoire of tools and strategies consistent with these new understandings.[16]

Inviting Adaptive Expertise and Generative Problem Solving

In contrast to a conception of teaching as fidelity to preexisting instructional strategies, we hold the view that for practice to become truly responsive to the learner needs and varied contexts of teachers' work, teachers must become adaptive and generative in their use of specific practices.

Teachers work best when they are authorized to flexibly adapt ideas and practices to their specific circumstances. When teachers view their work as ongoing inquiry, they can work together to co-design, implement, and study the effects of educational innovations and how to make them work within particular authentic, richly complex contexts.[17]

Our own work attests to the ways that empowered teachers can help to generate knowledge and instructional solutions. We have collaborated with communities of educators over the past twenty years and more to iteratively develop, try out, and refine the Reading Apprenticeship Framework and models and tools for student and teacher learning. Working closely with teachers ensures that our work is informed by teachers' experiences and expertise, and that the challenges teachers and students face when engaging with new instructional practices enter into the very early processes of designing new materials and approaches for professional development and classrooms.[18]

Researchers since McLaughlin and Berman in the 1970s have recognized that context matters—that, for example, implementing Reading Apprenticeship in a high school chemistry class will be different from implementing it in a community college chemistry class. As Victoria Gillis argues,[19] disciplinary literacy calls for adaptation rather than mere adoption of existing literacy strategies. Innovation and adaptation are expected and are, in fact, required by the integration of literacy and disciplinary practice. Similarly, Cynthia Coburn and her colleagues have described and elaborated the idea of teacher ownership of education reform.[20] Since teachers are the orchestrators of classroom practices and interactions, the extent to which they own the process of change and the ideas and principles underlying their work in the classroom, that is the extent to which change will actually occur.

To recognize, and authorize, teacher ownership of Reading Apprenticeship, we have developed the term *flexible fidelity* as a way to talk with our practitioner colleagues about what good adaptation of Reading Apprenticeship instruction and professional development looks like: Flexible fidelity to the Reading Apprenticeship model embodies the core principles of the model while making adaptations to particular contexts. To foster adaptive expertise, we refer teachers and professional development facilitators back to the Reading Apprenticeship Framework as a touchstone, and we ask them to inquire of themselves and each other how they are weaving the core principles of Reading Apprenticeship into their work. We invite them to engage in ongoing reflection on their practice.[21] We emphasize the centrality of the inquiry stance for classroom and professional learning. And we ask them to stay focused on who is doing the work of reading and comprehending in the class—they or their students. Ongoing examination and reflection with the Framework as a touchstone is thus key to navigating with flexible fidelity, in particular contexts. What we are after, ultimately, is teacher professionalism and generativity, as teachers participate knowledgeably in ongoing innovation and the development of improving practice.

A recent interaction with a middle school teacher illustrates the power of teacher ownership in this work of fostering engaged academic literacy and learning. In her classroom, a new student transferred in from a neighboring school that had not been participating in Reading Apprenticeship. She asked the student if he knew how to Talk to the Text, and he shook his head. One of her students said, as though to take the newbie under his wing, "You'll get used to it. Talking to the Text is what we do here." Another student piped up, "It's not just what we do here, it's *all* we do here. It's our culture."

Outcomes of Our Studies

We value the considerable intelligence and resourcefulness of the young people and adult learners we serve and aim to empower these students to take on more engaged, confident, competent, and literate identities in their various worlds of school, community, and work. Because of this mission, we have continuously gathered evidence to measure the impact of our inquiry-based professional development practices on teachers' knowledge, their classroom practices, and their students' learning. In one multiyear study of subject area teachers who participated in a Reading Apprenticeship professional development network, we examined the impact of these inquiry methods on twenty nine participating teachers' knowledge growth and change over two years.[22]

Additionally, we carried out close case studies tracing the changing thinking, instructional planning, and classroom practice of eight of these teachers. Data included interviews with teachers at the beginning and end of each of the two years; teachers' written reflections and evaluations; and audio- and videotapes of teachers engaging in reading process analysis, text analysis, analysis of students' reading processes, and collegial conversations about practice during professional development meetings. We also collected classroom artifacts such as lesson plans, assignments, and student work. Growth in students' reading engagement and comprehension was measured through pre-post surveys and a standardized test of reading comprehension at the beginning and end of each year.

In this study, we found that participating teachers became more aware of the complex ways in which they themselves made sense of a variety of texts, and they gained new appreciation for the reading difficulties students may face. They also developed a language for talking about invisible comprehension practices, which are, at times, difficult to articulate. They came to understand, by reading in the company of colleagues who may approach texts very differently, that their own ways of reading are learned conventions that can and must be taught to students. In turn, these changes helped teachers create classroom environments that were characterized by high student engagement and self-direction, high expectations for student performance, frequent collaboration between and among teachers and students, and high accountability on the part both of teachers and of students for student learning. Moreover, this pedagogy was *motivated from within* by teachers who now understood what reading entails and what texts demand, and who had the means to assist students in gaining this kind of strategic knowledge for themselves.

Importantly, students in these classrooms came to see reading as an active and strategic process. Taken as a group, students in these urban classrooms, behind their age-mates nationally on a standardized measure of reading comprehension, gained substantially more than a year's expected growth.[23] More recently, we have tested the inquiry-based Reading Apprenticeship professional development model with the rigorous methods of randomized controlled trials. In one such trial, we designed a study to examine the effects of the professional development model on teachers' ability to integrate disciplinary literacy practices into science teaching in high school biology classes, exploring the resulting changes in teacher knowledge and instructional practices, and changes in student achievement in science and reading. Schools were matched for demographics and student achievement, and teachers were randomly assigned to intervention and control groups. The study targeted schools serving high numbers of African American and Latino students as well as English learners and students from low socioeconomic groups. The study included multiple measures of teacher implementation and student learning over multiple time points to trace the linkages between the generative model of professional development in literacy for science teachers to these teachers' instructional practices and their students' engagement and learning in literacy and science.[24]

The results of the study were promising: Intervention teachers demonstrated greater use of metacognitive inquiry routines and greater support for science literacy learning, reading comprehension instruction, and collaborative learning structures compared to teachers in the control group. Students in the intervention classrooms performed better than control students on state standardized assessments in English language arts, reading comprehension, and biology. In addition, these students held more robust identities as science readers and learners, viewing themselves as more capable of rigorous science reading compared to students in the control group. This effect was even more profound for English learners.

In sum, the effectiveness of the methods of professional development we offer are supported by the knowledge base of the field of professional development and by our own studies, whether deep and textured or randomized and controlled.

Notes

1. Bransford, J. D., Brown, A. L., & Cocking, R. R. (Eds.). (1999). *How people learn: Brain, mind, experience, and school*. Washington, DC: National Academy Press.

   Desimone, L. M. (2009). Improving impact studies of teachers' professional development: Toward better conceptualizations and measures. *Educational Researcher, 38*(3), 181–199.

   Garet, M. S., Porter, A. C., Desimone, L., Birman, B. F., & Yoon, K. S. (2001). What makes professional development effective? Results from a national sample of teachers. *American Educational Research Journal, 38*(4), 915–945.

   Kennedy, M. (1998). *Form and substance in inservice teacher education* (Research Monograph No. 13). Madison: University of Wisconsin-Madison, National Institute for Science Education.

   Loucks-Horsley, S., & Matsumoto, C. (1999). Research on professional development for teachers of mathematics and science. *School Science and Mathematics, 99*(5), 258–271.

   Reed, D. K. (2009). A synthesis of professional development on the implementation of literacy strategies for middle school content area teachers. *Research in Middle Level Education Online, 32*(10), 1–12.

   Yoon, K. S., Duncan, T., Lee, S. W.-Y., Scarloss, B., & Shapley, K. (2007). *Reviewing the evidence on how teacher professional development affects student achievement* (Issues and Answers Report REL 2007 No. 033). Washington, DC: U.S. Department of Education, Institute of Education Sciences, National Center for Education Evaluation and Regional Assistance, Regional Education Laboratory Southwest.

2. Coburn, C. E. (2003). Rethinking scale: Moving beyond numbers to deep and lasting change. *Educational Researcher, 32*(6), 3–12.

   Darling-Hammond, L., Wei, R. C., Andree, A., Richardson, N., & Orphanos, S. (2009). *Professional learning in the learning profession: A status report on teacher development in the United States and abroad*. Dallas: National Staff Development Council.

3. Shulman, L. S. (1986). Those who understand: Knowledge growth in teaching. *Educational Researcher, 15*, 4–14.

   Shulman, L. S. (1987). Knowledge and teaching: Foundations of the new reform. *Harvard Educational Review, 57*, 1–22.

4. Abell, S. A. (2008). Twenty years later: Does pedagogical content knowledge remain a useful idea? *International Journal of Science Education, 30*(10), 1405–1416.

   Greenleaf, C. L., Litman, C., Hanson, T. L., Rosen, R., Boscardin, C. K., Herman, J., et al. (2011). Integrating literacy and science in biology: Teaching and learning impacts of Reading Apprenticeship professional development. *American Educational Research Journal, 48*(3), 647–717.

   Guskey, T. R., & Yoon, K. S. (2009). What works in professional development? *Phi Delta Kappan, 90*(7), 495–500.

   Kennedy, M. (1998). *Form and substance in inservice teacher education* (see note 1).

Loucks-Horsley, S., & Matsumoto, C. (1999). Research on professional development (see note 1).

Reed, D. K. (2009). A synthesis of professional development (see note 1).

vanDriel, J. H., Beijaard, D., & Verloop, N. (2001). Professional development and reform in science education: The role of teachers' practical knowledge. *Journal of Research in Science Teaching, 38*(2), 137–158.

5. Guskey, T. R., & Yoon, K. S. (2009). What works in professional development? (see note 4).

6. Boston, M. D., & Smith, M. S. (2009). Transforming secondary mathematics teaching: Increasing the cognitive demands of instructional tasks used in teachers' classrooms. *Journal for Research in Mathematics Education, 40*(2), 119–156.

Cohen, D., & Ball, D. (2000). *Instructional innovation: Reconsidering the story* (Working Paper). The Study of Instructional Improvement. Retrieved from http://www.sii.soe.umich.edu/documents/InstructionalInnovation.pdf

Schoenbach, R., & Greenleaf, C. (2009). Fostering adolescents' engaged academic literacy. In L. Christenbury, R. Bomer, & P. Smagorinsky (Eds.), *Handbook of adolescent literacy research,* (pp. 98–112). New York: Guilford Press.

7. Borko, H. (2004). Professional development and teacher learning: Mapping the terrain. *Educational Researcher, 33*(8), 3–15.

Fullan, M. (1991). *The new meaning of educational change.* New York: Teachers College Press.

Guskey, T. R. (2002). Professional development and teacher change. *Teachers and Teaching: Theory and Practice, 8*(3/4), 381–391.

Loucks-Horsley, S., & Matsumoto, C. (1999). Research on professional development (see note 1).

Richardson, V. (Ed.). (1994). *Teacher change and the staff development process.* New York: Teachers College Press.

8. Camburn, E., Rowan, B., & Taylor, J.E. (2003). Distributed leadership in schools: The case of elementary schools adopting comprehensive school reform models. *Educational Evaluation and Policy Analysis, 25,* 347–373.

Clark, K., & Borko, H. (2004). Establishing a professional learning community among middle school mathematics teachers. In M. J. Hoines & A. Fuglestad (Eds.), *Proceedings of the 28th Conference of the International Group for the Psychology of Mathematics Education* (Vol. 2, pp. 223–230). Bergen, Norway: Bergen University College.

Grossman, P., Wineburg, S., & Woolworth, S. (2001). Toward a theory of teacher community. *Teachers College Record, 103,* 942–1012.

McLaughlin, M. W., & Talbert, J. E. (2001). *Professional communities and the work of high school teaching.* Chicago: University of Chicago Press.

9. Desimone, L. M., Garet, M., Birman, B., Porter, A., & Yoon, K. S. (2002). How do district management and implementation strategies relate to the quality of the professional development that districts provide to teachers? *Teachers College Record, 104*(7), 1265–1312.

Fennema, E., Carpenter, T. P., Franke, M. L., Levi, L., Jacobs, V. R., & Empson, S. B. (1996). A longitudinal study of learning to use children's thinking in mathematics instruction. *Journal for Research in Mathematics Education, 27*(4), 403–434.

Kazemi, E., & Franke, M. L. (2004). Teacher learning in mathematics: Using student work to promote collective inquiry. *Journal of Mathematics Teacher Education, 7*, 203–235.

Little, J. W. (2001, September). *Inside teacher community: Representations of classroom practice.* Paper presented as an invited address at the biannual conference of the International Study Association on Teachers and Teaching, Faro, Portugal.

Little, J. W. (2002). Locating learning in teachers' communities of practice: Opening up problems of analysis in records of everyday work. *Teaching and Teaching Education, 18*, 917–946.

Shulman, L. S. (1986). Those who understand (see note 2).

Shulman, L. S. (1987). Knowledge and teaching (see note 2).

vanDriel, J. H., Beijaard, D., & Verloop, N. (2001). Professional development and reform (see note 4).

10. Ball, D., & Cohen, D. (1999). Developing practice, developing practitioners: Toward a practice-based theory of professional education. In L. Darling-Hammond & D. Sykes (Eds.), *Teaching as the learning profession: Handbook of policy and practice.* San Francisco: Jossey-Bass.

Guskey, T. R., & Huberman, M. (1996). *Professional development in education: New paradigms and practices.* New York: Teachers College Press.

Kennedy, M. (1998). *Form and substance* (see note 1).

Loucks-Horsley, S., Love, N., Styles, K. E., Mundry, S., & Hewson, P. W. (2003). *Designing professional development for teachers of science and mathematics.* Thousand Oaks, CA: Corwin Press.

Sparks, D., & Hirsh, S. (1997). *A new vision for staff development: Results-driven education, systems thinking, and constructivism.* Oxford, OH: National Staff Development Council.

Wilson, S. M., & Berne, J. (1999). Teacher learning and the acquisition of professional knowledge: An examination of research on contemporary professional development. *Review of Research in Education, 24*, 173–209.

11. Borko, H. (2004). Professional development and teacher learning (see note 7).

Darling-Hammond, L., Wei, R. C., Andree, A., Richardson, N., & Orphanos, S. (2009). Professional learning (see note 2).

Garet, M. S., Porter, A. C., Desimone, L., Birman, B. F., & Yoon, K. S. (2001). What makes professional development effective? (see note 1).

12. Pajares, M. F. (1992). Teachers' beliefs and educational research: Cleaning up a messy construct. *Review of Educational Research, 62*, 307–332.

Spillane, J. P. (1999). External reform initiatives and teachers' efforts to reconstruct their practice: The mediating role of teachers' zones of enactment. *Journal of Curriculum Studies, 31*(2), 143–175.

13. Desimone, L. M. (2009). Improving impact studies (see note 1).

Garet, M. S., Porter, A. C., Desimone, L., Birman, B. F., & Yoon, K. S. (2001). What makes professional development effective? (see note 1).

14. Zhang, J., Hong, H. Y., Scardamalia, M., Teo, C. L., & Morley, E. A. (2011). Sustaining knowledge building as a principle-based innovation at an elementary school. *The Journal of the Learning Sciences, 20*(2), 262–307.

15. Boston, M. D., & Smith, M. S. (2009). Transforming secondary mathematics teaching (see note 5).

Bransford, J., Derry, S., Berliner, D., & Hammerness, K. (2005). Theories of learning and their role in teaching. In L. Darling-Hammond & J. Bransford (Eds.), *Preparing teachers for a changing world* (pp. 40–87). San Francisco: Jossey-Bass.

Huberman, M. (1995). Networks that alter teaching: Conceptualizations, exchanges and experiments. *Teachers and Teaching: Theory and Practice, 1*(2), 193–211.

vanDriel, J. H., Beijaard, D., & Verloop, N. (2001). Professional development and reform (see note 4).

Whigham, M., Andre, T., & Yang, E. (2000, April). *Elementary and secondary teachers' beliefs about and instructional emphasis on the National Mathematics Education and Science Education Standards.* Paper presented at the annual meeting of the National Association of Research in Science Teaching, New Orleans, LA.

16. Greenleaf, C., & Schoenbach, R. (2004). Building capacity for the responsive teaching of reading in the academic disciplines: Strategic inquiry designs for middle and high school teachers' professional development. In D. S. Strickland & M. L. Kamil (Eds.), *Improving reading achievement through professional development* (pp. 85–96). Norwood, MA: Christopher-Gordon Publishers.

Loucks-Horsley, S., & Matsumoto, C. (1999). Research on professional development (see note 1).

17. Klingner, J. K., Boardman, A. G., & McMaster, K. L. (2013). What does it take to scale up and sustain evidence-based practices? *Exceptional Children, 79*(2), 195–211.

Ormel, B. B., Pareja Roblin, N. N., McKenney, S. E., Voogt, J. M., & Pieters, J. M. (2012). Research-practice interactions as reported in recent design studies: Still promising, still hazy. *Educational Technology Research and Development, 60*(6), 967–986.

18. Gutiérrez, K. D., & Penuel, W. R. (2014). Relevance to practice as a criterion for rigor. *Educational Researcher, 43*(1), 19–23.

Voogt, J., Laferrière, T., Breuleux, A., Itow, R. C., Hickey, D. T., & McKenney, S. (2015). Collaborative design as a form of professional development. *Instructional Science*, 1–24.

19. Gillis, V. (2014). Disciplinary literacy. *Journal of Adolescent & Adult Literacy, 57*(8), 614–623.

20. Coburn, C. E., & Stein, M. K. (2010). *Research and practice in education: Building alliances, bridging the divide.* Lanham, MD: Rowman & Littlefield Publishers.

21. Fenstermacher, G. D., & Richardson, V. (1993). The elicitation and reconstruction of practical arguments in teaching. *Journal of Curriculum Studies, 25*(2), 101–114.

Richardson, V. (1990). Significant and worthwhile change in teaching practice. *Educational Researcher, 19*, pp. 10–19.

22. Greenleaf, C., & Katz, M. (2004). Ever newer ways to mean: Authoring pedagogical change in secondary subject-area classrooms. In S. W. Freedman & A. F. Ball (Eds.), *Bakhtinian perspectives on language, literacy, and learning* (pp. 172–202). Cambridge, UK: Cambridge University Press.

Greenleaf, C., & Schoenbach, R. (2001). *Close readings: A study of key issues in the use of literacy learning cases for the professional development of secondary teachers.* Final report to the Spencer and MacArthur Foundations Professional Development Research and Documentation Program. Oakland, CA: Strategic Literacy Initiative, WestEd.

23. See note 22.

24. Greenleaf, C. L., Litman, C., Hanson, T. L., Rosen, R., Boscardin, C. K., Herman, J., et al. (2011). Integrating literacy and science (see note 4).

Assessment Tools

Reading Apprenticeship Teacher Practice Rubric

The Reading Apprenticeship Teacher Practice Rubric has six main goals, each with a number of subgoals. Teachers can focus in one or more of the goal areas, or they can reflect on their growth across the board as Reading Apprenticeship practitioners.

Goal 1: Reading Opportunities				
	4	**3**	**2**	**1**
Role of Reading				
Relationship of reading to other classroom learning activities	Essential to and deeply integrated	Supportive and related but not deeply integrated	Supplementary and related but not integrated	Peripheral; not typically or not integrated
Literacy goals and plans for reading instruction	Explicit and elaborate	Explicit	Very vague or narrow	Not explicit
Collaborative inquiry into how and why we read	Frequent and routine	Often	Occasional or not deliberate	Rare or absent
Frequency				
Assigned reading	Frequent and routine	Often	Occasional	Rare or absent
Volume				
All reading materials the teacher assigns per year	1,000 pages (equivalent of a standard textbook)	750 pages (equivalent of 3/4 of a standard textbook)	500 pages (equivalent of 1/2 of a standard textbook)	250 pages or fewer (equivalent of 1/4 or less of a standard textbook)
Accountability				
Teacher assessment of reading _comprehension_	Frequent and routine	Often	Occasional or often (but for completion only)	Rare or absent (or for completion only)
Teacher duplication of content from reading through lecture or presentation	Rare or absent	Occasional	Frequent	Frequent and routine
Student accomplishment of class expectations without reading	Rare or absent	Occasional	Frequent	Frequent and routine
Breadth[1]				
Assignment of multiple genres or text types	Frequent: five or more	Often: four	Occasional: three	Frequent and routine: zero to two

Frequent: In every, or nearly every, lesson.
Often: At least half but less than every lesson (two to three per week).
Occasional: Less than half of all lessons (one to two per week).
Rare or absent (zero to one per week).
[1] Teacher may expand breadth by using the range of genres or text types found in the textbook (e.g., graphs, data, visuals, narrative, exposition) or by supplementing with additional text types (e.g., lab materials, primary sources, newspapers, magazines, internet articles).

Goal 2: Teacher Support for Student Efforts to Comprehend Content From Text				
	4	**3**	**2**	**1**
Proximity of Support				
Student reading during class time	Frequent and routine	Often	Occasional	Rare or absent
Teacher mentoring and social support for reading and comprehending	Deliberate, frequent and routine	Deliberate and often	Occasional and informal, not deliberate	Rare or absent (or reading is independent)
Reading assigned outside of class time	Rare early in the year (may increase with student capacity)	Occasional, especially early in the year (may increase with student capacity)	Often	Routine (if any)
Teacher Support for Effort				
Student agency fostered by promoting and orchestrating *students' efforts* to solve problems and comprehend reading	Frequent and routine	Often	Occasional or informal (not deliberate)	Rare or absent
Teacher removal of student struggle by giving answers, solving comprehension problems, or presenting content	Rare or absent	Occasional	Often	Frequent and routine
Student Practice				
Work by students to comprehend content from text	Frequent and routine	Often	Occasional	Rare or absent
Formative Assessment of Efforts to Comprehend				
Teacher assessment of students' comprehension *during reading* to support students' efforts to *comprehend*	Frequent and routine	Often	Occasional (or assessment often occurs after reading, with a focus only on correct answers and completion)	Rare or absent (or assessment routinely occurs after reading, with a focus only on correct answers and completion)

Frequent: In every, or nearly every, lesson.
Often: At least half but less than every lesson (two to three per week).
Occasional: Less than half of all lessons (one to two per week).
Rare or absent (zero to one per week).

Goal 3:   Metacognitive Inquiry into Reading and Thinking Processes

	4	3	2	1
Metacognitive Conversation[2]				
"Reading" involves *talk* about metacognition—noticing and taking control of reading, thinking, and sense-making processes (in addition to talk about reading content)	Frequent and routine	Often	Occasional	Rare or absent
Characterization of metacognitive conversation about reading and thinking	Thematic, deeply integrated, central, pervasive	Deliberate but limited to particular activities or times	Informal, spontaneous, incidental	Rare or absent
Teacher Support				
Explicit modeling and instruction in tools, strategies, and routines to support metacognitive conversation about reading and thinking processes	Frequent and routine	Often	Occasional	Rare or absent
Explicit modeling and instruction of a range of reading and thinking processes used by self-monitoring, self-governing readers of the discipline	Ongoing and strategically scaffolded	Ongoing and scaffolded to some extent	Occasional	Rare or absent
Teacher modeling emphasizes reading and thinking processes rather than procedures	Frequent and routine	Often and ongoing to some extent	Occasional (or jump-start at beginning of year)	Rare or absent
Student Practice[3]				
Student practice of metacognitive reading and comprehension-monitoring routines, tools, and strategies	Frequent and routine	Often	Occasional	Rare or absent
Approach to Challenges				
Teacher encouragement of and support for students to grapple with challenging texts, tasks, and concepts	Frequent and routine	Often (or frequent with *limited* teacher support)	Occasional (or often with *little* teacher support)	Rare or absent
Accountability/Assessment of Metacognition				
Teacher collection and assessment of *students' reading and thinking processes*	Frequent and routine (ongoing assessment of metacognition with two or more measures)	Often (over time assessment of metacognition may become more intermittent or shift to content)	Occasional (or often assesses only content)	Rare or absent (or assesses only content)

Frequent: In every, or nearly every, lesson.
Often: At least half but less than every lesson (two to three per week).
Occasional: Less than half of all lessons (one to two per week).
Rare or absent (zero to one per week).

[2] If conversation focuses exclusively on confusions about and understanding of content, score as Goal 2, subgoal Student Practice.

[3] If routines focus on content and answers rather than on reading and thinking processes (e.g., double-entry reading logs focused on facts and examples), score as Goal 4, subgoal Instruction and Routines.

Goal 4: Specific Reading Comprehension Routines, Tools, Strategies,[4] and Processes				
	4	**3**	**2**	**1**
Instruction and Routines				
Explicit teacher instruction in a set of comprehension strategies and reading approaches used by experienced readers of the discipline	A robust set	A useful set	A limited set	A very limited set or no set
Instruction engages students in solving reading comprehension problems and challenges	Frequent and routine (across a large range of challenges, problems, texts)	Often (across a range of challenges, problems, or texts)	Occasional (or across a limited range of challenges, problems, or texts)	Rare or absent
Explicit Instruction and Modeling				
Frequency	Frequent and routine	Often	Occasional (or beginning of the year only)	Rare or absent
Focus	Flexible use across a range of texts and tasks	Flexible use	Use for demonstrating comprehension and correct form or procedures	Use for demonstrating correct form or procedures
Student Practice				
Student practice using comprehension strategies during reading of core texts to support sense making	Frequent and routine (during both guided and independent practice)	Often	Occasional (or typically after reading, to demonstrate comprehension)	Rare or absent (or only after reading, to demonstrate comprehension)
Accountability for Using Comprehension Strategies				
Accountable expectations that students use comprehension strategies during reading of core texts to support sense making	Frequent and routine	Often	Occasional	Rare or absent
Assessment of Comprehension Strategies				
Assessment, monitoring, reteaching, and guided practice in the use of comprehension strategies during reading of core texts to support sense making	Frequent and routine	Often	Occasional	Rare or absent

Frequent: In every, or nearly every, lesson.
Often: At least half but less than every lesson (two to three per week).
Occasional: Less than half of all lessons (one to two per week).
Rare or absent (zero to one per week).
[4] "Strategies" broadly include comprehension-supporting strategies and routines, disciplinary reading approaches, and approaches to monitoring and controlling attention, comprehension, and engagement. See Chapter Six in *Reading for Understanding*.

Goal 5:   Collaboration

	4	3	2	1
Frequency				
Student collaborative work	Frequent and routine	Often	Occasional	Rare or absent
Structures and Routines				
Characterization of routines and participation structures to support collaborative meaning making	Strategic, engineered, very routine, very productive, run smoothly	Deliberate, routine, productive, limited in number or purpose	Informal, incidental, infrequent	Rare or absent; may be pragmatic based on sharing resources
Teacher Support[5]				
Teacher modeling and mentoring students in participation and discourse norms; collaborative processes; and disciplinary reading, thinking, and discourse routines	Frequent and routine, substantial metacognitive conversation about how to collaborate	Often, some metacognitive conversation about how to collaborate	Occasional, may focus on task procedures	Rare or absent
Tools for Equitable Participation[6]				
Teacher use of routines, structures, and interventions that result in the participation of all students in small-group and whole-class activities	Frequent and routine	Often	Occasional	Rare or absent
Assessment and Accountability for Collaboration[7]				
Teacher assessment of group work for evidence of collaborative processes and learning	Frequent and routine	Often (emphasis may be on procedures or steps in task)	Occasional (emphasis may be on compliance or on-task behavior)	Rare or absent
Accountable expectations for contributions to the group and for the learning of individual members[8]	Frequent and routine	Often (may sometimes be assessed on individual contribution, product)	Occasional (generally assessed on individual work)	Rare or absent (always or almost always assessed on individual work)

Frequent: In every, or nearly every, lesson.
Often: At least half but less than every lesson (two to three per week).
Occasional: Less than half of all lessons (one to two per week).
Rare or absent (zero to one per week).
[5] For example, sentence frames for inquiry and disagreeing, modeling turn taking, coaching students in leadership roles.
[6] For example, randomized reporting out (popsicle sticks, names from a hat), itinerant mentoring, rotating group roles, turn-taking routines.
[7] For example, moves and monitors, makes notes about participation, supports self-assessment.
[8] For example, rubrics for self-assessment of group participation, group and individual grades; group grade dependent on all members achieving the set criteria.

Goal 6: Instruction that Promotes Equity				
	4	**3**	**2**	**1**
Teacher Agency				
Teacher perception of unwanted student behavior as malleable and subject to the influence of instructional decisions	Frequent and routine	Often	Occasional	Rare or absent
Instructional decision making guided by the question "Will this encourage or discourage this student from investing himself or herself in the learning process?"	Frequent and routine	Often	Occasional	Rare or absent
Teacher expression of confidence in his or her ability to positively influence student performance and engagement	Frequent and routine	Often	Occasional	Rare or absent
High Standards Supported by Differentiated Instruction[9]				
Literacy routines and assignments that engage all students in complex discipline-based literacy	Frequent and routine	Often	Occasional	Rare or absent
Teacher differentiation of instruction for groups and individuals using a broad array of modification and accommodation approaches	Frequent and routine	Often	Occasional	Rare or absent
Students gain proficiency and capacity in academic reading (on multiple measures)	All or nearly all, including most underprepared or underperforming students	Many, including many underprepared or underperforming students	Some, including mostly high-performing students	A few, including almost exclusively high-performing students
Routines and assignments are open-ended to promote participation and success of a wide range of students	Frequent and routine	Often	Occasional	Rare or absent
Negotiating Success[10]				
Teacher learning environment, practices, and policies motivate and support disengaged students	Frequent and routine	Often	Occasional	Rare or absent

Frequent: In every, or nearly every, lesson.
Often: At least half but less than every lesson (two to three per week).
Occasional: Less than half of all lessons (one to two per week).
Rare or absent (zero to one per week).

[9] For example, differentiation strategies might include selecting texts and designing units of study to support student interest and strengths; scaffolding complex tasks by, for example, chunking and using graphic organizers, sentence stems, or bookmarks; negotiating due dates, credit, task structure; engaging students in self-assessment and goal setting; explicitly teaching disciplinary reading comprehension strategies and approaches. Grouping strategies might include heterogeneous grouping to take advantage of peer mentoring and scaffolding, homogenous grouping for small-group mentoring and coaching, and groups based on reading levels. Formative assessment would respond to literacy growth over time.

[10] For example, strategies for engaging disinvested students might include highlighting progress, growth, and strengths; negotiating credit and due dates; supporting self-assessment; being available outside of class for instructional purposes to encourage students to seek help; explicitly teaching good-student skills; finding opportunities for less-experienced students to show their expertise; rewarding incremental steps toward success; engineering flexible groups to leverage interest and social connections.

Reading Apprenticeship Student Learning Goals

Student Learning Goals let students in on all the ways they can expect their reading and learning to grow in a Reading Apprenticeship classroom. They also allow the teacher and students to monitor growth.

How to Use Student Learning Goals

The learning goals are organized in sets that parallel the dimensions of the Reading Apprenticeship Framework.

Social Dimension: Collaborating in a Community of Readers and Writers Goals

These goals may be introduced as a set after the Setting Norms for Learning activity (*Reading for Understanding*, Box 3.4), for example, with students invited to highlight those they intend to focus on.

Personal Dimension: Building Personal Engagement Goals

This set of goals may be introduced after the Personal Reading History activity (*Reading for Understanding*, Box 3.9), for example, with students invited to highlight those they intend to focus on.

Metacognitive Conversation: Making Thinking Visible Goals

This short set of goals may be introduced after students have been introduced to metacognition with nonreading activities that illustrate their ability to think about their thinking. (See Chapter Four in *Reading for Understanding*, particularly Box 4.2 and Classroom Close-Up 4.1.)

Cognitive Dimension: Using Cognitive Strategies to Increase Comprehension Goals

After students have been introduced to a number of the reading strategies, it may be effective for them to read over the list of cognitive goals, to Talk to the Text (annotate the list with their questions and ideas), and to notice how many of these goals they are already working on and which ones they are curious about.

Knowledge-Building Dimension: Knowledge-Building Goals

As with the cognitive goals, these are best introduced with a Talk to the Text activity after students have experienced a number of them, so that they can be impressed with those they have already learned and anticipate others.

Customized learning goals are provided for four subject areas: science, history, literature, and mathematics. In each subject area, the set of goals is the same in the social and personal dimensions and for metacognitive conversation. The learning goals vary somewhat by subject area in the cognitive dimension and are entirely discipline specific in the knowledge dimension.

If students have selected goals to focus on, from time to time they will want to reflect on how successfully they are meeting their goals and perhaps focus on new goals.

At the end of a course, students can select a small subset of goals (e.g., two in each of the five categories) in which they think they have made progress—progress that they can document with early and later work samples, or with metrics like the amount of time they are able to stay focused on their reading or the number of pages they are able to complete now, compared with at the beginning of the course.

Students may also enjoy simply checking off *all* the goals they feel they have accomplished or grown in using. Teachers report that the goals make students feel successful (and even surprised by how much they have learned).

Student Learning Goals: Science

Collaborating in a Community of Readers and Writers

Contributing to Our Community	I contribute to maintaining a classroom community that feels safe, where everyone is able to take risks and grow.
Collaborating Effectively	I work with partners and groups in ways that are both respectful and risk-taking.
Participating Thoughtfully	I make my thinking count in discussions, as a speaker and a listener. I share my reading confusions and understandings to get and give help. I listen and learn from the reading confusions and understandings of others.
Building a Literacy Context	I understand and use the shared literacy vocabulary of our classroom.
Being Open to New Ideas	I appreciate and evaluate alternative viewpoints.
Developing a Literacy Agenda	I read to understand how literacy opens and closes doors in people's lives.
Sharing Books	I talk about books I am reading to involve others in what the books have to offer.
Writing to Communicate	I write to communicate my ideas to others.

Building Personal Engagement

Knowing My Reader Identity	I am aware of my reading preferences, habits, strengths, weaknesses, and attitudes—my Reader Identity.
Practicing	I put effort into practicing new reading strategies so that they become automatic.
Digging In	I am increasing my confidence and persistence for digging into text that seems difficult or boring.
Building Silent Reading Fluency	I read more smoothly and quickly, so I get more pages read.
Building Oral Reading Fluency	I read aloud more fluently and expressively.
Increasing Stamina	I set and meet stretch goals to read for longer and longer periods.
Increasing Range	I set and meet stretch goals for extending the range of what I read.
Choosing Books (SSR+)	I use tools I have learned for choosing a book that's right for me.
Taking Power	I read to understand how what I read applies to me and gives me power.
Reflecting on My Evolving Reader Identity	I reflect in discussions and in writing on my growth as a reader—my evolving Reader Identity.
Writing to Reflect	I use writing to step back and think about what I am learning.

Making Thinking Visible

Monitoring	I monitor my reading processes and identify problems.
Repairing Comprehension	I know what strategies to use to get back on track.
Talking to Understand Reading	I talk about my reading processes to understand them better.
Writing to Understand Reading	I write about my reading processes to understand them better.

Using Cognitive Strategies to Increase Comprehension: Science

Setting a Reading Purpose	I set a purpose for reading a text and keep it in mind while I read.
Choosing a Reading Process	I vary my reading process to fit my reading purpose.
Previewing	I preview text that is long or appears to be challenging, to mobilize strategies for dealing with it.
Identifying and Evaluating Roadblocks	I identify specific reading roadblocks and decide what to do.
Tolerating Ambiguity	I tolerate ambiguity or confusion in understanding a text while I work on making sense of it.
Clarifying	I work to clear up a reading confusion—whether it is a word, a sentence, an idea, or missing background information that I need to find.
Using Context	I use context to clarify confusions by reading on and rereading.
Making Connections	I make connections from texts to my experience and knowledge.
Chunking	I break difficult text into smaller pieces to better understand the whole.
Visualizing	I try to see in my mind what the author is describing. I read and represent scientific content and ideas in drawings, graphs, flowcharts, and other visuals.
Using Mathematics	I read and create numerical representations to help clarify complex scientific text and ideas.
Questioning	I ask myself questions when I don't understand. I ask myself questions about the author's idea, story, or text, and I know where to find the answers—whether in my mind, the text, other texts, other people, or a combination of these. I ask inquiry questions when something I read makes me want to know more. I take a "convince me" stand and ask questions about the evidence presented to support a scientific claim.
Predicting	I use what I understand in the reading to predict what might come next.
Organizing Ideas and Information	I use graphic organizers to sort out ideas or items of information to see how they are related.
Paraphrasing	I restate a sentence or an idea from a text in my own words.

Getting the Gist	I read and answer in my own words the question, "What do I know so far?"
Summarizing	I boil down what I read to the key points.
Sequencing	I order events in time to understand their relationships. I keep track of how scientific processes unfold.
Comparing and Contrasting	I make comparisons to identify similarities and differences.
Identifying Cause and Effect	I find conditions or events that contribute to or cause particular outcomes.
Using Evidence	I use evidence to build and support my understanding of texts and concepts.
Rereading	I reread to build understanding and fluency.
Writing to Clarify Understanding	I write about what I think I know to make it clearer to myself.

Building Knowledge: Science

Mobilizing Schema	I use my relevant networks of background knowledge, or schema, so that new information has something to connect to and is easier to understand.
Building and Revising Schema	I add to and revise my schema as I learn more.
Synthesizing	I look for relationships among my ideas, ideas from texts, and ideas from discussions.
Writing to Consolidate Knowledge	I use writing to capture and lock in new knowledge.

Building Knowledge . . . About Text: Science

Text Structure	I use my knowledge of text structures to predict how ideas are organized. I know to look for the predictable ways science text is structured: classification and definition, structure and function, process and interaction, claim and evidence, and procedure. I know that visuals and numerical representations are particularly powerful ways to convey complex scientific text and ideas.
Text Features	I use my knowledge of text features like headings and graphics to support my understanding.
Text Density	Because I know that science text is often tightly packed with new terms and ideas, I preview and reread it. Because I know that science text is often tightly packed with new terms and ideas, I chunk and restate the chunks in familiar language to keep track of the gist as I read.
Point of View	I use my understanding that authors write with a purpose and for particular audiences to identify and evaluate the author's point of view.

Building Knowledge . . . About Language: Science

Word Analysis	I use my knowledge of word roots, prefixes, and suffixes to figure out new words.

Referents	I use my knowledge of pronouns and other referents to find and substitute the word that a pronoun or other word is standing for.
Signal Words and Punctuation (Text Signals)	I use my knowledge of signal words and punctuation to predict a definition, results or conclusions, examples, sequence, comparison, contrast, a list, or an answer. I know to look for the text signals that go with different scientific text structures.
Contextual Redefinition	I know that when familiar terms are used in unfamiliar ways, I can redefine them in context to clear up confusion.
Sentence Structure	I use my knowledge of sentence structure to help me understand difficult text. Because science textbooks often use passive voice, I know to restate sentences in active voice to keep track of the subject and action. Because science textbooks often use complex sentence constructions, I know to find the logical connecting words between ideas.
Word-Learning Strategies List	I use strategies to learn new words in the texts I read.

Building Knowledge . . . About the Discipline of Science

Scientific Documents	I know how to read or represent diverse scientific documents: reports, data tables and graphs, illustrations and other visuals, equations, textbooks, and models.
Scientific Sourcing	I source a science document, set of data, or piece of evidence as a step in evaluating its authority or reliability.
Scientific Labels	I know that using scientific names and labels is a shortcut for communicating precisely about scientific processes and structures.
Scientific Inquiry	Knowing that scientific inquiry involves cycles of questioning, making observations, and explaining and evaluating observations helps me read science investigations and describe my own.
Scientific Evidence	I know that scientific claims must be supported by evidence that is carefully collected, evaluated, and reported so that others can judge its value.
Scientific Explanation	I can write a scientific explanation that makes a claim about observations of the natural world and convincingly defends the claim with evidence.
Scientific Corroboration	I know that corroborating findings in science is a way to find out how likely they are to be true.
Scientific Understanding	I know that for scientific understanding to evolve, science moves forward using best evidence and information even though these may be proved incomplete or wrong in the future.
Conceptual Change	I monitor my schema to decide whether compelling evidence about scientific claims changes my personal understanding of the natural world.
Scientific Identity	I am aware of my evolving identity as a reader and consumer of science.

Student Learning Goals: History

Collaborating in a Community of Readers and Writers

Contributing to Our Community	I contribute to maintaining a classroom community that feels safe, where everyone is able to take risks and grow.
Collaborating Effectively	I work with partners and groups in ways that are both respectful and risk-taking.
Participating Thoughtfully	I make my thinking count in discussions, as a speaker and a listener. I share my reading confusions and under-standings to get and give help. I listen and learn from the reading confusions and un-derstandings of others.
Building a Literacy Context	I understand and use the shared literacy vocabulary of our classroom.
Being Open to New Ideas	I appreciate and evaluate alternative viewpoints.
Developing a Literacy Agenda	I read to understand how literacy opens and closes doors in people's lives.
Sharing Books	I talk about books I am reading to involve others in what the books have to offer.
Writing to Communicate	I write to communicate my ideas to others.

Building Personal Engagement

Knowing My Reader Identity	I am aware of my reading preferences, habits, strengths, weaknesses, and attitudes—my Reader Identity.
Practicing	I put effort into practicing new reading strategies so that they become automatic.
Digging In	I am increasing my confidence and persistence for digging into text that seems difficult or boring.
Building Silent Reading Fluency	I read more smoothly and quickly, so I get more pages read.
Building Oral Reading Fluency	I read aloud more fluently and expressively.
Increasing Stamina	I set and meet stretch goals to read for longer and longer periods.
Increasing Range	I set and meet stretch goals for extending the range of what I read.
Choosing Books (SSR+)	I use tools I have learned for choosing a book that's right for me.
Taking Power	I read to understand how *what* I read applies to me and gives me power.
Reflecting on My Evolving Reader Identity	I reflect in discussions and in writing on my growth as a reader—my evolving Reader Identity.
Writing to Reflect	I use writing to step back and think about what I am learning.

Making Thinking Visible

Monitoring	I monitor my reading processes and identify problems.
Repairing Comprehension	I know what strategies to use to get back on track.
Talking to Understand Reading	I talk about my reading processes to understand them better.
Writing to Understand Reading	I write about my reading processes to understand them better.

Using Cognitive Strategies to Increase Comprehension: History

Setting a Reading Purpose	I set a purpose for reading a text and keep it in mind while I read.
Choosing a Reading Process	I vary my reading process to fit my reading purpose.
Previewing	I preview text that is long or appears to be challenging, to mobilize strategies for dealing with it.
Identifying and Evaluating Roadblocks	I identify specific reading roadblocks and decide what to do.
Tolerating Ambiguity	I tolerate ambiguity or confusion in understanding a text while I work on making sense of it.
Clarifying	I work to clear up a reading confusion, whether it is a word, a sentence, an idea, or missing background information that I need to find.
Using Context	I use context to clarify confusions by reading on and rereading.
Making Connections	I make connections from texts to my experience and knowledge.
Chunking	I break difficult text into smaller pieces to better understand the whole.
Visualizing	I try to see in my mind what the author is describing.
Listening for Voice	I listen for the author's voice to help me engage with a text.
Questioning	I ask myself questions when I don't understand. I ask myself questions about the author's idea or text, and I know where to find the answers—whether in my mind, the text, other texts, other people, or a combination of these. I ask inquiry questions when something I read makes me want to know more.
Predicting	I use what I understand in the reading to predict what might come next.
Organizing Ideas and Information	I use graphic organizers to sort out ideas or items of information to see how they are related.
Paraphrasing	I restate a sentence or an idea from a text in my own words.

Getting the Gist	I read and answer in my own words the question, "What do I know so far?"
Summarizing	I boil down what I read to the key points.
Sequencing	I order events in time to understand their relationships.
Comparing and Contrasting	I make comparisons to identify similarities and differences.
Identifying Cause and Effect	I find conditions or events that contribute to or cause particular outcomes.
Using Evidence	I use evidence to build and support my understanding of texts and concepts.
Rereading	I reread to build understanding and fluency.
Writing to Clarify Understanding	I write about what I think I know to make it clearer to myself.

Building Knowledge: History

Mobilizing Schema	I use my relevant networks of background knowledge, or schema, so that new information has something to connect to and is easier to understand.
Building and Revising Schema	I add to and revise my schema as I learn more.
Synthesizing	I look for relationships among my ideas, ideas from texts, and ideas from discussions.
Writing to Consolidate Knowledge	I use writing to capture and lock in new knowledge.

Building Knowledge . . . About Text: History

Text Structure	I use my knowledge of text structures to predict how ideas are organized.
Text Features	I use my knowledge of text features like headings and graphics to support my understanding.
Point of View	I use my understanding that authors write with a purpose and for particular audiences to identify and evaluate the author's point of view.

Building Knowledge . . . About Language: History

Word Analysis	I use my knowledge of word roots, prefixes, and suffixes to figure out new words.
Referents	I use my knowledge of pronouns and other referents to find and substitute the word that a pronoun or other word is standing for.
Signal Words and Punctuation (Text Signals)	I use my knowledge of signal words and punctuation to predict a definition, results or conclusions, examples, sequence, comparison, contrast, a list, or an answer.

Contextual Redefinition	I know that when familiar terms are used in unfamiliar ways, I can redefine them in context to clear up confusion.
Sentence Structure	I use my knowledge of sentence structure to help me understand difficult text.
Word-Learning Strategies List	I use strategies to learn new words in the texts I read.

Building Knowledge . . . About the Discipline of History

Historical Documents and Artifacts	I know how to identify and use diverse types of historical documents and artifacts.
Primary and Secondary Sources	I know the differences between primary sources and secondary sources.
Document Sourcing	I source a document or account to evaluate its credibility and point of view by identifying who wrote it, when, why, and for what audience.
Document Corroboration	I compare documents or accounts to look for evidence that what is written is credible and to find other points of view or perspectives.
Chronological Thinking	I know how to order events and assess their duration and relationships in time.
Historical Schema	I actively work to build my schema about particular times and places and how they differ—the geography, people, customs, values, religions, beliefs, languages, technologies, and roles of men, women, children, and minority groups.
Historical Contextualization	I use my historical schema to understand what it was like in times and places that I cannot personally experience.
Historical Cause and Effect	I use my understanding of cause and effect to identify historical relationships and impacts.
Historical Record and Interpretation	I understand that history is a combination of what can be observed, how it is observed, what can be interpreted, and how it is interpreted.
Historical Argument	I can write an historical argument that convincingly interprets the available evidence by making claims, supporting those claims with evidence, and explaining my reasoning.
Historical Identity	I am aware of my evolving identity as a reader of and actor in history.

Student Learning Goals: Literature

Collaborating in a Community of Readers and Writers

Contributing to Our Community	I contribute to maintaining a classroom community that feels safe, where everyone is able to take risks and grow.
Collaborating Effectively	I work with partners and groups in ways that are both respectful and risk-taking.
Participating Thoughtfully	I make my thinking count in discussions, as a speaker and a listener. I share my reading confusions and understandings to get and give help. I listen and learn from the reading confusions and understandings of others.
Building a Literacy Context	I understand and use the shared literacy vocabulary of our classroom.
Being Open to New Ideas	I appreciate and evaluate alternative viewpoints.
Developing a Literacy Agenda	I read to understand how literacy opens and closes doors in people's lives.
Sharing Books	I talk about books I am reading to involve others in what the books have to offer.
Writing to Communicate	I write to communicate my ideas to others.

Building Personal Engagement

Knowing My Reader Identity	I am aware of my reading preferences, habits, strengths, weaknesses, and attitudes—my Reader Identity.
Practicing	I put effort into practicing new reading strategies so that they become automatic.
Digging In	I am increasing my confidence and persistence for digging into text that seems difficult or boring.
Building Silent Reading Fluency	I read more smoothly and quickly, so I get more pages read.
Building Oral Reading Fluency	I read aloud more fluently and expressively.
Increasing Stamina	I set and meet stretch goals to read for longer and longer periods.
Increasing Range	I set and meet stretch goals for extending the range of what I read.
Choosing Books (SSR+)	I use tools I have learned for choosing a book that's right for me.
Taking Power	I read to understand how *what* I read applies to me and gives me power.
Reflecting on My Evolving Reader Identity	I reflect in discussions and in writing on my growth as a reader—my evolving Reader Identity.
Writing to Reflect	I use writing to step back and think about what I am learning.

Making Thinking Visible

Monitoring	I monitor my reading processes and identify problems.
Repairing Comprehension	I know what strategies to use to get back on track.
Talking to Understand Reading	I talk about my reading processes to understand them better.
Writing to Understand Reading	I write about my reading processes to understand them better.

Using Cognitive Strategies to Increase Comprehension: Literature

Setting a Reading Purpose	I set a purpose for reading a text and keep it in mind while I read.
Choosing a Reading Process	I vary my reading process to fit my reading purpose.
Previewing	I preview text that is long or appears to be challenging, to mobilize strategies for dealing with it.
Identifying and Evaluating Roadblocks	I identify specific reading roadblocks and decide what to do.
Tolerating Ambiguity	I tolerate ambiguity or confusion in understanding a text while I work on making sense of it.
Clarifying	I work to clear up a reading confusion, whether it is a word, a sentence, an idea, or missing background information that I need to find.
Using Context	I use context to clarify confusions by reading on and rereading.
Making Connections	I make connections from texts to my experience and knowledge.
Chunking	I break difficult text into smaller pieces to better understand the whole.
Visualizing	I try to see in my mind what the author is describing.
Listening for Voice	I listen for the author's voice or the voices of characters to help me engage with a text.
Questioning	I ask myself questions when I don't understand. I ask myself questions about the author's idea, story, or text, and I know where to find the answers—whether in my mind, the text, other texts, other people, or a combination of these. I ask inquiry questions when something I read makes me want to know more.
Predicting	I use what I understand in the reading to predict what might come next.
Organizing Ideas and Information	I use graphic organizers to sort out ideas or items of information to see how they are related.
Paraphrasing	I restate a sentence or an idea from a text in my own words.

Getting the Gist	I read and answer in my own words the question, "What do I know so far?"
Summarizing	I boil down what I read to the key points.
Sequencing	I order events in time to understand their relationships.
Comparing and Contrasting	I make comparisons to identify similarities and differences.
Identifying Cause and Effect	I find conditions or events that contribute to or cause particular outcomes.
Using Evidence	I use evidence to build and support my understanding of texts and concepts.
Rereading	I reread to build understanding and fluency.
Writing to Clarify Understanding	I write about what I think I know to make it clearer to myself.

Building Knowledge: Literature

Mobilizing Schema	I use my relevant networks of background knowledge, or schema, so that new information has something to connect to and is easier to understand.
Building and Revising Schema	I add to and revise my schema as I learn more.
Synthesizing	I look for relationships among my ideas, ideas from texts, and ideas from discussions.
Writing to Consolidate Knowledge	I use writing to capture and lock in new knowledge.

Building Knowledge . . . About Text: Literature

Text Structure	I use my knowledge of literary genres and subgenres to predict how ideas are organized.
Text Features	I use my knowledge of text features such as chapter titles, stage directions, and dialogue to support my understanding.
Point of View	I use my understanding that authors write with a purpose and for particular audiences to identify and evaluate the author's point of view.

Building Knowledge . . . About Language: Literature

| Word Analysis | I use my knowledge of word roots, prefixes, and suffixes to figure out new words. |
| Referents | I use my knowledge of pronouns and other referents to find and substitute the word that a pronoun or other word is standing for. |

Signal Words and Punctuation (Text Signals)	I use my knowledge of signal words and punctuation to predict a definition, results or conclusions, examples, sequence, comparison, contrast, a list, or an answer.
Contextual Redefinition	I know that when familiar terms are used in unfamiliar ways, I can redefine them in context to clear up confusion.
Sentence Structure	I use my knowledge of sentence structure to help me understand difficult text.
Word-Learning Strategies List	I use strategies to learn new words in the texts I read.

Building Knowledge . . . About the Discipline of Literature

Literary Genres	I can identify and use diverse literary genres and subgenres.
Literary Themes	I recognize universal literary themes—such as good versus evil, ideal versus flawed behavior, and psychological growth and change—and I know how to trace their development.
Literary Structures	I understand how different literary structures—such as plot, stanza, and act—organize and contribute to the meaning of a piece of literature.
Literary Commentary	I recognize how literature may incorporate or promote social, historical, economic, political, and cultural commentary, either transparently or through figuration such as irony, allegory, and symbolism.
Literary Movements	I can identify how a piece of literature is affected by literary movements such as transcendentalism, romanticism, realism, and feminism.
Narrative Voice	I understand narrative voice (first-person, third-person, third-person omniscient, unreliable narrator) and authorial voice, including relationships between author and narrator.
Language Choices	I can identify and use imagery, tone, dialogue, rhythm, and syntax to shape meaning.
Literary Inquiry	I understand that literature invites inference and interpretation within and across texts and experiences. In discussions and in writing, I offer and also consider others' evidence-based inferences and interpretations.
Literary Writing	I can use my understanding of literary genres, structures, language, and voice to write a range of forms.
Literary Identity	I am aware of my evolving identity as a reader and writer of literary forms.

Student Learning Goals: Mathematics

Collaborating in a Community of Readers and Writers

Contributing to Our Community	I contribute to maintaining a classroom community that feels safe, where everyone is able to take risks and grow.
Collaborating Effectively	I work with partners and groups in ways that are both respectful and risk-taking.
Participating Thoughtfully	I make my thinking count in discussions, as a speaker and a listener. I share my reading confusions and understandings to get and give help. I listen and learn from the reading confusions and understandings of others.
Building a Literacy Context	I understand and use the shared literacy vocabulary of our classroom.
Being Open to New Ideas	I appreciate and evaluate alternative viewpoints.
Developing a Literacy Agenda	I read to understand how literacy opens and closes doors in people's lives.
Sharing Books	I talk about books I am reading to involve others in what the books have to offer.
Writing to Communicate	I write to communicate my ideas to others.

Building Personal Engagement

Knowing My Reader Identity	I am aware of my reading preferences, habits, strengths, weaknesses, and attitudes—my Reader Identity.
Practicing	I put effort into practicing new reading strategies so that they become automatic.
Digging In	I am increasing my confidence and persistence for digging into text that seems difficult or boring.
Building Silent Reading Fluency	I read more smoothly and quickly, so I get more pages read.
Building Oral Reading Fluency	I read aloud more fluently and expressively.
Increasing Stamina	I set and meet stretch goals to read for longer and longer periods.
Increasing Range	I set and meet stretch goals for extending the range of what I read.
Choosing Books (SSR+)	I use tools I have learned for choosing a book that's right for me.
Taking Power	I read to understand how what I read applies to me and gives me power.
Reflecting on My Evolving Reader Identity	I reflect in discussions and in writing on my growth as a reader—my evolving Reader Identity.
Writing to Reflect	I use writing to step back and think about what I am learning.

Making Thinking Visible

Monitoring	I monitor my reading processes and identify problems.
Repairing Comprehension	I know what strategies to use to get back on track.
Talking to Understand Reading	I talk about my reading processes to understand them better.
Writing to Understand Reading	I write about my reading processes to understand them better.

Using Cognitive Strategies to Increase Comprehension: Mathematics

Setting a Reading Purpose	I set a purpose for reading a text and keep it in mind while I read.
Choosing a Reading Process	I vary my reading process to fit my reading purpose.
Previewing	I preview text that is long or appears to be challenging, to mobilize strategies for dealing with it.
Identifying and Evaluating Roadblocks	I identify specific reading roadblocks and decide what to do.
Tolerating Ambiguity	I tolerate ambiguity or confusion in understanding a text while I work on making sense of it.
Clarifying	I work to clear up a reading confusion, whether it is a word, a sentence, an idea, or missing background information that I need to find.
Using Context	I use context to clarify confusions by reading on and rereading.
Making Connections	I make connections from texts to my experience and knowledge.
Chunking	I break difficult text into smaller pieces to better understand the whole.
Visualizing	I try to see in my mind what the text is describing. I read and create numerical representations to help clarify complex mathematical text and ideas.
Questioning	I ask myself questions when I don't understand. I ask myself questions about the text, and I know where to find the answers—whether in my mind, the text, other texts, other people, or a combination of these. I ask inquiry questions when something I read makes me want to know more.
Predicting	I use what I understand in the reading to predict what a reasonable answer might be.
Organizing Ideas and Information	I use graphic organizers to sort out ideas or items of information to see how they are related.
Paraphrasing	I restate a sentence or an idea from a text in my own words.

Getting the Gist	I read and answer in my own words the question, "What do I know so far?"
Summarizing	I boil down what I read to the key points.
Sequencing	I order the steps in solving a problem.
Comparing and Contrasting	I make comparisons to identify similarities and differences.
Identifying Cause and Effect	I find conditions or events that contribute to or cause particular outcomes.
Using Evidence	I use evidence to build and support my understanding of texts and concepts.
Rereading	I reread to build understanding and fluency with mathematical language and processes.
Writing to Clarify Understanding	I write about what I think I know to make it clearer to myself.

Building Knowledge: Mathematics

Mobilizing Schema	I use my relevant networks of background knowledge, or schema, so that new information has something to connect to and is easier to understand.
Building and Revising Schema	I add to and revise my schema as I learn more.
Synthesizing	I look for relationships among my ideas, ideas from texts, and ideas from discussions.
Writing to Consolidate Knowledge	I use writing to capture and lock in new knowledge.

Building Knowledge . . . About Text: Mathematics

Text Structure	I use my knowledge of text structures to predict how ideas are organized.
Text Features	I use my knowledge of text features like headings and graphics to support my understanding.
Text Density	Because I know that mathematics text is often tightly packed with new terms and ideas, I preview and reread it. Because I know that mathematics text is often tightly packed with new terms and ideas, I chunk and restate the chunks in familiar language to keep track of the gist as I read.

Building Knowledge . . . About Language: Mathematics

| Word Analysis | I use my knowledge of word roots, prefixes, and suffixes to figure out new words. |
| Referents | I use my knowledge of pronouns and other referents to find and substitute the word a pronoun or other word is standing for. |

Signal Words and Punctuation (Text Signals)	I use my knowledge of signal words and punctuation to predict a definition, results or conclusions, examples, sequence, comparison, contrast, a list, or an answer.
Contextual Redefinition	I know that when familiar terms are used in unfamiliar ways, I can redefine them in context to clear up confusion.
Sentence Structure	I use my knowledge of sentence structure to help me understand difficult text.
Word-Learning Strategies List	I use strategies to learn new words in the texts I read.

Building Knowledge . . . About the Discipline of Mathematics

Conceptual Categories*	I can identify the purpose for and use different areas of math knowledge such as number, algebra, functions, geometry, statistics and probability, and modeling.
Mathematical Reasoning	I can think interchangeably about a math problem in abstract and quantitative terms. I monitor the reasonableness of the relationship between my abstract and quantitative thinking.
Mathematical Representation	I can read and represent mathematics with words, formulas, and mathematical symbols. I can read and create diagrams, tables, graphs, and flowcharts for mathematical purposes.
Mathematical Language	I understand the precise nature of mathematical language and use it to communicate exactly.
Problem Identification	I can read and identify "the problem" in a math problem.
Problem Solving	I make conjectures about and evaluate alternative approaches to a problem and then monitor the reasonableness of a solution approach as it proceeds.
Accuracy	I understand that in mathematics there may be alternate approaches to a solution, but only one correct answer. I check that the final solution makes sense and all computation is correct.
Pattern Application	I look for mathematical structures, approaches, and patterns that I can apply to the solution of new problems.
Mathematical Explanation	I can write to communicate my understanding of mathematical concepts, arguments, models, problems, and solutions, using appropriate language and forms.
Mathematical Identity	I am aware of my evolving identity as a reader and user of mathematics.

*These conceptual categories are drawn from the Common Core State Standards for Mathematical Practice.

Curriculum-Embedded Reading Assessment (CERA) Guidance and Tools

The Curriculum-Embedded Reading Assessment (CERA) is a formative assessment that measures literacy growth. The CERA offers teachers a rich picture of students' awareness of their reading processes and abilities to make sense of regular classroom reading materials.

Guidelines for Administering the CERA

Most students will be unfamiliar with a reading assessment that asks them to report on their own reading processes in both internal and external metacognitive conversations. Teachers find that explaining the CERA rationale and routine to students is an important first step.

How Is the CERA Administered?

The assessment can be given in one class period or less. Because it is not timed, teachers can adjust its timing to meet the needs of their students.

1. *Introduce the Assessment:* Explain the role of literacy in your classroom.

2. *Individual Reading:* Students read a piece of text and Talk to the Text (annotating the text with their responses and reading processes).

3. *Individual Writing:* Students respond to a series of prompts about the piece and their reading processes.

4. *Whole Class Metacognitive Conversation:* The class discusses reading and problem-solving processes and adds to the class Reading Strategies List.

5. *Scoring:* The teacher scores the student work using the CERA rubric.

6. *Using the Data:* The teacher sets new literacy instruction goals based on the data.

7. *Self-Assessment:* Students may reflect on their CERA work and set personal literacy goals.

How Often Is the CERA Administered?

You may give a CERA for your own purposes. The amount of time between the pre-assessment and post-assessment will depend on what the teacher hopes to learn. For example, a CERA might be given at the beginning and end of a year, grading period, or unit:

- Per year, to assess long-term growth.

- Per grading period, to gauge progress on academic literacy goals.

- Per unit or even a single week of instruction, when a new literacy strategy is introduced and practiced. For example, if the focus for that period of time has been asking and answering questions about reading, the CERA can be administered to see how well students are using this technique.

Text Selection and Question Development

Select a short, self-contained passage (a page or less) from a textbook, a supplementary text, or core curricular materials. For example, you might choose the introduction to a chapter, a primary source document, or a piece of literature from an anthology. The text should be representative of the content and challenge level of regular course materials that you use but should not be something you will actually assign either in class or for homework.

Students answer different kinds of questions on the CERA. A set of Individual Writing Prompts is included, and teachers also customize a few (four to six) comprehension questions that will provide a good snapshot of students' understanding of the specific text selected for students to read.

Materials and Preparation

Make a copy of the text for each student. Leave plenty of blank space around the text for note making. Also reproduce the writing prompts for students.

CERA Lesson Plan and Rubric

1. Introducing the assessment

- Give the first CERA early in the year, prior to significant instruction in metacognitive conversation, and then periodically as you deem necessary, to monitor student growth throughout the year.

- Before giving the CERA, establish purposes for supporting and assessing literacy growth. Explain that this assessment is designed to give you information that will help you teach students to become stronger readers in the discipline. Explain that the class will complete assessments like this periodically, as you monitor their progress and growth.

- Ask students to do their best. To elicit their best work, it can help to assure them that you will grade their effort and evidence of their literacy growth.

Explain the overall process: they will read and annotate a piece of text and then respond to a set of questions at the end.

2. Individual reading (ten to twenty minutes, depending on the text)

   • Have students write their names on both the text and the questions, and ask them to use pen for their writing.

   • Ask students to read the text silently and individually and talk to the text. If you have not introduced the Talking to the Text routine, explain that you want them to mark the text and make notes about their reading— for example, to underline words and write in the margins any questions, comments, clarifications, and predictions they have.

   • If students finish early, ask them to go back over their writing and see whether they want to add any other reflections, comments, questions, and confusions.

3. Individual writing (about ten minutes)

   • Ask students to respond to the written prompts (in pen) when they finish reading and Talking to the Text.

   • Encourage students to write a good summary that shows what they understood of the reading.

   • Be sure to explain that their answers to the questions after the summary will help you see what is confusing about the text and what they know how to do to make sense of texts as they read. Encourage students to take time to respond thoughtfully to the questions so that you can learn about them as readers. It can be helpful to assure students that you will grade this on effort and thoughtful answers that help you understand how they approach reading.

4. Whole class metacognitive conversation (five to fifteen minutes)

   • Ask students to review their Talking to the Text and responses to the questions and choose one or two things to share.

   • Invite students to share something they noticed about their reading— something they figured out, a confusion or a challenge in the reading. (You may need to model an example or two from your own reading.)

   • You might ask:

      What did you mark or comment on in the text?

      What did you do there? What was going on in your thinking?

How did doing that help your reading?

- Add to the class Reading Strategies List (or introduce the term *meta-cognition* and start a Reading Strategies List now if this is the class's first metacognitive conversation).

- Take a moment to appreciate students for sharing their thinking. Explain that this is one of many conversations that will help you learn how to help them become stronger readers of the discipline over the year.

- You might offer students a minute or two to write a brief reflection on what they learned from the CERA process and discussion.

5. Assessing student work

- Use the descriptors in the CERA Rubric to assess students' academic literacy.

6. Using the data to set and adjust literacy instruction goals

- Once you have a sense of what your students know how to do as they read, you can begin to set instructional goals. For example:

   Many students begin by not marking the page much at all. It will be difficult to see what they know how to do as they approach reading. The first step for students on this end of the rubric is to learn to Talk to the Text and make their thinking visible to you and to themselves.

   For students who are marking the text, you will want to assess the breadth of their repertoire of strategies and knowledge (about the content and the world, text, language, and disciplinary practices) that support reading.

- With this information, you can consider next steps for modeling and practicing reading processes.

- As you gather data from new CERAs, you can adjust your disciplinary literacy goals and instruction to respond to students' changing abilities and needs, helping them to develop disciplinary reading habits that will support stronger comprehension and growing independence over time.

7. Self-assessment

- You might offer students an opportunity to read their work, review the rubric, and set literacy goals. You may also want to share your observations about their strengths and literacy instructional goals for the next period of time.

Curriculum-Embedded Reading Assessment (CERA) Individual Writing Prompts

Please respond to the following questions (in pen).

Part I. Summary

1. In your own words, write a short summary (one or two sentences) of this piece.

Part II. Reading Process

2. What kinds of things were happening in your mind as you read this?

3. What did you do that helped you to understand the reading?

4. What questions or problems do you still have with this piece?

Part III. Self-Assessment

5. How easy or difficult was this piece for you? (circle one)

   pretty easy   not too hard   pretty hard   too hard

6. How well would you say you understood this piece?

Part IV. Comprehension Questions *(teacher to supply for the given text)*

7.

8.

9.

10.

Curriculum-Embedded Reading Assessment (CERA) Rubric

Overview	Noticing Reading	Focusing on Reading	Taking Control of Reading
Evidence of student's overall control of reading processes	Few or no marks on the page along with vague responses to process questions and confused answers to comprehension questions. Teacher gains little insight into student's reading process, what is confusing, or how to support the student.	Marks on the page and responses to questions give insight into student's reading process and comprehension. Teacher gathers important information about problems student encountered and next steps for supporting the student.	Substantial marking on the page and elaborated answers to questions give detailed information about student's reading process and comprehension. Teacher is able to develop rich ideas for instruction and how to support student's reading comprehension.

Metacognitive Conversation	Noticing Reading	Focusing on Reading	Taking Control of Reading
Student writes about reading process to monitor comprehension and get back on track	ANNOTATIONS ON THE TEXT Few or no marks to give evidence of strategic or thoughtful reader interaction with the text; for example: • Sparse underlining with no written comments. • Whole paragraphs highlighted with no indication of important ideas or questions. • Marks limited to a single type of interaction, such as underlining unfamiliar words.	Marking indicates some reader interaction with the text; for example: • Some limited strategic marks focused on one or more strategies, such as making connections, asking questions. • Comments in margins are generalized responses, such as "boring," "cool," or "me too." • Comments and marks identify specific problems, such as "What?" connected to a highlighted section.	Marking indicates substantial reader–text interactions focused on problem solving and building understanding; for example: • A variety of marks for varying purposes, such as highlights, circles, underlines. • Strategic marking of main ideas, text signals. • Purposeful comments that clarify, ask and answer questions, make connections, summarize.
	RESPONSES TO CERA QUESTIONS Summary misses the main idea or indicates confusions, yet student indicates text was "easy" and he or she understood it "well."	Summary indicates identification of the main ideas.	Summary indicates understanding of the main ideas and may connect to larger themes.
	Process responses offer little evidence of strategic reading; for example, the response is vague, no problems or confusions are identified, strategies are vague— "I just read it."	Process responses indicate some evidence of what is seen in the marking and annotating; for example, student thought about what a key term meant.	Process responses use literacy vocabulary to specifically describe reading processes.
	Taken together, responses suggest student is unaware of reading difficulty.	Taken together, responses indicate an awareness of roadblocks and processes. Student identifies at least one comprehension problem either solved or unsolved.	Taken together, responses demonstrate student is aware of confusions and able to apply strategies to get back on track.

Using Cognitive Strategies	Noticing Reading	Focusing on Reading	Taking Control of Reading
Student uses strategies to focus on reading and take control: *Setting reading purpose* *Choosing reading process* *Previewing* *Identifying and evaluating roadblocks* *Tolerating ambiguity* *Clarifying* *Using context* *Making connections* *Chunking* *Visualizing* *Listening for voice* *Questioning* *Predicting* *Organizing ideas and information* *Paraphrasing* *Getting the gist* *Summarizing* *Using evidence*	**ANNOTATIONS ON THE TEXT** Few or no marks give evidence of strategic interaction with the text.	Specific areas of the text are marked and commented on as roadblocks or confusions.	Marks and comments connect to one another; for example, an underline of a key term is connected to a definition; a section underlined is related to a summary note or question.
	Marks, if any, indicate a single strategy, such as underlining only key words or highlighting everything indiscriminately.	Marks indicate the use of one or more literacy strategies but may not lead to solutions. Marks may appear "practiced." For example, many questions are asked but not all seem useful, purposeful, or strategic, and few are answered.	Multiple strategies are in use, possibly signaling student's attempt to resolve a persistent confusion.
	Comments, if any, indicate general confusion or reactions— such as "Huh?" or "Why am I reading this?"—and do not draw attention to specific problems to be solved.	Comments focus on the text and reader response, but not on identifying roadblocks and problems.	Comments clarify problems or answer questions posed by student.
	RESPONSES TO CERA QUESTIONS Summary does not clearly demonstrate comprehension.	Summary identifies main ideas.	Summary clearly states main ideas, which may also be marked in the text.
	Process responses do not identify roadblocks or problems to solve.	Process responses relate to marks and annotations on the text and describe at least one strategy used or problem solved.	Process responses relate to marks and annotations on the text and demonstrate the use of multiple strategies to solve problems.
	Taken together, responses indicate student is unable to use strategies to get back on track.	Self-assessment demonstrates understanding of challenges and how to get back on track.	Self-assessment demonstrates understanding of main ideas and awareness of how reading problems were solved.

Building Knowledge	Noticing Reading	Focusing on Reading	Taking Control of Reading
Student mobilizes, builds, and revises schema about: *Content and the world* *Texts* *Language* *Disciplinary discourse and practices*	**ANNOTATIONS ON THE TEXT** Marks indicate little or no attention to developing word knowledge; for example, student highlights all long words, or words—such as proper nouns— that do not interfere with comprehension.	Marks indicate a focus on understanding; for example, student highlights words that have importance for comprehension of the big ideas in the text.	Marks indicate several strategies for word learning and attention to syntax and context clues; for example, in addition to words, context clues are highlighted; margin notes indicate word analysis.
	No indication that student is reading beyond word level to attend to sentence and context clues.	Some indication that student is reading beyond word level and attending to sentence and context clues.	Student reads beyond word level, attending to range of sentence and context clues.

RESPONSES TO PART I. SUMMARY AND PART II. READING PROCESS QUESTIONS

Summary indicates student is not connecting to relevant background knowledge or has limited schema about the author's ideas or theme; for example, "This was about reading and how he hated it."	Summary reflects general understanding and unelaborated referencing of the author's ideas or themes; for example, "This is about how going to jail made him want to learn how to read."	Summary reflects strong understanding and references the author's ideas and themes; for example, "Learning to read may have been the most important turning point in his life."
Reading process responses do not reference text genres or text structures nor visuals and formatting features as guides to reading.	Reading process responses indicate awareness of text genres and text structures and visuals and formatting features; for example, student references the introduction.	Reading process responses indicate use of text genres, text structures, visuals, and formatting features to solve problems and build understanding of the text; for example, "I figured out that I could understand the graph better if I reread the paragraph that referred to it."
Reading process responses either indicate no attention to word learning and language or responses to language are generalized; for example, "It had lots of hard words."	Reading process responses may describe clarifying a difficult word or phrase or using text signals to understand a sequence, for example.	Reading process responses indicate ways that student learned new words or solved complex syntax problems. Student may use new vocabulary from the text in his or her summary in ways that reflect understanding.
Reading process responses do not indicate awareness of discipline-specific discourse or practices.	Reading process responses indicate some awareness of discipline-specific discourse or practices; for example, "The reporter told this in a way that makes immigrants seem bad."	Reading process responses reflect comfort recognizing and using disciplinary discourse and practices; for example, "I saw that this was a scientific argument, so I knew to look for whether the evidence supported the explanation."

Reading Apprenticeship Metacognitive Funnel

The metaphor of a metacognitive funnel helps students and their teachers recognize that attention during reading can shift, developmentally deeper over time and within a single reading event.

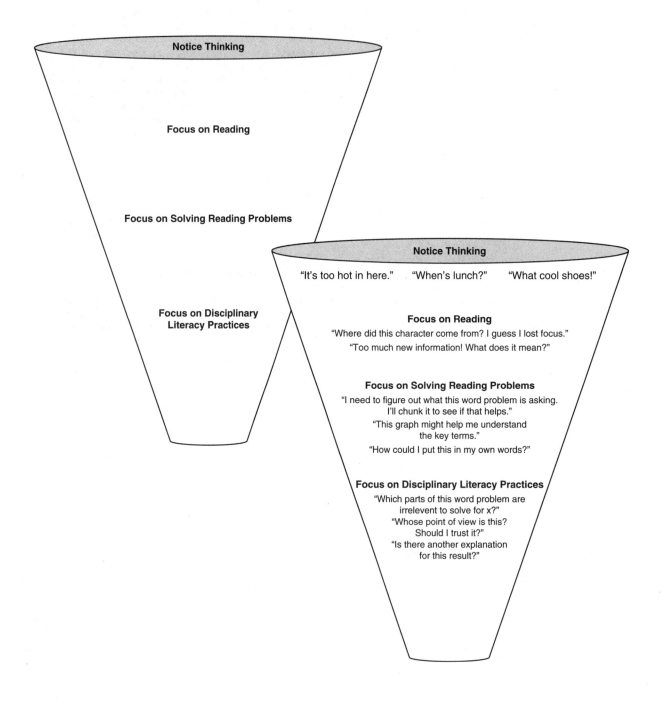

What Does a Reading Apprenticeship Classroom Look Like?

Teachers can use this snapshot of a Reading Apprenticeship classroom as a reflection tool, for lesson planning, and with colleagues for peer observations. It can also serve as a guide for administrators' classroom walk-throughs. Three characteristics of a Reading Apprenticeship classroom are paramount: a focus on comprehension, a climate of collaboration, and an emphasis on student independence.

A Focus on Comprehension

- Reading Apprenticeship is embedded in subject area learning: students develop strategies, identify and use text features, build topic knowledge, and carry out discipline-based activities while reading course-related materials.

- The work of comprehending reading materials takes place in the classroom; the teacher scaffolds the learning and serves as model and guide.

- The work of comprehending is metacognitive; how readers make sense of text is as important as what sense they make of it.

A Climate of Collaboration

- Class members draw on each other's knowledge, serving as resources to make sense of text together.

- Class members respect and value problem-solving processes: classroom norms support risk taking, sharing knowledge and confusion, and working together to solve comprehension problems.

- Grouping arrangements support collaboration and inquiry: students work independently, in pairs, in small groups, and as a class, depending on the task and the text.

- A shared vocabulary to describe reading processes and text features is evident in classroom talk, materials in use, and materials on display.

An Emphasis on Student Independence

- Students are agents in the process of reading and learning: they actively inquire into text meaning; their own and others' reading processes; the utility of particular reading strategies; and their preferences, strengths, and weaknesses as readers.

- Students are expected and supported to read extensively: course-related materials are available on various levels, and accountability systems are in place to ensure that students read large quantities of connected text.

- Over time, students are expected and able to do more reading, make more sophisticated interpretations, and accomplish more work with texts with less support from the teacher during class time.

Other Things to Notice

Reading Apprenticeship classrooms can also be recognized by a number of other classroom characteristics, including how materials and student groupings are used; the types of learning activities students undertake; and the roles of the teacher, students, and classroom talk in the learning environment.

Materials

- What materials are present? How are they being used?

- What kind of work is displayed in the classroom? On the walls? On the board?

- What do these displays indicate about how reading is approached and the role it plays in the class?

Groupings

- How is the classroom arranged?

- What kinds of groupings are students in as they carry out classroom tasks?

- What do these arrangements offer students as learning environments?

Tasks and Activities

- What activities are the teacher and students engaged in?

- What activities seem to be routine in this classroom?

- Who is doing the work of reading and comprehending?

Teaching and Learning Roles

- What roles do the teacher and students play in classroom activities?

- Does the teacher model, guide, and collaborate in comprehension as well as give instructions, assign, and question students?

- Do students pose questions and problems as well as respond to questions about course readings?

- Do all members of the classroom community collaborate in comprehension, share their knowledge and experience, inquire?

Classroom Talk

- What does the teacher say—to the class, to small groups, to individual students?

- What do the students say—to the teacher, to each other?

- What do the teacher and the class talk about?

- What kind of language is being used?

NOT Reading Apprenticeship

This table highlights some common ways implementation can fall short of what Reading Apprenticeship is.

NOT Reading Apprenticeship	Because Reading Apprenticeship *IS*. . .
Organization of Instruction	
Instruction is organized so that students mainly take notes from PowerPoints and lectures.	Reading Apprenticeship requires students' active engagement. Students, not the teacher, do the intellectual work.
When reading happens in class, teachers read to students, ask individual students to read aloud to the class, or orchestrate round-robin or popcorn reading.	In class, all students read—more and to themselves—with the goal of digging into challenging academic texts. They use their peers as resources for solving reading problems or confusions.
Discussion takes place mostly between the teacher and the whole class (or a few students with the rest of the class not talking).	Students actively discuss in pairs or small groups. Whole class discussion more typically follows small group discussion in the form of group share-outs and reflection.
Tasks can be completed by scanning the text for the answer or not reading at all, (as when the requested information calls for personal connections or has been explored in a class discussion).	Tasks *require* students to read closely, and to think.
Implementation of Routines and Strategies	
The role of the social and personal dimensions is equated with icebreakers.	Students build recognition of their own agency and the power of collaboration.
Teachers perform the metacognitive routines, for example, the Think Alouds and Talking to the Text, and students listen.	Students carry out metacognitive routines independently and in collaboration. Teachers occasionally model a new routine or use for a routine, *briefly*.
Metacognitive conversation/routines do not go beyond pro forma, general interactions with text; for example, to notice a personal connection or identify an unfamiliar word.	Metacognitive conversation/routines serve the purposes of disciplinary learning; for example, restating the passive voice of science texts to keep track of the subject and action.
Reading strategies are posted in a fixed list.	Reading Strategies Lists become diverse, depending on the reading purpose (for example, Previewing Strategies List, Word-Learning Strategies List, Reading Poetry Strategies List), and are revisited as is opportune.
Cognitive strategies like questioning and summarizing are used as checks on content attainment only. Teachers ask most of the questions.	Reading Apprenticeship changes the classroom conversation, with discussion of "how did you figure that out" holding equal space with "what's the answer." Students ask most of the questions.
Administrative Support and Progress Monitoring	
Reading Apprenticeship is offered as a one-time "training."	Reading Apprenticeship professional learning incorporates regularly scheduled time for teachers to meet in teams or learning communities.
Administrators evaluate classes for Reading Apprenticeship "compliance" with a checklist of surface-level behaviors.	Teams of administrators and teachers plan and conduct literacy rounds using Reading Apprenticeship protocols that encourage ongoing improvement.

Index